NIHIL OBSTAT:
Rev. Msgr. Glenn D. Gardner, J.C.D.
Censor Librorum

IMPRIMATUR:
† Most Rev. Charles V. Grahmann
Bishop of Dallas

February 25, 2002

The Nihil Obstat and Imprimatur are official declarations that the
material reviewed is free of doctrinal or moral error. No implication is contained therein that those granting the Nihil Obstat and
Imprimatur agree with the contents, opinions, or statements
expressed.

Cover Photo

The Hubble telescope reveals the heart of the Whirlpool Galaxy.
Photo Credit: NASA and the Hubble Heritage Team (STScI/AURA).
Acknowledgment: N. Scoville (Caltech) an T. Rector (NOAO).
Used by permission.

Acknowledgments

The Scripture quotations contained herein are from the *New Revised
Standard Version Bible: Catholic Edition* copyright © 1993 and 1989
by the Division of Christian Education for the National Council of
the Churches of Christ in the U.S.A. Used by permission. All rights
reserved.

Send all inquiries to:
Thomas More® Publishing
An RCL Company
200 East Bethany Drive
Allen, Texas 75002-3804

Telephone: 800-264-0368 / 972-390-6400
Fax: 800-688-8356 / 972-390-6560

Visit us at: **www.thomasmore.com**
Customer Service E-mail: **cservice@rcl-enterprises.com**

Printed in the United States of America

Library of Congress Control Number: 2002102193

7483   ISBN 0-88347-483-2

2 3 4 5 6   07 06 05 04 03

God *for* Grownups

God
for
Grownups

Virginia Smith

ThomasMore®
— *An RCL Company* —
Allen, Texas

Dedication

This book is dedicated with profound gratitude
to all who have been my teachers:
those who actually came attached to classrooms,
those whose role has been parent,
relative, colleague, or friend,
and particularly those who entered my life
disguised as students.

"The question about the spiritual life is a very challenging question. It touches the core of life. It forces you to take nothing for granted . . . neither good nor evil, neither life nor death, neither human beings nor God."

—Henri Nouwen *(Embraced by God's Love)*

"Nothing is more practical than finding God, that is, than falling in love in a quite absolute way. What you are in love with, what seizes your imagination, will affect everything. It will decide what will get you out of bed in the morning, what you do with your evenings, how you spend your weekends, what you read, who you know, what breaks your heart, and what amazes you with joy and gratitude. Fall in love, stay in love, and it will decide everything."

—Pedro Arrupe, S.J. *(National Catholic Reporter)*

Contents

Foreword

This book should be compulsory reading for every adult Christian. Ideally, it should be placed in every church pew as a companion to the hymnal or missalette. Certainly, it addresses a felt need that all of us in varying degrees experience: a lamentable lack in our faith development.

Religious education is seen as highly desirable for those of Sunday school age, yet it usually ceases to be valued once they have grown up. Theology, being one of the sciences, is commonly considered the exclusive domain of scholars, and so the knowledge of God for ordinary adults remains restricted to what they learned in their youth. While adults eagerly advance to a mature knowledge in the areas of sexuality, politics, and business, their God-knowledge remains stunted. The majority who acquire any knowledge about God after their youth often do so only while attending grownup Sunday school, listening to the brief weekly lessons from the pulpit.

This critical volume systematically approaches this regrettable poverty by examining the nature of God in the Bible, first in the Hebrew Testament, and then in the Christian Testament. The author then wisely widens her readers' understanding of God beyond that of the Jewish and Christian revelations. All divine revelation is an elevation, and this book's use of a variety of rich sacred sources is legitimately based on our Christian belief that in addition to speaking in the Bible, the Holy Spirit has also enlightened humanity in various places at various times. Virginia Smith raises the readers' perceptions of God by her inclusion of concepts of the Divine Mystery contained in the other great religions, in Islam and those of the Far East.

Finally, the author brings to the writing of this book her artistic skills as a teacher. She weaves humor and a sense of enjoyment into her content, using a commonplace language that makes her material accessible and entertaining for all readers. Her artistry cleverly holds our attention as our minds are opened to embrace a new cosmically larger, more loving and compassionate God. In the process, *God for Grownups* helps launch us into a lifelong love affair with our faith.

—Edward Hays
Author,
Prayers for a Planetary Pilgrim

You Are Here Because . . .

As the ever-present shopping mall sign points out with annoying regularity, "You are here." Here, in this case, is the opening paragraph of a book you must have thought would be of some use to you, or you would never have opened it. The precise reason why you are here is nobody's business but your own. But whatever that reason is, and contrary to what you may believe, I can tell you that you're not alone.

Years spent with both end-stage adolescents and all-age adults in either a formal or informal educational arena have convinced me that there is a need for a book of this sort. Again and again, I encounter what I've come to regard as the great Catholic inadequacy issue. Persons whose self-esteem is alive and well in many areas of their lives suddenly revert, at least metaphorically, to preschoolers who want nothing more than to climb into bed and pull the covers over their heads. However, with these hapless souls, the yen beckons, not because they're afraid of the dark, but because they feel they're in the dark about (of all things) their religion.

During my tenure as a parish director of religious education (DRE), it fell to me to conduct preparatory sessions with parents prior to their children's reception of the sacraments of Reconciliation and Eucharist. Early on, I would blithely toss out this dictum derived from Vatican II's *Declaration on Christian Education (Gravissimum educationis)*: "Parents are, in fact, the first and foremost educators of their children within a family atmosphere animated with love, providing a well-rounded formation" (3). I quit lobbing this bomb into the crowd upon noticing the number of faces that markedly blanched and the number of eyes that opened extraordinarily wide.

Had I hit them with the news that they would need to memorize Thomas Aquinas's *Summa Theologica* (Christian Classics, 1948, 1981) in its entirety before the next meeting, they could scarcely have exhibited greater shock. Having no wish to set the entire room hyperventilating, I commenced a more nuanced approach.

As I discovered, it wasn't that these highly responsible parents *would* not take on such a role; it was that many were totally convinced they *could* not. If there is truth to the adage that we cannot share with another that which we do not ourselves possess, these folks saw themselves as living proof of this unhappy premise.

Was their self-assessment correct? Yes, no, and maybe. Some simply lacked confidence, never having been asked to assume the primary role in their children's religious development, but were perfectly capable of doing the job. Others might not have been quite so well equipped but, with help, could do what was required. Others were right; they were abysmally unqualified.

Those who fell with a dull thud into this group were, by and large, not responsible for the situation in which they reluctantly found themselves. *But most thought they were!* And therein lies the crux of the issue, not to mention a major source of this sense of Catholic inadequacy I alluded to above.

Parents of school-age children are merely the examples of choice here. Some appear regularly at weekend liturgies and are active parishioners who contribute in a variety of valuable ways to their faith communities. Others maintain minimal affiliation; some, none at all. Quite a few are in their late teens or twenties whose apparent disinterest in religion masks a deep and abiding thirst for something to believe in which does not require them to put their intellects on hold or check their secular knowledge at the door. From there, the ages range from thirty to ninety and up. Almost nothing else about them is the same, but common to all is the pervading embarrassment over their real or imagined absence of instruction in matters religious.

Some of their discomfort is, unfortunately, justified. It is not unusual to find individuals who hold advanced degrees in their chosen fields, yet harbor what amounts to a second grade (pre-First Communion) religious education. Living as we do in a century where the speed of innovation and change revs up on a daily basis, such a situation is not only sad, it's risky. How can even the most intelligent be expected to deal responsibly with what was once termed "future shock" from a Catholic Christian stance if this stance is either unknown or misunderstood? Forming a core collection of beliefs and practices on which to base one's life with little or no in*form*ation is asking a lot.

How did things come to such a pretty pass? Should we long for the "good old days" when everybody seemed to know what it meant to be Catholic? Let's review.

The Good Old Days (Before Vatican II)

Return with me now to those wonderful days of yesteryear, where we encounter, not the Lone Ranger, but *The Baltimore Catechism* (Tan Books and Publishers, 1977). This is going to brand me the last living dinosaur, but I remember it well. I was a public school kid who got weekly doses of that venerable volume during Saturday morning catechism classes. For all its flaws, this *Catechism* did have some things going for it.

Catechists were frequently not much older than their students and not much better versed. One of those who tried to keep my fidgety feet flat on the floor on those long-ago Saturdays is a member of my current parish. At the time, of course, I thought she was a genuine grownup when, in fact, she must have been in her late teens . . . early twenties at the outside. Training? I doubt that she received much, but she really didn't need much. The task before her lay almost entirely in coaxing from us verbatim answers to her questions straight out of the book. Did we "get it"? Probably not a lot. Did anybody care? Probably not a lot. But we certainly knew how to answer questions like:

- Who made you? God made me.
- Why did God make you? God made me to know, love, and serve him in this world and to be happy with him in the next.

To the extent that we were able to fire back the prescribed pat answer to the proper question, all was right with our catechetical world.

That approach wasn't all bad. It put something dependable, if inadequate, between our ears for future use. It also provided a very real sense of what it meant to be Catholic. There was a rather comforting "one for all and all for one" feeling to it that helped define our place in the church and beyond, as well as our understanding of God and his expectations (God was definitely a him).

But even then, it wasn't enough. Simplistic answers to complex questions would be hauled up by inquiring minds sooner or later and found wanting. Then what? The arrival of that day for some simply brought the conclusion that religion was childish, something they had outgrown and would possibly need to replace later in life with . . . well, who knew what? Others clung with the desperation of the drowning to these early "certitudes" because they *were* religious and, therefore, invested with some kind of sanctity, which could only be tampered with under the threat of serious sin, probably mortal. Long after they had a number of academic achievements to show for themselves, they still harbored (usually secretly) those dutifully memorized answers from long vanished catechism classes.

As often happens when revisiting "the good old days," we discover that selective memory has warped our vision somewhat. The era of *The Baltimore Catechism* probably wasn't quite so uncomplicated as some remember.

Stiff Winds of Change (Vatican II)

Then, in on the wings of a snow white dove (if this symbolism suits you) flew the Holy Spirit. Not surprisingly, the winds of change thus generated resulted in the tossing about of long-held practices, the whipping up of theological debate, and, to borrow from our Islamic friends, a dervish-like whirl of new ideas.

The figure at the center of the maelstrom was a most unlikely champion, Pope John XXIII. Angelo Roncalli was elected to the papacy in October 1958 by a conclave seeking an appropriate successor to Pius XII, who had occupied the Chair of Peter for nearly twenty years (1939–1958). Roncalli's seventy-seventh birthday was hovering on the horizon when the papal lot fell to him, making it highly unlikely that his would be either a long or important reign. The first assessment proved correct. John XXIII was pontiff for less than five years, succumbing to cancer in June 1963. The second appraisal missed its mark by a wide margin. John's papacy not only was important, but is now seen as one of the most momentous of the twentieth century. This son of the soil from a small Italian village, elevated to his church's position of primacy in the waning years of a long life, did nothing less than change the world, not just his world, not merely the Catholic world, and not even exclusively the Christian world, but the world at large, pole to pole.

John XXIII, you see, not quite three months into his papacy, announced his intention of convening an ecumenical council, which would become known as the Second Vatican Council, or Vatican II. In effect, all the church's bishops had not met in council (such a convocation is what constitutes an ecumenical council, as opposed to the gathering of diverse Christian traditions we usually associate with the term) for roughly four hundred years. The Council of Trent, Catholicism's response to the Protestant Reformation, met off and on for eighteen years (1545–1563).

Assembling during the period known as the Counter Reformation when the church was under attack from a number of camps, the bishops at Trent reacted as might have been expected: they went into defensive mode, battening down the hatches, shoring up the defenses, and securing the fortress against further assaults. The canon (official list) of biblical books was declared, although in practice it had been widely accepted for centuries. The rubrics of the Mass and sacraments were defined, assuring a more universal code of practice. And this is just for starters. Pared down to the essentials, Trent gave birth to the church most Catholics knew and often loved until Vatican II. After Vatican II, when objections to change were frequently buttressed with, "It's always been that way," *always* usually meant since Trent, whether the speaker was aware of it or not.

The intent of John XXIII was to throw open the windows of Trent's fortress church and let in lungsful of ecclesiastical fresh air. Lest I be remiss, let me insert here that there was one major council between the sixteenth and twentieth centuries. If there's a Vatican II, it stands to reason there must have been a Vatican I somewhere along the way. Convened in December 1869, it met in final session less than nine months later, closing in September 1870, when the Franco-Prussian War made it difficult for the bishops to travel. Vatican I is remembered primarily for issuing a dogmatic constitution on the church which defined papal primacy and infallibility. (I'd bet you thought that was done many centuries earlier!)

Getting back to Pope John's fresh air project, it was his objective to open to review and possible revision all that came under the purview of Catholic belief and practice. He sensed that the "barque of Peter," like most vessels long at sea, now had a great many barnacles attached to its hull. Some practices had outlived their time. Once very meaningful to earlier generations, they resonated little if at all with late twentieth-century believers and remained more out of force of habit than anything else. The situation was akin to that described by Anthony de Mello, S.J., in his fable "The Guru's Cat" (*The Song of the Bird*, Image Books, 1984):

> When the guru sat down to worship each evening, the ashram cat would get in the way and distract the worshipers. So he ordered that the cat be tied during evening worship. After the guru died, the cat continued to be tied during evening worship. And when the cat expired, another cat was brought to the ashram so that it would be duly tied during evening worship. Centuries later, learned treatises were written by the guru's scholarly disciples on the liturgical significance of tying up a cat while worship is performed.

It's not unlike our own homes. Many of us have drawers, cabinets, closets, basements, garages, and attics that contain a peculiar assortment of items we no longer have any need for but haven't the heart to discard. In extreme cases, we can't even remember their original purpose.

Not everything can or should be classified a barnacle, of course. At the core of Catholic belief and practice are those elements which define us, which are the heart and soul of Catholicism and are, therefore, nonnegotiable. While acknowledging this to be so, Pope John wanted even these reexamined to see if, perhaps, they could be expressed in a manner more suitable, more intelligible to those whose life experience was either largely or entirely post-World War II.

During his days as a Vatican emissary, living in such dissimilar milieus as Bulgaria, Turkey, France, and Venice, Angelo Roncalli developed an expansive worldview. This perspective extended beyond political and cultural considerations to religious traditions as well since his work brought him into negotiations among Latin rite (Roman) Catholics, Eastern rite Catholics, and Orthodox Christians. He was also acutely aware of the attempted genocide of European Jews during Hitler's Third Reich.

As a result, it was crystal clear to John XXIII that the world that came out of World War II in 1945 was a vastly different place than the world that plunged into conflict in 1939. For better or worse, that prewar world was gone forever. For better or worse, it was the postwar world, a world in which nearly everything had changed, that humanity was now forced to contend with. To do this, old dogs, young dogs, all dogs had to learn new tricks in almost every area of life.

The pace of day-to-day life, revved up to previously unknown speeds during the war years, showed no sign of slowing. If anything, it was steadily climbing. More and more demands were made on ever more limited time slots. Personal and professional day planners became more or less permanent extensions of people's hands, and the blocks of time recorded in these books quickly filled to overflowing. Time became the most valuable commodity one possessed, and, needless to say, the prioritizing of this precious asset became a necessary life skill. That which was irrelevant or inconsequential would not be around long.

Could this fate befall religious faith as well? Pope John thought so. If modern Catholics could see no reason to allocate valuable time and effort to the practice of their faith, inevitably it would fall by the wayside. Oh, it would probably continue on some perfunctory level for a generation or two, again out of force of habit. But in due time, like an engine badly in need of refueling, it would slow, then stop.

Postwar Catholics needed to be shown in ways meaningful to them why this ancient faith should not only remain part of their lives, but be central to them. It was Pope John's hope that Vatican II would take the critical first steps in that direction:

- culling out that which had outlived its usefulness,
- restoring valuable rites and observances far older than Trent which had fallen into disuse but whose restoration would prove a boon to the modern church, and

- restating essential beliefs and practices in such a way that they would be grasped and retained in contemporary minds and hearts.

The council did accomplish much along these lines over three short years (October 1962–December 1965). In the end, sixteen documents were promulgated:

- four major constitutions, two pastoral and two dogmatic;
- nine decrees, including the *Decree on the Apostolate of the Laity;*
- three declarations, among them the landmark *Declaration on the Relationship of the Church to Non-Christian Religions.*

The papal signature on each was that of Paul VI who was elected to continue the council and the work of his predecessor after Pope John's death in June 1963, months before even the earliest of the council documents was finalized.

Collectively, the Vatican II documents at least partially achieved John's dream, closing the Counter Reformation fortress chapter of Catholic history and opening one more in keeping with the post-World War II years of the late twentieth century and beyond. And so the "interim" pope of whom so little was expected left an enviable legacy to his church and the wider world as well, his more insightful vision leading to more focused direction. As Bill Huebsch reminds his readers in *Praying with Pope John XXIII* (Saint Mary's Press, 1999):

Some writers and biographers have created the impression that Pope John XXIII was a simple peasant priest, raised suddenly and without preparation to the papacy. . . . Some have even thought of him as an innocent but bumbling fellow, out of touch with protocol and tradition. It is more accurate, however, to recognize that Pope John XXIII knew precisely who he was and what he was doing. . . . Pope John had faith. He had faith in the church, a common enough phenomenon in the pre-Vatican II period of Catholic history. But more important, he had faith in Christ, who is beyond the church. This wider faith in Christ allowed Pope John to see the church with a fresh perspective and with enough distance that he could judge it according to the Gospel and call it to renewal.

Renewal?

So the church was renewed, and everybody lived happily ever after? Well, not quite. In fact, not even close. Major change more often than not results in major confusion. Upheaval is followed almost instantaneously by uproar. Upon occasion it's followed by schism, where one or more factions pull away from the parent group and set out on their own. Fortunately, with the possible exception of France's Archbishop Marcel Lefebvre and his dissident followers, this didn't occur after Vatican II. Nearly everything else did, however.

Unless you were born before 1950, you really have no frame of reference for grasping the Catholic mindset during those first post-Vatican II days, especially the initial chaotic decade. Like any other historical period, secular or religious, it's one thing to read about it or even be told about it by those who were there; it's quite another to live through it.

Some opted for oversimplification, consigning everything before Vatican II to the archives of antiquity and accepting everything that emerged from the council as modern manna from heaven. Others took a diametrically opposite approach, vigorously defending any and all pre-Vatican II practices and staunchly refusing to accept anything that remotely smacked of Vatican II origin. The former group forgot that the church, like any venerable institution, is always at her best drawing on the finest assets from all eras of her considerable history, including the most recent. The latter group also forgot that the church is always at her best drawing on the finest assets of her considerable history, including the most recent.

Both camps meant well. Both made understandable blunders. The council's proponents, in their zeal to implement every single one of its directives instantaneously, cleaned the church's house with a vengeance, often dispatching items to the ecclesiastical garage sale long before anything existed to replace them. The council's opponents made every attempt to hold the fort with little consideration as to whether or not the particular "fort" they happened to be defending at the moment was worth the trouble. Needless to say, there was a yawning chasm separating the two groups and little attention paid to designing, let alone building, bridges. Volumes could be (and have been) written on these tumultuous years, but for our purposes here, it mostly boils down to "Why should you care?"

Why Should You Care?

The principal reason you should care is that all the ecclesiastical whoop and holler described above has mightily affected you whether you've been mindful of it or not. It has contributed remarkably to that Catholic inadequacy I wrote about a few pages above. Now don't misinterpret what I'm about to say. I'm an unabashed Vatican II aficionado, so much so that I view the council as the single greatest religious event of the twentieth century—not Catholic religious event exclusively, but religious event in the broadest possible sense of the word. But it wasn't perfect, and neither were the earnest-to-enthusiastic souls who worked their darnedest to get council dictums up and running.

As noted above, elements which probably really should have been disposed of were dispatched before anything much existed to replace them. Music fell victim to this industrious zeal practically overnight, wrenching us from the likes of Bach and Franck to what I used to term the "Row, row, row your boat" school of liturgical music. The culture shock was considerable. Before long, two saving graces emerged: the work of a new generation of immensely talented composers began to make its way onto the liturgical scene and, eventually, the glorious music of our past began to reappear. It would seem we've begun to find our way, and the path ahead holds great promise.

Another field that fell victim to precipitous, if well-meaning, haste was religious education, which encompassed both Catholic schools and parish programs, customarily called C.C.D. (Confraternity of Christian Doctrine). Granted, a lot needed to be done in this area. But, as any educator knows, entirely new courses of study are not envisioned one day and magically appear in classrooms the next. Quite the contrary. The time lag between concept and completion can be lengthy.

As a consequence, a number of years elapsed during which religion teachers and catechists were forced to deal with less than optimal materials. If those doing the instructing were struggling, it stands to reason that those being instructed were struggling as well. If the late

1960s and most of the 1970s were formative years for you and if you've found yourself dealing with the dreadful Catholic inadequacy syndrome, you may be putting two and two together and coming up with, *It's not my fault!* And you're right! Maybe it's nobody's fault individually and everybody's fault collectively. Who knows? And, to be honest, who cares? Assessing blame achieves nothing. The consequences of the outcome are what matter.

Although most would be reluctant to come out as bluntly as a bishop I heard speak on this topic at a national conference, he may not have been far off the mark. Said he: "The result was that we raised a generation of religious illiterates." If you're a member of the generation of which he speaks, don't take offense. *IT'S NOT YOUR FAULT!* (Is that Catholic inadequacy starting to recede even a little?)

What in the end proved true for music rescued the floundering field of religious education as well. Innovative and extremely competent religious educators were tapped by practiced publishers, resulting in a spate of new programs for every age level—as today's parish director of religious education might put it, from womb to tomb. Although a satisfactory religious education involves a good deal more than the availability of trustworthy classroom materials, these tools do at least make such training a possibility.

By this time, you may be protesting, "I'm not a member of that generation. I'm younger (or older). But I'm just as aware of a lack of grounding in my faith. What about me? Am I to blame? Do I get this Catholic inadequacy thing dumped in my lap?" Of course not!

Education is always a work in progress. It's never completed, and it's never flawless. This should come as no surprise to anyone who recalls with even minimal accuracy long hours spent in high school and/or college classrooms. Experiences ran the gamut from delectable to detestable and every variation in between. As is the case with secular studies, some came away far more challenged and enlightened than others.

So why not simply chalk it up to experience and move on with whatever you managed to carry away from those catechism/C.C.D./religious education classes? Because you wouldn't dream of doing this in most other fields of endeavor, knowing that it would somehow incapacitate you in today's fast-moving, high-tech world. You recognize the need to delve deeper, wander more widely merely to stay abreast of the constant changes around you. To use one of the current buzz terms, it's a "need to know," and on some level, you may sense it in the domain of religion as well. It may be nothing more than a hunch that there's a lot more to this than you have yet explored or experienced. Or it may be the disconcerting premonition that, if all this "God stuff" you keep hearing about is even half as important as it sounds, you should be paying considerably more attention to it. In either case, you'd be right.

Defining Moments Up the Ante

September 11, 2001, provided one of those rare moments when the world seemed to skid to a stop and focus its total attention on a single event. The remembrance of those horrific happenings is seared into the collective memory and recorded in surprising detail in those personal data banks tucked between the ears of everyone who heard of them, even young children. Making sense of such a catastrophe seems imperative and, at the same time, not entirely possible. Still, there is an almost gut-wrenching need to try.

Priorities get reordered in a hurry. What's important? What's vital? What's required for life? Faith, family, friends rise to the top of the pecking order like corks in a stormy sea. Knowing what to do regarding family and friends comes fairly naturally: bolster sagging relationships; repair broken ones; reestablish connection where neglect has taken its toll; above all, make certain those dear to us realize beyond question exactly how dear they are.

But faith? This may prove more difficult, especially if we haven't recently—or ever—dug down deep to find its roots. What grounds us? What do we really believe? Why? Can we center our lives on it? Would we want to? Who is God? *Where* is God at times like these? What do other great religious traditions—in this case, Islam—truly believe, as opposed to what we may wrongly presume? Where do we stand on common ground? Where must we agree to disagree?

It quickly becomes apparent that we need to know our own faith well, both in order to find our way through great tragedies without succumbing to despair and in order to move toward a world in which such calamities are no longer possible. Mature Catholic Christians can and should be firm in an informed faith and unshaken in their confidence in God even while joining others in a common grief and mourning. Our mantra may well be, "Thank God for God!"

What's with God, Anyway? Our Need to Know

The schools of thought regarding the existence of God or the importance of God in our lives are as diverse as those who raise the questions. Responses to the former range from, "Do you mean to tell me you still believe in God?" to "Nothing makes sense unless one acknowledges a great mind behind it all." On the latter point (which assumes some notion of God's existence), replies run from, "Something or someone is out there, but has little or nothing to do with me," to "God is the focal point of life, intimately involved in all its aspects." If you're reading this book, I suspect you harbor some conception of God, but everything else might easily be up for grabs.

Life would certainly be easier if God would just drop by for a personal visit (actually, that's what we believe happened when Jesus was born), present you with a copy of his autobiography and resumé, and then hold a Q & A seminar after you'd read them. At that point, you'd stand at least a chance of not only knowing something *about* God, but in fact *knowing* God.

Well, I'm sorry to have to break this to you, but it doesn't work this way. Although *everything* depends on our grasp of God, those of us who inhabit the planet at the moment are only the latest in a long line of mortals to grapple with the enigma and come up short. Face it. We are never going to get an adequate grip on God. Big surprise! How many of the very human beings in our lives do we comprehend completely? How well do we do scrutinizing ourselves? When was the last time someone you thought you knew very well said or did something which caught you completely by surprise? When was the last time *you* said or did something you couldn't believe you'd said or done?

The more years I rack up, the clearer Jesus' words on this matter become to me: "Do not judge, and you will not be judged" (Luke 6:37a). He didn't forbid us to make value judgments; we can and should do that. He simply cautioned that we are entirely incapable of comprehending, let alone judging, others—even ourselves. Paul underscored the same point:

"But with me it is a very small thing that I should be judged by you or by any human court. I do not even judge myself. I am not aware of anything against myself, but I am not thereby acquitted. It is the Lord who judges me" (1 Corinthians 4:3–4). If we must necessarily concede our inability to fully fathom even those most closely entwined in our lives, we should find it an easy segue to the recognition that we will never come even remotely close to grasping God (remembering that God is the creator and we are the created makes that a tad more palatable).

This does not, however, mean that we shouldn't try. We may have to settle for "grope" when we'd be eminently more comfortable with "grasp," but "grope" is all we're likely to get this side of the Great Divide, and it really has more going for it than you might think. Whatever the topic at hand, we pretty much grope our way through life. All our lives, we feel around our surroundings, trying to get a better handle on them and attempting to improve our skills at dealing with them. We're probably never going to know all there is to know about anything, even the subject matter in which we have the most aptitude and interest. But we keep trying; we keep learning; we keep running to get up to speed and stay there.

Learning to know about God and know God (which are two rather different things) is often frustrating. We're torn between, "We can't know anything" (a view espoused by some Far Eastern religions), and "We can know everything; we're just not trying hard enough" (a view espoused by those with a rather exalted view of the capability of the human brain). In between lies a huge amount of floundering as humanity, individually and collectively, strives to know what *can* be known and, even more challenging, to wrap finite intellectual resources around the infinite.

Suppose you drew the unlikely assignment of interviewing God. How would you begin? If it fell to me, I'd open with, "Tell us a little bit about yourself." Improbable interviews aside, does God ever do this in the real world? The three major Near Eastern religions (Judaism, Christianity, and Islam) all conclude that it's happening all the time.

ASIDE TO THE READER: Now that we have reached the point where God will be referred to on a regular basis, I need to apprise you of the pronoun problem. God, except when incarnate in Jesus, has no specific gender. References to God should reflect this neutral nature. But the English language makes this impossible since it contains no single neutral pronoun other than "it," which leaves something to be desired when describing real, live beings, human or divine. In tiptoeing around the dilemma, several techniques are sometimes used:

- inserting the noun *God* or its equivalent wherever a pronoun might (or should) be used—but this becomes so grammatically awkward after a while that it's just plain annoying;
- concocting such contrivances as "s/he" to indicate both/and—but this unravels when there arises the need for a noun as the object of a sentence or phrase ("s/him" doesn't work and is just plain strange);
- recognizing the limitations of language, any language, heaving a hearty sigh of resignation, and resorting to *he* and *him* as a concession; then, moving on to more pressing matters.

In this undertaking, we'll go with the last option as likely to cause the least mischief.

What Do We Know, and How Do We Know It?

That which can be known about God is called revelation. God's disclosure of himself to his human creatures is effected through any number of avenues. Among the most common are:

- creation: the natural condition on this planet and beyond;
- sacred writings: primarily the books of the Hebrew and Christian Scriptures;
- secular writings: everything from philosophy to fiction may reveal something of God; a prime example might be Fyodor Dostoevsky's classic, *The Brothers Karamazov*;
- those who share our human condition and who, because they are made in the image of God (more on this later), to some extent reflect God;
- and, for Christians, the ultimate revelation, Jesus, God incarnate (enfleshed).

Seldom, if ever, is revelation expeditious or effortless. Humanity has collected insights gradually over the whole of its history, a process which continues and will still be in progress when the sun sets on the final day of human history. God will never be entirely revealed to us in this life, which is just as well. Were we capable of fully comprehending God, then God would no longer be God.

On the other hand, it's terribly important to bear in mind that no words of Jesus, no words anywhere in Scripture ask us to believe blindly. Among our many gifts is rational thought, and we are not only permitted but expected to utilize it to its fullest extent. Unless we have a much too exalted perception of its capabilities, we don't have to worry about catching up with God anytime soon.

And This Leaves Us?

You are here conceivably because you identify with bits and pieces, dribs and drabs, of what's been said so far. This being the case, what can you reasonably expect from this book?

What not to expect comes easier:

- This is not a handy, dandy guide to all things religious.
- Neither is it a magic answer book replete with easy answers and quick fixes—there's no such thing.
- Nor is it a sure cure for a chronic case of Catholic inadequacy.

This said, what you *can* expect is an engaging journey through time as we examine what our forebears have learned and passed down to us and what they picked up along the way that spoke to them of God and what God was trying to tell them (revelation).

Some of this will be seen through the eyes of our far distant ancestors, some through the eyes of our Hebrew/Israelite/Jewish religious "grandparents," some through the eyes of Jesus, and some through the eyes of great religious traditions which are neither Jewish nor Christian. Such a sojourn may bring us finally to a more thoughtful awareness of where we are right now, how we got here, and what the implications of this may be for ourselves and the people we love, our associates and those for whom we assume responsibility . . . and for God's wider world in which we all live.

CHAPTER ONE

As It Was in the Beginning, Is Now, and Ever Shall Be

A young girl took her mother by surprise with the inevitable question, "Where did I come from?" Although she had hoped she wouldn't have to deal with the issue for a few more years, the mother dutifully put her work aside, sat down, and explained procreation on a par with the child's age and intellectual capacity. Pleased with her willingness to tackle difficult subject matter, the mother asked, "Now do you see?" to which her daughter replied, "I guess so. My friend at school comes from Minnesota, and I just wondered where I came from."

We're all curious about our origins, and sometimes we don't have much more luck getting a handle on the answer than the bewildered little girl. This puts us in good company, however. *Where did we come from?* is one of the Three Great (B-I-G) Questions which have been in the minds and on the lips of humans since that long-ago day when they were first capable of even the most rudimentary thought:

- Where did we come from?
- What are we doing here?
- Where are we going?

Every component of human life is inextricably tied to one or more of these basic queries. From humankind's ongoing attempts to deal with these questions come varying worldviews and concepts of God that will doubtless continue to grow and develop until the curtain falls on the final act of human history. Even then, those who follow us will still be grappling. Perhaps the last words heard will be, "But . . . ," "What if . . . ?" "Why . . . ?" "If that's true, then . . ." Controversy involving the "Big Three" will never end if for no other reason than every time we manage to solve one piece of the puzzle, it leads directly to a whole assortment of issues we didn't know enough to even ask about before.

The more we learn, the more aware we become of how little we really know. Some would say, myself included, that this suggests we are dealing with an infinite mind so far beyond our own noticeably finite intellects that there's no hope of bridging the yawning gap. True enough, but this doesn't mean we shouldn't go as far as we can. We live today as the recipients of our forebears' endeavors. In our time, we make our contribution and pass the accumulated knowledge on to those who will be the next inhabitants of planet earth.

Even though we live with the certainty that we will never entirely solve the mysteries suggested by the "Big Three," inquiring into them can be both fascinating and engrossing, not to mention extremely profitable. Although they can be approached from a number of perspectives, e.g., scientific or sociological, the twin realms of philosophy and religion may have the most to tell us.

The Bible Says . . .

The sacred writings of many of the earth's peoples hold a vast treasure of thought regarding the *where-what-when* triad. Certainly, the Hebrew and Christian Scriptures do. But before we can begin to plumb their depths, we need to have the proper tools in hand. Leaving aside for the moment the writings of other religious traditions, let's focus on how to perceive our own. Is there a recommended procedure? Indeed there is, and a popular name for it is the historical-critical method. Lest that sound ominously pedantic and plodding, stay the course a page or two, and it will begin to make sense.

First, we need to hit the rewind button and roll back in time to 1943. The Chair of Peter was occupied by Pius XII, and most of the earth's surface was engulfed in history's most horrific global conflict, World War II. Little wonder that an extraordinary encyclical promulgated that year received something less than the attention it merited. The encyclical was *Divino afflante Spiritu* ("On promoting biblical studies"). Although this document is frequently cited as the springboard of contemporary Catholic Scripture scholarship, it actually observed the fiftieth anniversary of a similar encyclical, *Providentissimus Deus* ("On the study of Holy Scripture"), penned by Leo XIII in 1893, the same pope who established the Pontifical Biblical Institute in 1909. But it is Pius XII's contribution that is generally credited with plunging Catholicism into the modern age of Scripture scholarship.

At this point, you'll have to forgive me if I yield to the temptation to take the road already nicely paved rather than carve a new one out of the verbal wilderness. I addressed this issue in the *Scripture from Scratch* Facilitator's Manual (St. Anthony Messenger Press, 1991), and inasmuch as I said there what I want to say here, I'm simply going to make the most of it here:

> Following centuries of using Saint Jerome's Vulgate (Latin) version of the Scriptures as the starting point for all biblical investigation, researchers were now free, even encouraged, to bypass Jerome's fifth-century work in favor of the much older Hebrew, Aramaic, and Greek manuscripts. (Although no original manuscript exists for any biblical book, Old Testament or New, texts of these books do exist in their original languages.)
>
> Not only did Pius XII open avenues of opportunity to translators, but he swung open the door leading to a variety of areas in biblical study. He stated categorically that a genuine understanding of the biblical books was impossible without considering the time period and culture from which they sprang, the type of literature the writers used, the audience for whom the books were originally intended, and the authors' intent in selecting particular themes.
>
> As soon as World War II ended and world conditions became somewhat stabilized, modern Catholic biblical study began in earnest. The 1960s brought the twentieth century's bellwether event for Catholics. Pope John XXIII changed the face of the church forever by convening the Second Vatican Council. To this

day, many Catholics view Vatican II primarily as the source of earthshaking changes in liturgical practice. Most of these were set down in the *Constitution on the Sacred Liturgy*.

Of equal importance in the eyes of Scripture enthusiasts, however, was the *Dogmatic Constitution on Divine Revelation (Dei verbum)* which underscored Pius XII's earlier teaching and expanded it even further. Regarding the use of the Bible for prayer and study by all Catholics and the availability of modern translations, the document reads:

> Access to sacred Scripture ought to be open wide to the Christian faithful. For this reason the Church, from the very beginning, made her own the ancient translation of the Old Testament called the Septuagint; she honors also the other Eastern translations, and the Latin translations, especially that which is called the Vulgate. But since the Word of God must be readily available at all times, the Church, with motherly concern, sees to it that suitable and correct translations are made into various languages (22).

Again emphasizing the approach to Scripture outlined in *Divino afflante Spiritu*, the council fathers said:

> Seeing that, in sacred Scripture, God speaks through men in human fashion, it follows that the interpreter of sacred Scriptures, if he is to ascertain what God has wished to communicate to us, should carefully search out the meaning which the sacred writers really had in mind, that meaning which God had thought well to manifest through the medium of their words.
>
> In determining the intention of the sacred writers, attention must be paid, *inter alia*, to "literary forms for the fact is that truth is differently presented and expressed in the various types of historical writing, in prophetical and poetical texts," and in other forms of literary expression. Hence the exegete must look for that meaning which the sacred writer, in a determined

situation and given the circumstances of his time and culture, intended to express and did in fact express, through the medium of a contemporary literary form. Rightly to understand what the sacred author wanted to affirm in his work, due attention must be paid both to the customary and characteristic patterns of perception, speech and narrative which prevailed at the age of the sacred writer, and to the conventions which the people of his time followed in their dealings with one another (12).

One more citation from *Dei verbum* helps the essentials of the Catholic approach to Scripture truly to emerge:

In order that the full and living Gospel might always be preserved in the Church the apostles left bishops as their successors. They gave them "their own position of teaching authority." This sacred Tradition, then, and the sacred Scripture of both Testaments, are like a mirror, in which the Church, during its pilgrim journey here on earth, contemplates God from whom she receives everything, until such time as she is brought to see him face to face as he really is. . . .

Sacred Tradition and sacred Scripture, then, are bound closely together and communicate one with the other. . . . Sacred Tradition and sacred Scripture make up a single sacred deposit of the Word of God, which is entrusted to the Church (7, 9, 10).

This sampling of the council document provides several insights into the mind of the church today respecting the Bible:

- The Bible is intended to be available to all the faithful.
- Translations should be invitingly readable and constantly updated as more and newer data become accessible.
- Understanding of biblical writings *must* take into consideration the times and circumstances in which they were composed, plus such related factors as their

literary style, the sources utilized, the culture, and the audience originally intended.

- For Catholics, the Bible does not stand as the sole source of divine revelation. The church stands today, as it consistently has, on the twin pillars of Scripture and Tradition, seeing in each the reflection of the other.

Historical Criticism

Motivated by the strong support of popes and bishops, Catholic Scripture experts moved rapidly to put the church in the forefront of contemporary Bible research. Today, Catholicism can take its proper place among other Christian traditions in the various areas of biblical endeavor.

The umbrella approach, which gained great favor among Catholic scholars as well as those from a number of mainline Protestant denominations, came to be called *historical criticism*. But for many average Catholics getting their first taste of Scripture scholarship, the word *criticism* is a stumbling block. Tending to associate the word more with fault finding than with examination, some back away from what seems to them an exercise in picking the Bible to pieces. In reality, the historical-critical method seeks to do what both Pope Pius XII and Vatican II recommended: analyze and evaluate the sacred books from as many angles as possible in order to extract every potential nuance of meaning. Historical criticism, then, is correctly viewed as a detailed investigation. To assess it as a hostile attempt at correction is to miss its meaning entirely. Quite a diversity of specialized studies falls under the historical-critical umbrella.

The thirst for biblical knowledge seems far from being slaked, and the church's Scripture pros are doing an admirable job of providing a continuing stream of commentaries, diction-aries, concordances, atlases, magazines, books, and computer formatted materials on any and all matters biblical.

Sadly, the majority of these works were not yet available when the initial biblical fervor burst upon the church immediately following Vatican II—solid, reputable materials were assembled as fast as possible, but not fast enough for some. Under the sincere but often erroneous assumption that a Bible study is a Bible study is a Bible study, large numbers of Catholics joined groups whose basic approach to the sacred books was fundamentalist—very far from that taken by the Church.

Again it should be stressed that the Catholic manner of viewing the Bible today is shared by a number of mainline Protestant traditions. Scripture professionals from many backgrounds are working together in this ecumenical age. Much of the unraveling of our common thread is past, thankfully, but interested parties on all sides agree that nothing is gained by ignoring honest differences or failing to address them. Such differences are real and must be acknowledged. It is therefore essential that every attempt be made to honor those beliefs which are strongly held by others while holding to our hearts those which are dear to us, all the while trusting that the Holy Spirit will in time overcome our divisions.

Having clearly established the church's endorsement of the historical-critical method of contemporary biblical research, it would be beneficial to examine a few of the areas of specialized study.

Form Criticism

Most of us are veterans of high school and/or college literature courses of one kind or another, so literary criticism should seem reasonably familiar. Simply put, it's the fine art of discovering what kind of book you're reading. Does it make a difference whether we realize that a work we believed to be history is in reality historical fiction? Obviously, it makes a *huge* difference. Our expectations will be totally different.

Margaret Mitchell's *Gone with the Wind* (reprint: Scribner, 1996) provides a familiar model. Did America experience a divisive war in the 1860s? Sadly, yes. Did General Sherman's forces make a devastating march through Georgia? Sadly, yes again. Did Rhett Butler and Scarlet O'Hara brave Atlanta's flames? Extremely doubtful. They are fictional characters placed is a historical setting. If we fail to grasp that very essential point, we are doomed to misread much of the story.

The Bible is often presumed to be a book. It's an understandable mistake because it does, after all, look like a book, feel like a book, sit on the shelf like a book. But this has only been the case since the fifteenth century when Johannes Gutenberg invented movable type. Originally, the "books" of the Bible were preserved orally, then consigned to papyrus or parchment scrolls, then to codices, the forerunners of modern books. Whatever the format, the crucial concept here is that there were many, many of them. This is what the word *Bible* means: "the books" or, my own preference, "a little library."

Like all libraries, except those of an extremely specialized nature, the Bible contains all manner of literary types; among them historical accounts, letters, satires, philosophy, song lyrics, poetry, proverbs, fiction, and myths. Fiction and myths? *In the Bible?* It's not as much of a surprise (or shock) as you might think, and we'll talk about it at length in the next chapter (ensuring that you will definitely read the next chapter).

Literary Criticism

"These five major concerns of elementary literary criticism—the words, the characters, the story or thought line, the literary form, the relation between form and content—can help the reader to enter the world of a written text and understand it more thoroughly than ever before." Wise words from Daniel J. Harrington, S.J., whose *Interpreting the New Testament: A Practical Guide* (Michael Glazier, 1979) has long been a valuable resource for Bible buffs. He continues: "To proceed without an initial understanding of the text's raw material (its words) is to court a final misunderstanding."

All too true, but easier said than done. A word in one language is not always the same word in another. There may not even be a corresponding word in the language into which the translator is moving the text. No two languages ever translate precisely word for word into one another. Not only do they not have the same kinds of words very often; they don't have the same number. And then there are all those idiomatic expressions. Every language has them, and English may well contain the mother lode. "I'm at the end of my rope." "Pitch it in File 13." "Put the pedal to the metal." How can these and hundreds like them be translated in such a manner that the possibility of correct interpretation is maximized and the possibility of distortion minimized? Dealing with "the text's raw material" is vital to the process of perception but can be excruciatingly difficult.

Textual Criticism

Again I turn to Harrington because nobody says it better:

> We have no manuscript of a biblical book written directly by its author. The texts that we do possess derive from the originals (or autographs) through a number of intermediary copies. And with each copying, the possibility and indeed the likelihood of mistakes or alterations entering into the manuscript tradition grow. Textual criticism seeks to produce a text as close to the original as is humanly possible.

If a number of copies of a particular biblical book still exist, chances are almost nil that they will be identical. A word, a phrase, a clause, a sentence, an entire passage may be present in some but not in others. Was this intentional? Accidental? The work of a sleepy scribe? The work of an editor with a personal agenda which may be furthered by tweaking the text a tad? Did someone decide to correct grammar or improve style? Was something added, or something deleted?

Just deciphering the text may be daunting. Ancient Hebrew was written without vowels. Sometimes, the context of the passage will make the choice obvious, but not always. If English were written only in consonants and you were faced with *bd*, what would you opt for? Bad? Bed? Bid? Bode? Abode? Abide? Bead? Bud? It would depend, of course, on the sense of the sentence. But if it's not immediately apparent from that, then what? The textual critic's lot is not an easy one.

It would seem reasonable to suppose that the older the manuscript is, the greater weight should be placed on its reliability on the grounds that it is closer in time to the original. Often, that's a valid supposition, but sometimes not. The older may have been copied from one manuscript less than carefully. The younger may have been copied from another manuscript meticulously.

In making these and a host of other judgment calls, the textual critic must be deeply sensitive to the tone of the original author and what he was trying to convey.

Source Criticism

This discipline is closely related to the first of the three great questions: Where did we come from? Here it probes a biblical book and asks: Where did it come from? Was there an earlier version of this work? For instance, some scholars believe that the gospel of Matthew we know today had a forerunner, which no longer exists, proto-Matthew. Has this book borrowed liberally from another or others? Today, it is accepted with virtual certainty that both the gospels of Matthew and Luke used Mark's earlier work extensively. Are influences at play here which have no biblical foundation whatever? The Genesis flood story is remarkably similar to the Mesopotamian Gilgamesh legend. Does this present a problem?

Neither Mark nor Luke was one of Jesus' inner circle of Twelve. Where did they get their material, especially Mark, since he was first out of the chute? Who did they talk to about what? The biblical era wasn't that different from our own. Literary works don't simply appear. They have writers, and sources. Because Christians believe the biblical books to be inspired, they sometimes act as though they thought the Bible fell fully formed, leather bound, and gilt-edged out of heaven into the waiting hands of Jesus' followers. That was not the scenario, and as yet, we don't know everything we'd like to about what was. Meanwhile, the source critics are on the case.

Historical Criticism

Devotees of this scholarly pastime spend their time asking: What really happened? Harrington again: "Historical criticism studies a narrative purporting to convey historical information to determine what actually happened insofar as this is possible."

We've already seen that not all, and quite possibly none, of the gospel writers were Jesus' companions and eyewitnesses to the events they describe. Even assuming some were on the scene, over thirty years had elapsed before any gospel writer put quill (or brush) to scroll. Memories can do tricky things in three or more decades. Paul wrote earlier, for the most part in the 50s, but he wasn't an eyewitness either. And this is just the relatively short Christian era.

Consider the sweep of some two millennia which makes up the Hebrew Scriptures (Old Testament). Consider as well that many of their oldest traditions were preserved orally for centuries, passed by word of mouth from generation to generation before finding their way into written form. Consider that there is a four-hundred-year silence between the end of the Book of Genesis and the opening of the Book of Exodus. And consider that the writers were not intent upon writing history in the first place. Why would anyone choose to be a historical critic?

Christians tend to zero in on Jesus. How much do we know, can we know about him as a historical figure? None of the gospels presents his biography nor intends to do so. There's that yawning silence between the episode in the Temple when Jesus was twelve that Luke tells us about and the start of Jesus' public ministry when he was roughly thirty. We'd love to fill in those eighteen years, but we can't.

It's easy to swing to either one end of the pendulum or the other, to say: "If the Bible says it, I'll take it at face value," or "There's absolutely nothing reliable in those archaic pages." The truth, as usual, lies somewhere in the middle ground, ground historical critics are covering with a fine-tooth comb.

Redaction Criticism

Back to Harrington:

> Redaction criticism proceeds from the realization that the New Testament writers' choice of material, [Harrington confines himself in this book to the Christian Scriptures] the order in which they placed what they had collected, and the alterations they made in the traditional material were determined to some extent by their theological outlooks. . . . The redaction critic wants to know what these traditional materials meant for the biblical writer and for the community in which he lived and for which he wrote, and why they have been modified. Redaction criticism is obviously the child of source criticism and form criticism.

It may be easier to see this area of study in action in the gospels than anywhere else because in these four accounts we have a somewhat similar story line. Take the infancy narratives as examples:

- Why does the earliest gospel, Mark, contain no reference to Jesus' birth?
- Did the author know nothing about it?
- Did he believe it to be of little consequence to his audience?
- Or did it simply not fit into his plan for the document he planned to write? (Mark virtually invented, probably inadvertently, the specialized literary form called gospel.)
- Why do we hear of singing angels, shepherds, census, mangers, and so on, only from Luke?
- Why magi, slain infants, and Egyptian sojourns only from Matthew?
- Why does John bypass Jesus' human birth almost entirely in favor of establishing his divine origins?

A redaction critic has a field day with all these whys and an infinite number of others.

Who Wrote the Bible?

By this time, you may well be wondering what happened to the notion that the Bible is divinely inspired. Well, it hasn't gone away, but, like a good many other religious ideas, it may require rethinking. It's not a matter of one almighty author versus a slew of human ones. There's a little more to it than that.

When I was a child, I remember seeing what must have been a fairly popular piece of religious art gracing the walls of homes I visited. It depicted a bearded man writing on a scroll. Over his shoulder hovered a rather large and formidable angel. *Hovered* is probably the wrong word as the angel had a death grip on the wrist of the writer, leaving no doubt where the material being written actually originated. I believe the bearded man was alleged to be Matthew, apostle and evangelist. However, the illustration made it abundantly evident that, whoever he was, he was merely a tool in the hand of a higher power—literally. It was as though God, finding it inconvenient being a disembodied spirit from time to time, set about locating a body to borrow long enough to write a book. As silly as it sounds, it's not far from commonly held belief.

To explain what we as a church do perceive inspiration to be, I turn to Margaret Nutting Ralph's *And God Said What?* (Paulist Press, 1986). If it seems as though I'm dragging in a host of collaborators in the course of this book, I am. My devious design, if indeed it is such, is to introduce you to extraordinary writers whom you may never have met so that, when you're looking for trustworthy names to help you with a special topic or you encounter these names while browsing either the Internet or "for real" bookstores, they will be old friends. You can't go wrong collecting an armchair library of these authors' works.

Well, before I was inspired to take off on that little side trip, we were addressing biblical inspiration. Ralph has this to say:

> Instead of thinking of inspiration as something that occurred between God and one writer, it is better to think of inspiration as occurring between God and each member of the community. The Bible, from beginning to end, is the product of God's acting in and through his people. God's inspiration, God's acting in the hearts and minds of his people, was present at every stage of the growth process which resulted in the Bible. At the time of the event it was God's inspiration which allowed the people to experience and interpret the event as a religious event. Those who were moved to speak and write about their religious experiences were inspired. Those who were moved to pass on, reinterpret and make contemporary the lessons from the past were inspired. The communities which accepted and responded to these written works, integrating them into their worship services and establishing them in a unique place of honor in their religious traditions, were inspired. A reader today who reads Scripture, who finds that it speaks to his or her heart, who allows it to take root, to form conscience, and to shape action is also inspired. God acts in and through his people; he breathes in and with them; he inspires them. The Bible is a fruit and a channel of inspiration.

Biblical inspiration, then, runs both more broadly and more deeply than is usually thought. It's not a matter of taking each individual word verbatim from the page and making it infallibly *the Word*. The perilous shoals of translation alone make this an impossibility even if it were a desirability, which it is not. To make thoughts, and the exact terminology in which they are expressed, sacrosanct is to restrict, even eliminate theological and secular growth and development. Not for us is the dubious perspective of a woman who, faced with a newer English translation, made her own firm stance clear, "If the King James Version was good enough for Saint Paul, it's good enough for me!"

Back to the Big Three

Having completed a somewhat lengthy side trip through methodology, we are now better equipped to examine these Big Three Questions. Nonetheless, a disclaimer of sorts is still necessary. The Bible is not a magic answer box, containing the answers to every question the human mind can form. The conviction is that the answers are in there somewhere if we just know where to look, just know how to understand what we're reading, just know the coded language which will reveal it all. Returning again to our academic "lit" courses, we recall that it is unreasonable to expect any literary work to be something it was never intended to be. The Bible is not the be all and end all of God's revelation, nor does it ever make this claim. The hallowed books it contains are among our greatest treasures, but God is revealed in other ways as well, i.e., Tradition, creation, the people around us, sacraments, and prayer. Therefore, an inquiry into the Big Three Questions should lead us to seek clues wherever and however God is revealed.

Where Did We Come From?

Other questions begin to surface almost before we get the big one out of our mouths:

- Did prehistoric people have any sense of a force, a mind, a being greater than themselves? How do we know?
- Did these same people possess some notion that there is more to life than what we are living here and now? How do we know?
- Were prehistoric people really people?
- When, how, and where did the first humans come into being?

- What defines a human being, and how does this differ from other life forms on our planet?
- Is the fact that we exist at all merely random chance, or were we specifically created?
- *If* we were created, by what—or whom?
- If we were created by someone, does this imply that we are responsible to someone?
- Is it possible to know this someone? If so, how?
- Is it possible to have a relationship with this someone? If so, what?
- Who am I, and what is humanity, in respect to this someone?
- *Who am I?*

What Are We Doing Here?

If the first question has us running around in tight little circles making high, squeaky noises, the second is worse:

- Does life have a purpose, or did we, like the fictional Topsy, just grow?
- Does it matter how we live our lives?
- Are some choices preferable to others? Why? What are the criteria?
- How is morality defined, and what constitutes a moral existence?
- Is ethical behavior a relative matter?
- Is there such a thing as objective truth? If so, can we know what it is?

Most theological discourse in any religion comes down to a search for the meaning of life. The conclusions drawn from contemplating these questions and others like them in large part determine religious belief and practice no matter where in the world it is found.

Where Are We Going?

As Peggy Lee once inquired in plaintive melody: "Is that all there is? Is that all there is? If that's all there is, my dear, then let's keep dancing . . . and have a ball if that's all . . . there . . . is." It's the wistful sigh, breathed down the long corridor of time. Well?

- Where do we go from here? Anywhere? Nowhere?
- Is what we regard as death in reality the supreme birth experience?
- Are mortals ultimately immortal?
- If so, what kind of existence can be expected beyond this one?
- Will we endure as individuals or become one with some sort of world soul?
- What is the ultimate value of human life?

These inquiries merely prime the cerebral pump. Trust me, others will pop up faster than dandelions in spring. But for now, let's tear a fresh page from the pad and see what we can "create."

CHAPTER TWO

In the Beginning, God

T
hese four deeply profound words open the Book of Genesis in two current English translations, the *Revised English Bible* *(REB*, Oxford University Press, 1998) and the *New Jerusalem Bible (NJB*, Doubleday, 1985). Not only is it hard to envision phraseology more expressive, there is a strong temptation on my part to wish they'd stopped right there. All we really know about where we came from is contained in this one splendid assertion: "In the beginning, God!" All else is commentary—many, many words uttered and/or written over millennia in an always inadequate attempt to explain: "In the beginning, God!"

"Mything" the Point

People of all times and places have spent a good deal of time thoughtfully addressing the issue of origin. In and of itself, this is not particularly surprising since it's the first of the Big Three Questions. It's how they've done it that may initially raise an eyebrow or two. If all realms and religions, civilizations and clans, possess an ancestral account of their beginnings, we'd expect them to be vastly different, and we'd be right. We might also expect them to take a number of diverse literary forms, and we'd be wrong. Surprisingly, each and every one is the same genre—it's a myth.

Now wait a minute; surely this can't be true of the Genesis accounts. They're in *the Bible!* True enough, but didn't we agree earlier that biblical truth can and does take many literary forms? Perhaps, but if we allow for the possibility of biblical myths, are we not also allowing for the possibility that scriptural creation stories aren't true? If we are, it's because we're "myth"ing the point of this literary device. Myths are always true; they just aren't factual. Myths hold within them some of the most profound truths of God and nature, but rarely are they data based.

Once we stop hyperventilating and really think about it, it soon becomes clear why the tales of human origin have long been interwoven with mythical elements. Our "Just the facts, Ma'am" culture shakes its head disbelievingly when asked to place its trust in that which cannot be scientifically documented. And this is not always a bad thing. Technological tools such as space probes, satellites, and the Hubble telescope have taught us more in the past few decades about the universe and its possible origins than all of prior human history. The term "Big Bang" is familiar even to children and serves to begin the search for the real story behind the foundation of creation. But we're a long way from possessing the whole story even now.

Imagine what it was like for ancient peoples whose ideas of their universe were very different indeed. They believed in creation, of course. How could they not? It surrounded them on every side; they were intimately part and parcel of it every waking hour. In many ways, it determined how their lives were lived. But where did it come from? How did it get here? What, if anything, was behind it all? Specific details were unknown. Eyewitness accounts were a little sparse as well. How best, then, to at least try to illustrate this undeniable truth? How about incorporating what *is* known into a story? Great idea! Everybody loves stories. What's more, they *remember* them and retell them generation after generation.

Telling the Story

The Book of Genesis opens that section of the Bible known either by the Hebrew name Torah (variously translated *instruction* or the *Law*) or the Greek Pentateuch (five books). Along with Exodus, Leviticus, Numbers, and Deuteronomy, Genesis records the most primitive Judeo-Christian lore. Here are found narratives that existed for centuries before finding their way into writing.

Western minds place little stock in oral tradition. Memory, perhaps, returns to childhood birthday parties and a game of "Telephone" involving the transmission of a single sentence from lip to ear all around the room. When the last person repeated aloud the whispered message received, it rarely bore any resemblance to the original transmission. We then dismiss this form of communication as untrustworthy, never stopping to consider that for preliterate societies, the spoken word, often memorized, was the only means of preserving the story of a family, a village, an entire people.

Many modern Bibles preface the first chapter of Genesis with a subhead reading either "Primeval" or "Prehistory." This subsection continues from Genesis 1:1 to 11:26 and includes the tales of creation, humanity's fall, the great flood, and the Tower of Babel—a heritage as old as the people themselves, a heritage rich in truth but short on verifiable certitudes.

Source critics have identified four principal strands of tradition within the Torah accounts. Peter Ellis in *The Men and the Message of the Old Testament* (Liturgical Press, 1976) has assigned a color to each source and laid out passages from the Torah so that the color coding indicates how they were assembled during the writing process. Why so many sources? Was oral tradition unreliable after all? Actually, it's only natural that variants would occur among the Israelite tribes when we remember that the rapid transit and instant communication we take for granted today were not so much as imagined during the bulk of human history.

Faced with differences, sometimes contradictions, the scribal editors had three choices:

- include one version and discard the other,
- merge two accounts into a single story line (the flood story),
- lay both renderings into the text side by side (the creation accounts).

Suddenly, the reality that there are two stories of creation and that they bear no resemblance to one another is more easily reconciled. They couldn't be more different, but they both have deeply religious truths embedded within them.

Seven-Day Week = 365-Day Year

Genesis' first chronicle of creation is set within the framework of a seven-day week. Historical criticism suggests to Catholics and mainline Protestants that this is a literary device, not a scientific premise.

Maintaining that this explanation of the planet's origins is to be taken literally is known as "creationism." This view is generally held by more evangelical congregations.

"In the beginning, God . . ." affirms from the first phrase of the first sentence of the first chapter of the first book of the Bible that there is an intelligence whose capabilities we cannot begin to fathom behind everything that is. Although I rarely think of the Nobel Prize winning physicist Albert Einstein as a stand-up comic, I laugh out loud whenever I run across this comment attributed to him: "The probability of life originating from accident is comparable to the probability of the unabridged dictionary resulting from an explosion in a printing shop."

Using the seven-day week as a sort of flow chart which would accommodate the other necessary elements was a stroke of genius. Those who would first hear it and later read it would be almost sure to get it. It's a universally familiar concept. How better to bring colossal events within the scope of human vision than to situate them in an every-day (in this case, seven-day) setting.

An almost identical technique was used by the late astronomer Carl Sagan. In *The Dragons of Eden* (Random House, 1978), Sagan set about telling those of us unaccustomed to dealing in light years what the known history of the universe would look like if laid out in a hypothetical calendar year. He didn't mean to imply that all of creation and all of human history took place in a year but only that it's easier to see the relativity of time spans when they're displayed on a common calendrical grid. These few samplings from Sagan's "calendar" demonstrate the point.

Carl Sagan's "Cosmic Calendar"

- January 1   Big Bang
- May 1   Origin of the Milky Way galaxy
- September 9   Origin of the solar system
- September 14   Formation of the earth
- September 25   Origin of life on earth
- December 1   Significant oxygen atmosphere begins to develop on earth

- December 19   First fish and vertebrates
- December 21   First insects; animals begin colonization of land
- December 22   First amphibians; first winged insects
- December 23   First trees; first reptiles
- December 24   First dinosaurs
- December 26   First mammals
- December 27   First birds
- December 28   First flowers; dinosaurs become extinct
- December 29   First primates
- December 30   First hominids; giant mammals flourish
- December 31   10:30 P.M.—First humans
               11:00 P.M.—Widespread use of stone tools
               11:46 P.M.—Domestication of fire
               11:59 P.M.—Extensive European cave painting
               11:59:20—Invention of agriculture
               11:59:50—First dynasties of Sumer and Egypt
               11:59:51—Invention of the alphabet
               11:59:56—Birth of Jesus
               11:59:59—Renaissance in Europe
- January 1 A.M. (first second)—Today's world

Rearranges one's thinking, doesn't it? For me, it utterly destroys any notion of ancient history. In the overall scheme of things, we haven't really been on the scene long enough to have any! And if, as some scientists believe, Sagan's hypothetical year in actuality encompasses roughly fifteen billion years, even the longest human life is barely a breath. Wow!

This is what the first biblical creation account intends as well—to make us go, "Wow!" God should be wowing us on a regular basis. If this isn't happening, something's wrong. That something may well boil down to the simple, if embarrassing, conclusion that we just aren't paying attention. A phrase that surfaces frequently in biblical writing is "Fear of the Lord." *Fear* in this case might better be translated "awe." We don't cower in fright before our God; rather, we drop to our knees in awe. Awe is merely another term for wow.

Creation or Creationism

This is all well and good, but it still doesn't entirely spell out why we believe firmly in both creation and its creator while opting for a nonliteral interpretation of the biblical accounts. If we take a closer look at the text, it may be more evident.

If a people's worldview is a major factor in determining their religious outlook, then the first thing that needs to be established is that the ancient Israelites saw their surroundings much differently than we do today. They can be excused for an error or two inasmuch as they lacked the space probes, satellites, and Hubble telescope spoken of earlier. While this is said tongue in cheek, it's no less true. One of my Scripture professors pounded this idea into us with such force that I still remember it more or less verbatim: "The first thing you need to do when studying the Bible, especially the Old Testament, is shed your twentieth-century American skin." By this he meant that if we impose on people of other times and places the standards and learning of our own, we will not only be wholly unfair to them but doom ourselves to misinterpretation as well. They dealt with what was known *then*, not what is common knowledge *today*. Before we make some condescending comment intended to reveal our obvious superiority, we might do well to bear in mind that some centuries down the line, others will have to cut us some slack on the grounds that we simply didn't know any better.

No Israelite Astronauts

People of the ancient Near East didn't seek their place in the universe—they were the universe. The earth itself was perceived as flat, supported by pillars whose foundations were sunk into the depths. This below-ground realm came to be known as *Sheol* or the nether (under) world. The earth's pillars are mentioned in a number of biblical books, among them 1 Samuel 2:8, Job 9:6, and Psalm 75:4.

Arching over the earth was a dome called the firmament (see Job 37:18, Psalm 19:2, Sirach 43:10, Ezekiel 1:22, 23, 26, and Daniel 12:3). The firmament was very real and would have ended a prospective astronaut's career in a matter of seconds. Across it traveled the sun by day and the moon by night. Through it the stars shone and precipitation fell.

Above the firmament was the Abode of the Gods (plural)—eventually to the Hebrew mind, God (singular). While we smile at such a primal picture of earth and its immediate neighbors, notice how much of the terminology, hence the thinking, remains with us today. We still speak of the four corners of the earth, fully aware that these are nowhere in evidence. Dawn is sun*rise;* dusk, sun*set.* In *Prayers for a Planetary Pilgrim* (Forest of Peace Publishing, 1988), Edward Hays proposes that these pivotal times of day be christened morning and evening turn-around:

> And night could be called "look-out," as we see before us the billions
> of stars and those limitless vistas of the universe. . . . Look-back,
> as day might be called, turns our attention away from our larger
> destination and gives us an opportunity to look at that massive
> nuclear-powered star we call the sun. It is the engine that propels
> our cosmic colony of planets, the solar system, out into the darkness
> of space. We rely so fully on its majestic power and seemingly
> endless endurance that we have made this daystar divine, or at
> least a symbol of that mystery we call by countless names.

Should you stand outside your parish door of a Sunday morn and inquire of those entering the general geographical locale of hell, rare would be the person whose index finger would not point emphatically down. Conversely, if you were to ask directions to heaven, those same fingers would unswervingly reverse course and call your attention to that which lies above—whatever that might turn out to be. Now this works very well while we remain in the flat earth mode where "up" is predictably up, and "down" is predictably down. It loses something, however, as soon as the idea of a sphere orbiting a star moving with a solar system comes into play. Which end is up?

Still, the call of vintage imagery continues to exert its pull in ways both subtle and traditional. Ecclesiastical architecture has long favored exterior spires and steeples which tend to lead the eye—guess where? Gothic churches, for all their stately beauty, abound in interior arches and windows, all of which point—you guessed it. Even in secular parlance, the realms above are regularly referred to as "the heavens."

If you sense here an uphill battle, you're right. And it may not even be a battle worth fighting. The human mind doesn't do well with abstracts when it comes to this sort of thing. One picture is worth a thousand theologians. So there's nothing really wrong with imagery, even outmoded imagery, providing we recognize it for what it is: *imagery!* As a friend used to say when we were overestimating the importance of a bit of television footage we were shooting, "It's only a movie." Right! It's only a picture, an image. As long as we keep fumbling our way toward a clearer understanding of the reality behind the image (and maybe acquiring a newer, more accurate image along the way), we'll be all right.

And when we read, "And God said, 'Let there be a dome in the midst of the waters, and let it separate the waters from the waters' " (Genesis 1:6), we don't swing to one end of the illustrative pendulum and declare that it's nonsense and has nothing to tell the modern world, or to the other end and assert that it must literally have happened exactly that way. We allow the text to speak as what it really is, a means of explaining a great truth within the boundaries of the information available at the time, not as a science text which it most decidedly is not.

God Creates Everything

"In the beginning, God" really does say it all when it comes to our origins. But since it was submitted earlier that great truths undergird these age-old myths, perhaps we should look at a few.

The first is the heart and soul of this first biblical narration. God creates *everything!* Note the verb tense. While past tense is probably more commonly used, it sends entirely the wrong message. Creation isn't over. As I write this, it is April. The first insect has yet to take the first bite out of the fresh new leaves adorning every tree and shrub. The crabapple tree in the backyard is so laden with pink petals that it bends toward the ground to let us see them better. Each spring shower seems to rain green paint, so emerald is the grass the next morning.

Creation a thing of the past? Not likely when it is creation that first conveyed God's message to us that death is never the end; wherever death seems to be having the last word, as during winter, stay tuned; more life, greater life is on the way. Edward Hays would have us see it this way in *The Gospel of Gabriel* (Forest of Peace Publishing, 1996):

> [Creation] was and continues to be the first inspired Scripture.
> Creation contains not simply a prophecy of the resurrection, but

proof of it! Creation's revelation is simple, but profoundly hopeful: nothing dies; it only changes form. Energy, the basic ingredient from which everything is made, cannot be destroyed or killed. . . . The pascal mystery of the passion, death, and resurrection is written boldly across all of creation for those with eyes to see.

For all we know, creation may be endless. It's what God "does for a living." Through the eye of the Hubble telescope as it eavesdrops on portions of the universe humans have never before been privy to, we have actually witnessed the birth of stars. And the number of these stars is legion. Once more, the notions we may hold more from habit than any real commitment come in for a reality check. Our ancestors may be excused for thinking themselves the center of the universe. So far as they knew, they were. So if something were to happen which would demolish the world they knew, that would be the end of everything. Some of this thinking continued to hold sway as the new millennium dawned, causing a collective holding of breath among those who feared it would signal the end of the world, the end of everything.

Today, far from seeing ourselves as the center of the universe, we can barely find our little blue marble in space on a celestial map. Will there someday be an end to our world? There most assuredly will be when that great furnace that is our daystar, the sun, inevitably cools. Scientists, thankfully, assure us that it's good to go for quite a while, so we can relax on this score. We're probably a greater danger to ourselves than any exterior force could ever be. Regardless of when or how it happens, when our home planet reaches the end of its run, who is to say that new stars, other planets may not be coming into being. Will they support life? Only God's endlessly creative mind knows. But one constant will remain: God creates everything.

Creation Is Good

Beyond the simple truth that creation is lies the deeper awareness that creation is *good*. Seven times during the theoretical seven-day week (seven being the perfect number according to ancient Near Eastern belief), observations of this nature are made: "And God saw that the light was good" (Genesis 1:4a); "And God saw that it was good" (Genesis 1:10b, 12b, 18b, 21b, 25b); and finally, "God saw everything that he had made, and indeed, it was very good" (Genesis 1:31a). Does this have any real significance, or is it merely an exercise in redundancy? In reality, it could scarcely be more significant, but before exploring this, allow me to step outside the text long enough to explain that the a/b designations attached to the Genesis verses above constitute the standard manner of designating the first or last part of a particular verse.

Meanwhile, back at creation, the issue of whether it is inherently good or evil has ceaselessly colored religious thought and continues to do so today. Implied in the determination of which of those elements is dominant in creation is which of those elements is dominant in human nature. Given a choice (and we face dozens daily), are we more predisposed to virtue or vice? When we individually or collectively blow it badly, those among us who take a dim view of the human condition mutter, "What did you expect?" while those who subscribe to the Genesis vision are more inclined to murmur quietly, "We can and should do better."

Stewardship = Responsibility

"Then God said, 'Let us make humankind in our image, according to our likeness; and let them have dominion over the fish of the sea, and over the birds of the air, and over the cattle, and over all the wild animals of the earth, and over every creeping thing that creeps upon the earth' " (Genesis 1:26). This passage has habitually been rendered something like, "We're in charge; it all belongs to us, and we can do anything we darn well please." Only in recent years have we been brought to the realization that we are intended to be less proprietors than stewards of our lush and lovely planet.

Stewardship is light on privilege, heavy on responsibility. Stewards are seen more as managers in both testaments, and occasionally the term is translated this way: "And the Lord said, 'Who then is the faithful and prudent manager whom his master will put in charge of his slaves, to give them their allowance of food at the proper time?' " (Luke 12:42).

Western civilization especially comes late to care for the environment. Others have seen their ecological duties earlier and more clearly. When the United States government wished to purchase a great swath of land in the Northwest during the 1850s, Chief Seattle made an eloquent and urgent plea to the American president. In part, he said:

> Every part of this earth is sacred to my people. Every shining pine needle, every sandy shore, every mist in the dark woods, every meadow, every humming insect. All are holy in the memory and experience of my people. We know the sap which courses through the trees as we know the blood that courses through our veins. We are part of the earth and it is part of us. . . .
>
> Will you teach your children what we have taught our children? That the earth is our mother? What befalls the earth befalls all the [children] of the earth. This we know: the earth does not belong to man; man belongs to the earth. All things are connected like the blood that unites us all. Man did not weave the web of life; he is merely a strand in it. Whatever he does to the web, he does to himself. One thing we know; our god is also your god. The earth is precious to him, and to harm the earth is to heap contempt on its creator. . . .
>
> We love this earth as a newborn loves its mother's heartbeat. So, if we sell you our land, love it as we have loved it. Care for it as we have cared for it. Hold in your mind the memory of the land as it is when you receive it. Preserve the land for all children and love it, as God loves us all (*The Good Earth*, Sacred Heart League, 1990).

To Life!

The traditional Jewish toast "To life!" would make a fitting finale to the first creation story. What God ultimately creates is life in myriad forms, all of them intricately related and completely dependent on God for existence. There is, then, order in creation. All subsequent religious questions will bear directly or indirectly on the meaning of life. How should it be defined? What is its value? How long does it last? How should it be lived? The initial attempts to wrestle with such matters will be rudimentary, but they will develop over the centuries until the pages of the Christian Scriptures unfold a vista of life that never ends, that life once created is never destroyed. Precisely what does this mean? We're still working on it, and always will be. To life!

God: Creator, Not Creation

As much as we may revere creation, we do not worship it. If this seems both a strange and an obvious allegation, the veneration of nature in its many forms is among the oldest forms of religion. Adoration of the sun may have been the earliest and most common of these practices, for its indispensable character was impossible to ignore. Sun = life. No sun = death.

Until well into recorded history, those who dwelt in northern latitudes held religious celebrations at the time of the winter solstice. The centerpieces of these festivities were gigantic bonfires, lighting the dark sky of the long, long night as a reminder to the sun to return. Christians eventually came to observe the birth of Jesus near that time of year, thereby "baptizing" the Roman festival of Saturnalia by diverting attention from the rebirth of the sun to the birth of the Son.

Scheduled between December 17 and 23, this traditional holiday of the world's greatest super power during the early Christian era was characterized by the close of businesses, the temporary emancipation of slaves, the exchange of gifts, and a general air of revelry. I only mention this to illustrate the manner in which feasts long associated with one religious tradition are sometimes appropriated by another and given an entirely distinct identity.

Religions which worship elements of nature are termed "animist" because they believe in some type of supernatural spirit inhabiting and animating all living things (plant and animal life). Some extend this to nonliving things (stones, water, air, fire, etc.)

The God of Genesis as seen in the first creation account exists entirely apart from that which he has made. God has no need of any created thing. God *was* before creation came to be; God *is* while creation continues; God *will be* when creation is no more. God and only God is eternal. But the life God creates is immortal; in other words, it began at some point even if it will not end.

Science tells us that matter is never obliterated. It merely changes form. Christian theology tells us that human beings are never obliterated either though we see a somewhat singular future for them: eternal life with God (a concept which will take most of biblical history to unfold). Humanity, then, is immortal. As we hear in Preface I from the *Mass of*

Christian Burial: "The sadness of death gives way to the bright promise of immortality. For your faithful people life is changed, not ended. When the body of our earthly dwelling lies in death, we gain an everlasting dwelling place in heaven."

Even given this thrilling prospect, we need to bear in mind that we are created beings, and the God who is our creator exists above, beyond, and entirely apart from all created things. This doesn't mean that God has no interest in creation, no love for it, no interaction with it. It simply means that God has no need of it.

Thinking about Creation Has "Evolved"

In 1859, a major earthquake shook the world to its seismic core. Granted, it wasn't the kind of tremor that would have registered on the Richter scale, but it set off global upheaval nonetheless. It was the publication of Charles Darwin's *On the Origin of Species*. From its pages sprang the premise that has both captivated and confused all kinds of folks ever since, especially those of the religious and scientific communities. Some rejected it out of hand as balderdash and poppycock. Some embraced it unreservedly. Others either came down somewhere between the polar opposites or closed their eyes (and minds) to the prospect altogether. Unhappily, these attitudes remain basically unchanged a century and a half later.

How might we go about determining a reasonable position on this matter? The logical point of departure for God-centered people who think would almost have to be: How does what is known of God come into play here? What has God revealed about his nature that surfaces here? What attributes of God are conspicuous here?

ADMONITION: It is essential to take great care to see God as God has been revealed. Like any of us, God has certain traits because God is real. We may have the freedom to think, but we are not free to make up a God who suits us. As an unnamed wit once aptly observed, "We were made in the image of God and have been reversing the process ever since."

First and always foremost to my mind is God's benevolence. Unlike the many gods of the ancient polytheistic world, this God is on our side. This is not a hostile or even indifferent deity. Bottom line: It would be unfaithful to the nature of such a God to set up a situation in which we could not possibly succeed.

God is also truth. Wherever truth is found, whether in the religious or secular arenas, it must reflect God. Blend this quality with the loving kindness mentioned above, and another conclusion is unavoidable. It would betray God's nature to set up two parallel lines of "truth" which are incapable of interacting or interrelating, call one *Science* and one *Religion,* and essentially tell us, "Have fun, guys; pick one."

Confining ourselves to only these two attributes of revelation, we are led to one conclusion: Science and religion must somehow relate to one another. Attempting to ascertain this relationship and build on it has never been easy. A real marriage of the two has failed to result. The factions from time to time concede a certain cohabitation, but the more expected outcome has been separation, if not outright divorce.

Into this acutely dysfunctional state of affairs strides Professor of Theology John F. Haught, director of the Georgetown Center for the Study of Science and Religion, with a rejuvenating vision for the twenty-first century and beyond. In *God after Darwin: A Theology of Evolution* (Westview Press, 2000), Haught suggests that what is lacking in both of these competing ideologies is the notion of novelty, a necessary component of evolution and the essence of the unfolding of divine mystery. He argues that Darwin's disturbing picture of life, instead of being hostile to religion—as scientific skeptics and many believers have thought it to be—actually provides a most fertile setting for mature reflection on the idea of God. Two excerpts from Haught's work will serve to provide a taste of his assertions:

> As long as we think of God only in terms of a narrowly human notion of "order" or "design," the "atheism" of many evolution-ists will seem appropriate enough. Evolution does indeed upset a certain sense of order; and if "God" means simply "source of order," even the most elementary perusal of the fossil record will render this ancient idea suspect. But what if "God" is not just an originator of order but also the disturbing wellspring of novelty? And, moreover, what if the cosmos is not just an "order" (which is what "cosmos" means in Greek) but a still unfinished *process?*

Suppose we look carefully at the undeniable evidence that the universe is *still* being created. And suppose also that "God" is less concerned with imposing a plan or design on this process than with providing it with opportunities to participate in its own creation. If we make these conceptual adjustments, as both contemporary science and a consistent theology actually require that we do, the idea of God not only becomes compatible with evolution but also logically anticipates the kind of life-world that neo-Darwinism biology sets before us.

Haught moves aside from his principal flow of ideas to reflect:

As a Roman Catholic I learned from an early age that there can be no genuine conflict between scientific truth and religious faith. I consider it my good fortune to have been advised throughout my life that believers in God should not look to biblical texts or religious creeds for information of a scientific nature. For many Catholics and other Christians this simple instruction has been the source of both religious and intellectual liberation. By allowing us to distinguish clearly between the literal and religious senses of scripture, it implies that we do not have to place the cosmology of Genesis in a competitive relationship with Darwin's theory. The Bible is not trying to teach us science, but beneath and through its historically conditioned cosmological depictions it is inviting us to share a vision of ultimate reality that does not depend for its plausibility upon any particular view of nature. Throughout the past three thousand years, ideas about God have, in fact, outlived potential absorption into many different cosmologies.

Gardening with Genesis

Thus far, nothing has been said about the second account of creation recorded in Genesis 2:4b–3:24. This version is generally considered much older than the first and springs from a completely different oral tradition. Whereas the seven-day week story is usually attributed to what is called the priestly tradition and reflects a certain elegance of style, the Garden of Eden tale comes from what it known as the "J" or J(Y)ahwist

(German scholars spell Yahweh with a "J") strand—so called because Yahweh is the name by which God is known in this rendering. This, therefore, is part of the Bible's earliest lore, finding its way into writing perhaps during the reign of Solomon in the tenth century B.C.E. (Before Common Era). And within it nestle elements of a much older, prebiblical rendition. Gone is the lofty language of God proclaiming, "Let there be. . ."

Enter stage left Adam, Eve, the serpent, the garden, the tree, and all manner of enchanting characters not so much as alluded to in account #1. Lions and tigers and bears; oh my! What have we here?

You might say we have utopia, paradise not in a global setting, but in a very specific "garden in Eden, in the east" (Genesis 2:8a). Eden does itself mean "fertile garden." Across the Fertile Crescent stretching from Mesopotamia to Egypt where the earth congenitally thirsted and water was by far the most precious commodity, there could be no more readily accepted notion of Shangri-La than a luxuriant garden sustained by fresh, life-giving water. A water supply which flows freely rather than being drawn from wells or stored in cisterns is often called living water in biblical texts. Eden is, in effect, an oasis. The Islamic concept of paradise sounds very much like this. Islam, of course, arose in what is today Saudi Arabia. Whether or not Eden was patterned on an actual locale is open to conjecture, but again we need to keep in mind that we are reading a myth, one with allegorical overtones—and puns.

In Hebrew, *adam* means "man" or "human." This *adam* is "formed . . . from the dust of the ground" (Genesis 2:7a), *adamah*. Plays on words are almost always lost in translation. The woman's name is defined by the text: "The man named his wife Eve, because she was the mother of all living" (Genesis 3:20). Does the serpent represent evil incarnate? The wording does not say that. It simply states that it "was more crafty than any other wild animal that the Lord God had made" (Genesis 3:1a). And it talks! Inasmuch as this is a mythic scenario, this is acceptable.

Is This Story True?

Recalling that myths are always true, that they just aren't factual, what does the second creation account have to tell us? We'll turn first to Dianne Bergant, C.S.A., for some insights. "We all come from God. This is first and most important," writes Bergant in her *Scripture from Scratch* article, "You'll Never Believe What Happened in the Garden" (St. Anthony Messenger Press, 1097, 1997). Also, "Made from the rib of the man, the woman is no more inferior to him than the man is inferior to the dust of the ground from which he comes." And regarding the turning point of the story:

> The two were then driven out of the garden and prevented from returning to it. We sometimes interpret this expulsion as another punishment, but then again they did not do so well in that garden. They flirted with temptation; they ate from the wrong tree; they came to know shame; they tried to pass the blame for their transgression onto someone else. This was not their finest hour. The cherub with the fiery sword may have kept them from repeating their offenses, as often happens in myth, or from committing even more. Expulsion could be a blessing in disguise. This may not have been their finest hour, but it certainly was one of God's. For no other reason than the goodness of God, they were thrust into the real world and given another chance. The wages of sin is divine compassion. And this is what happened in the garden.

The credentials of our next scriptural "authority" may not be as impeccable as Sister Dianne's, but he's hard to surpass as a humorist. I call as my next witness Mark Twain, whose abbreviated *The Diary of Adam and Eve* (Random House, 1996) may not be one of his best known works but is certainly one of his most whimsical. In recounting the arrival of Cain, the first human child, Adam muses:

> We have named it Cain. She caught it while I was up country trapping. . . . It resembles us in some ways and may be a relation. That is what she thinks, but this is an error in my judgment. The difference in size warrants the conclusion that it is a different and new kind of animal . . . a fish, perhaps, though when I put it in the water to see, it sank, and she plunged in and snatched it out before there was opportunity for the experiment to determine the matter. I still think it is a fish, but she is indifferent about what it is, and will not let me have it to try. I do not understand this.

The coming of the creature seems to have changed her whole nature and made her unreasonable about experiments. She thinks more of it than she does any of the other animals, but is not able to explain why.

Written with Twain's usual tongue-in-cheek facetiousness, the diary nevertheless helps us see the folly of placing too literal an interpretation on what is a small literary gem. We're learning more about humanity's origins almost every day, courtesy of anthropologists like the family Leakey whose work in Tanzania's Olduvai Gorge is legendary, but we still have far more questions than answers, making such venues as myths and "diaries" entirely appropriate.

Finally, Harold S. Kushner weighs in on the subject. In *How Good Do We Have to Be?* (Little, Brown & Co., 1996), Rabbi Kushner invites us to approach the events of Eden from somewhat the same perspective as Sister Dianne:

I am suggesting that the story of the Garden of Eden is not an account of people being punished for having made one mistake, losing Paradise because they were not perfect. It is the story of the first human beings graduating, evolving from the relatively uncomplicated world of animal life to the immensely complicated world of being human and knowing that there is more to life than eating and mating, that there are such things as Good and Evil. They enter a world where they will inevitably make many mistakes, not because they are weak or bad but because the choices they confront will be such difficult ones. But the satisfactions will be equally great. While animals can only be useful and obedient, human beings can be good. The story of the Garden of Eden is not a story of the Fall of Man, but of the Emergence of Humankind.

And so, although humanity unquestionably knows a great deal more about its origins now than ever before, a lot of exploring and, doubtless, fumbling still lies ahead. Future generations coping with the question of where they came from will repeat after us as we repeat after generations past, "In the beginning God . . ."

CHAPTER THREE

One Central Theme

We move on to Big Question—B-I-G Question!—
Number Two: What are we doing here? This is the
question that will occupy our thoughts for the greater
part of this book. One frustrated father, upon being
asked what his offspring was taking up in college, replied with resignation, "Space." At the close of our allotted span on planet Earth, most of
us would like to have compiled a more impressive resume than that. You
might want to review at this point some of the questions posed relative to
the Big Question Number Two at the close of chapter 1.

In the quest for answers, we turn first and always to what has been
revealed to us about the nature of God. This may shed some light on who
we are as persons and what is expected of our human nature. Any
number of books could emanate from these two statements. For our
purposes here, we will concentrate primarily on the writings found in the
Bible, beginning with the Hebrew Scriptures.

You don't have those in your Bible? Sure you do. You're more
familiar with them as the Old Testament. Oh great! Another newfangled
notion thrown in to confuse the issue. Not really! The books of the
Hebrew Bible were, naturally, in existence and stood alone long before
the Christian era. They remain sacred in their own right to Jews today. To
label them "old" is somehow demeaning. There's at least an implication
that they are outdated or, at the very least, of less value than the "new"
Christian books. Increasingly, the more courteous—and more accurate—
terms Hebrew and Christian Scriptures or First and Second Testaments
are finding their way into broader acceptance.

For similar reasons, the traditional "B.C." ("Before Christ") and "A.D." (*Anno Domini*—"Year of the Lord") are giving way in some quarters to "B.C.E." and "C.E." ("Before Common Era" and "Common Era"). At a time when, thankfully, Scripture scholarship is increasingly interfaith, it only makes sense to use, where possible, terminology amenable to all parties concerned. It would be a mistake to read an anti-Jesus message into the use of these newer terms. There is absolutely no intent to downplay Jesus' role on either the secular historical or religious spiritual stage. The older terms are not strictly correct anyway as we now realize that Jesus was not born in the year that launches the Christian calendar but anywhere from four to seven years earlier. The use of "B.C." in this instance would give Jesus the strange distinction of having been born several years before Christ. There is more than one school of thought on this subject, but for the remainder of these pages, the newer nomenclature will be used, if for no other reason than to familiarize you with it.

Blood and Gore—Begats and More! (Do I Have To?)

Many are the Christians who, while enjoying a certain acquaintance with the gospels and the letters of Paul, have little or no connection to the Old Testament beyond the snatches heard during eucharistic liturgies. There may be several reasons for this:

- a mistaken belief that the significance of these books ended once Jesus came on the scene (Jesus didn't think so—see Matthew 5:17);
- an earnest endeavor to read the Hebrew Bible straight through from Genesis to Malachi, which often meets an untimely end (usually at about Leviticus);
- encounters with drawn-out genealogies (Who begat whom?) and bloody battles, which don't seem likely to advance one's spiritual life;
- the simple supposition that it's just too *hard!*

Whatever the reason, making another attempt is well worth the effort, largely because, as Christians, we cannot fully grasp what Jesus said and did without being grounded, even as he was grounded, in these books.

Granted, being faced with a two-thousand-year time span in a foreign culture can be daunting. A movie covering the entire First

Testament period would clean out every casting office on the planet. Hordes of people move through these pages. Not all are named, but among those who are, not one is called Fred or Amy. It's a nightmare. But don't despair. Help is on the way in the form of a handy-dandy little skeletal structure I've devised. All you have to be able to do is count to four. (For me, this qualifies as higher math!) Follow the bouncing bullet points:

- One central theme: Covenant
- Two central events: Exodus
                              Exile
- Three central characters: Abraham
                              Moses
                              David
- Four groups of books: Torah (Pentateuch)
                              Historical
                              Prophetic
                              Writings (Wisdom literature)

There now, that wasn't so hard. Of course, a certain amount of augmentation may be needed on each, and this is what the next few chapters are about, starting with:

One Central Theme: Covenant

If the canon (official list) of biblical books is comprised of works in a variety of literary forms attributed to numerous writers from a wide assortment of times and places, is it even possible to find some kind of common thread that will tie it all together? Thankfully, yes! From the long list of major themes, subtopics, and myriads of lesser motifs, one looms over all the rest: the notion of covenant.

If this announcement seems less than helpful, chalk it up to the fact that covenant is a term that does not find its way into contemporary usage all that often. It might be beneficial that we find out what it is before we can expect its biblical significance to dawn on us.

Accustomed as we are to legal contracts, we can barely imagine life without them. Whenever we do anything *important* involving ourselves and another party, a formal agreement is drawn up, generally by an attorney. If this document is agreed to, both parties sign, their signatures are attested to by witnesses, and copies are filed all over the place certi-fying that the compact has been made. Those exploring the branches of their family tree to see who might be hanging there are almost patheti-cally appreciative of this practice, facilitating as it does the verification of events long past. However, if their search takes them far enough out on that lineage limb, the paper trail will end.

As our computers spew out endless streams of paper, we find it incomprehensible that human history has been to a great extent pre- or nonliterate. Where writing did exist in the civilized world, the ability to do so was reserved to very few. Surprising to us, the goal of generalized literacy is quite recent.

Literate or not, there has always been a need to place some sort of official stamp on agreements of great import, and this is where the covenant ceremony saved the day. A covenant is a promise or an agreement which binds the parties entering into it. It is not entered into lightly as it sometimes seems in one of the few covenant ceremonies in general use today, the wedding. This is a solemn pact made, as my grandmother used to say, right out in front of God and everybody. This is the general idea; out of all those witnesses somebody should survive for the duration of the compact. That it must have something significant to tell us is affirmed by its appearance 289 times in the *New American Bible* translation (World Publishing, 1990).

You Will!—or—Will You?

Biblically speaking, it becomes necessary to tweak Grandma's maxim slightly. Throughout Scripture, covenants are entered into not so much in front of God and everybody as by God and everybody. This God which the Hebrew-Israelite-Jewish people gradually come to see as omnipotent (all powerful), omniscient (all knowing), and omnipresent (all present)—this God who possesses both the right and the capacity to thunder, "You will!" to human creatures instead is far more likely to inquire courteously, "Will you?"

It should be admitted that "You will!" renders a covenant impossible as one of the striking characteristics of a covenant is that it must be entered into freely and knowingly by both parties or the agreement is void. But "Will you?" leaves the decision squarely in the hands of humanity. God proposes; humanity disposes. This freedom to choose is one of the traits that separates our race from every other species sharing our world. We alone possess the independence to say *yes* or *no* to God. Regardless of what God would often prefer (and what we perversely just as often blame God for), the choice is ours. Even when the option we select ends in disaster, God respects our decision and ratifies it (which helps explain why no one can be permanently separated from God unless that is the choice freely made).

Free will may be the most astonishing gift (and greatest gamble) of God. We could just as easily have been created without it. We would, then, always have been true to our highest nature and never in danger of ruining our lives or dashing the hopes God has for us. This would make us little different from the other denizens of the earth, living out our nature automatically. As William J. O'Malley, S.J., reminds us in his wise and witty book *Why Be Catholic?* (Crossroad Publishing, 1993):

> No planet or crocus or lion can violate its nature. No planet gets fed up with whirling and puts on the brakes; no crocus refuses to take in nourishment; no lion can reject the hassle of dealing with its mate and become celibate. Only human beings can reject their programming . . . refuse to be human and act instead like clods, or vegetables, or beasts. . . . The key difference between humans and animals is conscience. As far as we know, no tiger goes into a village, gobbles a lamb, and lurches back into the forest mumbling, "Oh *God!* I did it *again!* I've got to get counseling."

We are seemingly designed to choose good freely, to interact ethically with one another freely, to serve God freely. If we are made in the image of God, perhaps free will isn't quite so complicated. Who among us is much interested in having people in our lives because they have to be there? How much would the love of friends and family be worth if there were no choice?

So crucial is freedom to a covenant that its absence nullifies the agreement. If this seems like way more than you ever needed to know about the idea of covenant, in fact, it isn't. Covenant is this important to discerning who God is and who we are in relation to him.

The First Inklings

The idea first surfaces in the prehistory section of the biblical library when Noah is told to build an ark to save himself and his family from the devastation to come. "But I will establish my covenant with you; and you shall come into the ark" (Genesis 6:18a). When the flood waters recede, the covenant is reaffirmed (Genesis 9:8–17). Here again we have a story which need not be taken literally in order to provide cogent lessons in what God expects of the human family. Almost certainly based on Mesopotamia's much older Gilgamesh legend, Noah's flood is just one of a host of deluge legends dotting the folklore of diverse cultures in the Northern Hemisphere, many of which could have had no contact with one another.

In their 1997 book *Noah's Flood* (Touchstone Books), Columbia University geologists William Ryan and Walter Pitman theorize that such tales in the Middle East might stem from a cataclysmic inundation of the Black Sea. The ultimate cause of such watery chaos would have been, they believe, the gradual thawing of the great glaciers at the end of the last Ice Age. Pouring into the then land-locked Black Sea at two hundred times the volume of Niagara Falls, this cataclysm would have set off devastation on a vast scale, causing those who lived along the shores to scramble to safety on higher ground.

Noted explorer Robert Ballard has had some success in locating concrete evidence of those long-submerged habitations on the floor of the sea with the aid of submersibles. A debacle of such proportions would surely be seared upon the collective memory, retold and embellished in the telling for centuries to come, eventually evolving into a morality tale of great force. The contrast between good and evil is drawn in broad strokes. Humankind is quite obviously deserving of "plenty of nothing," to borrow a phrase from George Gershwin.

Even so, in the end, God wishes to enter into a covenant relationship with less than perfect mortals. What does this say about God? What does it suggest about our individual and collective lives?

With the appearance of Abram (Abraham), the Genesis adventure takes a more historical turn. Abram will be treated in far greater detail in chapter 5, but for now, it suffices to say that this foundational figure is usually described as the first historical person to appear on the biblical stage (Genesis 11). With him, all manner of wheels are set in motion.

Abram is really the first to have dealings with God, a God he knows not at all. In working toward forming a relationship, God counts on covenant, a common practice in the ancient Middle East and one that would be familiar to Abram. The business between them involves the promise of land to Abram. To seal the agreement, God organizes a covenant ceremony (Genesis 15:7–21).

As we read this passage, it all seems very strange to us (and reminds us again why it is we seldom venture into this part of the Bible). Various animals are brought in, split in half, and the two parts are laid out on the ground. "When the sun had gone down and it was dark, a smoking fire pot and a flaming torch passed between these pieces" (Genesis 15:17). The party making the pledge (in this case, God) walked between the halves of the carcasses, tacitly implying by doing so: "If I fail to live up to what I have solemnly promised, may the fate of these animals befall me." (There is probably little basis for the rumor that this constitutes the first record of a split personality.)

One of the attributes of God being his entirely spiritual nature, this puts him at something of a disadvantage on occasions such as this when a body is definitely required. There will be many incidents in both testaments when the presence of God is made known, but God does not appear. These are termed *theophanies* from the Greek *theos*, meaning "God", and *phaninomai*, meaning "to appear." *Epiphany* has a similar Greek base and is nearly synonymous.

These manifestations of God take many forms, primarily from nature. The most recurrent is clouds, with fire being a close second. Remember, the fleeing Israelites being led during the Exodus by a pillar of cloud by day and a pillar of fire by night? (Exodus 13:21–22) The "smoking brazier/flaming torch" in the covenant ceremony is God's stand-in. (*Brazier* is translated "firepot" in some translations due to its frequently startling rendering on the part of unwary lectors.)

In Genesis 17:2–14, this covenant is reiterated, made more specific, and a vital component is added. "Every male among you shall be circumcised" (Genesis 17:10b), a visible sign of the agreement made. At this point, Abram's name is changed as well. Abram, the patriarch of a large extended family, becomes Abraham, "the ancestor of a multitude of nations" (Genesis 17:5b).

Names carried a significance which is foreign to contemporary cultures. They were chosen with great care as they were not so much what the person would be called as what the person would be. Thus, a change in name indicated a change in the person or the person's role or both.

This long-ago pact between God and Abraham lives on today at the heart of a number of disputes over land in modern Israel. When the Jewish state was established in 1947, there was no question where it would be located. No other plot of land anywhere on the globe was so much as eligible for consideration. *This* was the Promised (covenanted) Land—its long-time Palestinian inhabitants naturally disagreed. This highly emotional issue will not be satisfactorily dealt with anytime soon.

Promises from on High at Sinai

The Israelites were absent from that land, nonetheless, for some four hundred thirty years (Exodus 12:41a), a span of centuries spent, first in plenty, then in poverty in Egypt. A long biblical silence is all we possess from this period, additional evidence that the Bible is not a history text. So it is not the name of Abraham we generally associate with covenant but the name of Moses. Moses—Sinai—Covenant. It's nearly impossible to think of one without the others.

After shepherding the grumpiest bunch of ingrates you're likely to find out of the Egyptian pharaoh's clutches and safely (if you can call it that) to the far end of the Sinai peninsula, Moses deposited them lock, stock, and tent at the foot of Mount Sinai and said: "Let's take five!" (free translation). While the Israelites waited, Moses carved out a pair of stone tablets and began the laborious trek to the top of the mountain where he encountered God in, guess what? Another theophany:

> He said: "I hereby make a covenant. Before all your people I will perform marvels, such as have not been performed in all the earth or in any nation; and all the people among whom you live shall see the work of the LORD; for it is an awesome thing that I will do with you" (Exodus 34:10).

When Moses at last descended from the mountaintop, the tablets he had carried up contained the core of the covenant—the "Decalogue," or Ten Laws (Commandments). The ratification necessary to make the covenant binding on both parties had been secured following Moses' earlier encounter: "Moses came and told the people all the words of the

LORD and all the ordinances; and all the people answered with one voice, and said, 'All the words that the LORD has spoken we will do' " (Exodus 24:3).

This resolute declaration of faith was followed by that unfortunate incident with the golden calf (Exodus 32). At the forefront of this unhappy episode was, of all people, Moses' brother Aaron, the first high priest! Not only would we have expected better of someone in his position, we would have counted on him for a little more inventive alibi. How's this for one of the lamest excuses of all time: "So I [Aaron] said to them, 'Whoever has gold, take it off'; so they gave it to me, and I threw it into the fire, and out came this calf!" (Exodus 32:24). Oh, please! On this particular day, at least, Aaron was seemingly about three sandwiches short of a picnic. And him the newly anointed high priest! Things are not off to a promising start.

God didn't think so either, and it took considerable begging, actually downright groveling, on the part of Moses to keep God from chucking the entire arrangement. But the point is, he didn't. And as we follow the covenant thread through the books ahead, something even more staggering becomes clear: he never does. No matter how far the Israelites stray from their part of the bargain (and they will wander very far very often), God remains faithful to them. No matter how forgetful they become (and they will have some long memory lapses), God remembers. Even when they neglect God (They never phone; they never write!) and amble off after other gods, they are always invited to return and welcomed when they do.

This has got to be some of the best news to ever come our way. No matter what, God never gives up on us. We may comport ourselves less than admirably. Our conduct may cost us friends, family, position, and self-respect—yet God never gives up on us. It may appear to the world, and to ourselves, that we have done precious little with our lives, but we have up to and including the final breath we draw to turn all that around, because God never gives up on us.

Granted, all this theology isn't immediately apparent in the Book of Exodus, but it starts there and will expand and deepen over time. Our grasp of God, like our grasp of physics or music or psychology, requires time to broaden and deepen, to grow.

Another useful lesson from the golden calf fiasco is that the mighty aren't any more immune to doing something "dumb" than the rest of us. This lesson is coupled with another. Doing something unworthy of ourselves denotes a flaw, not a fatality (unless we make it one). Aaron redeemed himself nicely during his remaining years, and for most of Israel's priestly history, high priests took pride in being his direct lineal descendants.

All of us fall on our faces, at least metaphorically, an embarrassing number of times over our lifetimes. None of these is spiritually fatal as long as we have the shame-faced humility to spit out the dust, apologize with earnest intent not to repeat the blunder, and move on. I wish I could say we never do repeat the blunder, but unhappily we sometimes do, afflicted as we are with an Achilles heels of one type or another. But if our resolve to improve remains sincere, we can count on God to meet us considerably more than half way. Wait until we get to the parable of the forgiving father (prodigal son). There we'll find a father who actually runs to meet the returning playboy.

Some years ago while attending a conference in Spokane, Washington, I was housed along with the other participants at a large Jesuit facility. While there, I picked up a version of the "Stations of the Cross" written by a member of the local Jesuit community, a man so crippled by rheumatoid arthritis that he must have known a considerable amount about carrying crosses. I cannot now find that little book; nor can I come up with the author's name, but I will never forget a particular line from it. Jesus' walk to Calvary was written as though the reader were alongside, experiencing everything that Jesus experienced. When Jesus falls, slamming his face into the filth beneath him, he looks over at the reader (you, me) and encourages quietly, "Get up. Together we can still make something of your life."

No matter how flat we've fallen (and we're always harder on ourselves than on anyone else), no matter how many times we've missed the mark (which is what the word *sin* really means), we have no right to give up on ourselves. God never does.

Following the Thread

If it were possible in these circumscribed pages to follow the covenant between God and the people, we would see that it acts very much like a thread in a garment, sometimes laying on the surface of the cloth where it is visible to all, sometimes relegated to the back of the fabric, unseen but still holding the material together. It really is no exaggeration to say that the covenant gives cohesion to the entire canon of the Hebrew Scriptures, regardless of how diverse the individual books may be.

Nor does the thread disappear when we move into the pages of the Christian Scriptures. In one of Luke's exquisite canticles, the priest Zechariah, soon to be the father of John the Baptizer, proclaims:

> "Thus he [God] has shown the mercy promised to our ancestors, and has remembered his holy covenant" (Luke 1:72).

Mark, Matthew, and Luke all recount Jesus' words over the cup of wine at the Last Supper in one way or another:

> He said to them, "This is my blood of the covenant, which is poured out for many" (Mark 14:24).

> Then he took a cup, and after giving thanks he gave it to them, saying, "Drink from it, all of you; for this is my blood of the covenant; which is poured out for many for the forgiveness of sins" (Matthew 26:27–28).

> And he did the same with the cup after supper, saying, "This cup that is poured out for you is the new covenant in my blood" (Luke 22:20).

Common to all three renderings is the prominent reference to blood. If this makes you uncomfortable and you're making little muttering noises about remembering now why the Bible can be disquieting, repeat to yourself what my professor said about twentieth-century American skin.

Blood has been recognized as the life force since prehistoric times. Cro-Magnons painted lines of red on the bones of their dead to symbolize blood. Primitive people with no knowledge of anatomy whatever are crystal clear on this point: where there is blood, there if life; where blood has drained away, there is death. The ceremonies of ancient religions frequently included the drinking of blood, either from a sacrificial animal, or person, or the blood of enemies, a practice forbidden to the Israelites (Leviticus 7:26–27).

In Israelite practice, the blood of sacrificed animals was splashed upon the altar, thereby offering back to God the life force he gave. On special occasions, blood was also sprinkled on people. One such occasion was the covenant ceremony. Covenants were made in blood, signifying that they were living agreements intended to be lived out by the parties involved. Jesus, a devout Jew steeped in these age-old practices, breaks with tradition and institutes a new covenant in his own blood; he

- amends the covenant, something only God could do, thereby making a claim to divinity;
- repeals the prohibition on the drinking of blood in this one special instance;
- suggests that he will himself become a sacrifice.

As with so many beliefs and custom in his religious heritage, Jesus amplifies their significance without destroying it. We are heirs to this inheritance and remain, through baptism, covenanted people to this day.

In *Catholicism* (HarperSanFrancisco, 1994), Richard McBrien remarks: "What Jesus announced was not only a renewal of the Covenant with the people of Israel. His message was even more comprehensive than that. It would embrace the whole world."

And from the *2000 Catholic Almanac* (Our Sunday Visitor Press, 1999) comes: "The Mosaic (Sinai) covenant made Israel God's Chosen People on terms of fidelity to true faith, true worship, and righteous conduct according to the Decalogue. The New Testament covenant, prefigured in the Old Testament, is the bond people have with God through Christ. All people are called to be parties to this perfect and everlasting covenant, which was mediated and ratified by Christ."

The covenant thread remains unbroken by God although humanity has failed innumerable times. That thread will ultimately spool out in God's domain, where we will live in a covenanted relationship with him evermore. In a fractious world where nearly every institution and a disturbing number of people let us down at some point, it is comforting to be positioned on a looming mass of evidence that testifies: God never gives up on us.

Why are we here? One major reason appears to be in order that we may live out the days of time and eternity covenanted to the God we love, a God who for sometimes unfathomable reasons loves us as well.

CHAPTER FOUR

Two Central Events

N obody advances far into this life before discovering that it comes equipped with a seemingly inexhaustible succession of ups and downs, and they raise some of our most troubling questions. Can we piously ascribe them to the will of God? Does God "do that" to us, or are these peaks and valleys the consequence of choices made by our own free will or that of others. There are those mountaintop moments of the type Peter experienced at Jesus' transfiguration, "Lord, it is good for us to be here" (Matthew 17:4a). Then there are those desolate moments of the type Peter experienced in the hours following Jesus' arrest when he failed his beloved friend so miserably. If we had our "druthers," we'd take highs over lows every time, but life just doesn't work that way, not for individuals, not for nations.

Looking back over the century recently completed, most Americans would be able to see how our nation was profoundly impacted by turning points such as the two world wars, the Great Depression, and the Vietnam conflict. And so it was for the Israelites. Their history came to hinge on two climactic events, the Exodus and the Exile.

The "Ex" can be extended to extraordinary experiences capable of either enhancing or threatening their very existence. On the pinnacle stands the Exodus; in the pit lies the Exile. Following the Israelite tribes through the upheaval brought about by events both great and grim may tell us something about the God who was with them through it all and who continues to be with us "through it all."

Before hitting the Exodus trail, it should certainly be conceded that these are but two of hundreds, perhaps thousands, of happenings recorded in the biblical books, many of tremendous consequence. But these two are so pivotal that to bypass them is to leave gaping holes in the profile we're trying to draw of our God. They provide vital depth and perspective regarding the nature of God, plus some interesting insights into our own nature. This will be something of a departure from what we've discussed up to this point, but it couldn't be more appropriate as the word *exodus* means "departure." So, with "your loins girded, your sandals on your feet, and your staff in your hand" (Exodus 12:11a), let's set out.

Cecil B. de Mille versus *Reader's Digest*

The story of the Exodus is a long one, filling the entire biblical book of the same name. Needless to say, we can't cover it all here, and for our purposes, we don't really need that much detail. Besides, Cecil B. de Mille has already been there and done that. It's almost impossible to imagine anyone who has not seen his monumental epic with a cast composed of much of Western civilization. It's unrealistic to expect to dodge it on TV all the way through Holy Week. If it takes a few biblical liberties, it can at least be credited with familiarizing nearly everyone in the English-speaking world with the story, thus relieving us of the obligation of slogging through it here.

Nonetheless, for the benefit of those who may be a bit hazy on the sequence of the story, I shall borrow from myself, repeating here a sort of *Reader's Digest* condensed version of the main events. This originally appeared in *Scripture from Scratch*: "Exodus and Exile: Shaping God's People" (St. Anthony Messenger Press, 295, 1995).

- Captive people unable to gain their freedom—
  Israelites (Exodus 1)
- An unlikely hero whose misgivings about himself are shared
  by many—Moses (Exodus 2–4)
- An intransigent, despotic ruler who won't budge—
  Pharaoh (Exodus 6)
- Some fairly dramatic convincing of the ruler—
  Plagues (Exodus 7–11)

- The departure of nobodies bound for nowhere—
  Exodus (Exodus 12:31–13)
- The obligatory chase scene—Pharaoh's Chariots
  (Exodus 14:4–14)
- Adventures in water management—Red (Reed) Sea
  (Exodus 14:15–15:21)
- Sighs of relief; wails of discontent—Human Nature
  (Exodus 15:1–16:3)
- Fast food, Sinai style—Manna and Quail (Exodus 16:4–36)
- Laying down the Law—Decalogue (Ten Commandments)
  (Exodus 19–20)
- Idol minds are the Devil's workshop—Golden Calf
  (Exodus 32)
- Setting things right and journeying on—Covenant
  (Exodus 33)

From Slavery to Freedom and Back Again

The Exodus and the Exile act as literary bookends. Between them is encountered a major portion of Israelite history. As we shall see, they form a kind of mirror image of one another. The Exodus is the story of the journey from slavery to freedom. The Exile is the story of the journey from freedom back into slavery. This double-edged freedom/slavery sword will figure prominently into our review of these events. Other motifs from the Exodus resonate so deeply and universally that they continue to find their way into contemporary spiritual life. Among these are the desert experience, organized religion, moral and ethical legislation, and the land (that land of promise spoken of earlier).

In examining each of these, we are well advised to view them from two very different perspectives:

- What did they mean to Moses and the Israelites during the time of the Exodus (probably about the middle of the thirteenth century B.C.E., although the date is uncertain)?
- What do they mean to us in the twenty-first century? How can we be assured that the conclusions we draw are reasonable extensions of the original intention?

A good rule of thumb in interpreting any scriptural passage in light of a current societal question is to first situate it in its original time and place. This generally supplies a natural springboard to later eras and locales and gives at least some assurance that there's a line of connection between the two. Those whose only exercise is jumping to conclusions are likely to arrive at completely unfounded, sometimes downright silly, ones; i.e., the fact that the Israelites ate manna and quail in the desert indicates pizza had not yet been invented.

"Let My People Go"

The liberation of the Hebrew people, the focal point of the book, harkens back to something we already found in Genesis: free will. Human beings are created to think, speak, act, and live as free people. Americans should have no trouble absorbing this; the nation was founded on precisely this precept. But, as with free will, there are all manner of ways in which human freedom can be abused, and as history attests, nearly all of them have been exercised at one time or another.

Freedom, then, is not license, a total disregard for restraint. When that which I am entitled to as a member of the human family (*my* rights) collide with that which you are entitled to as a member of the human family (*your* rights), something's got to give. There arises a need for a mutually agreeable restriction of a legal or moral nature.

The law and order system so taken for granted today was absolutely unknown in most ancient societies. Community arbiters of order, such as police forces, did not exist. Furthermore, the separation of church and state so ingrained in our thinking would have bewildered our ancestors. There was no separation of secular from religious. These archaic ideas, which may be news to us, need to be filed behind our left ear and kept close at hand as the conversation moves closer to Sinai.

When the Sea of Reeds (near the site of the Suez Canal, so really not the Red Sea at all) closed over Pharaoh's armed forces, the chariots and charioteers, Moses might have been forgiven for beating Martin Luther King, Jr., to the punch with the line: "Free at last! Free at last! Thank God Almighty, I'm free at last." It doubtless didn't occur to him, and this is just as well because he'd have been oh, so wrong. The struggle was only beginning, and the worst of it lay ahead.

Freedom, the Exodus tells us, is always a work in progress. Never fully attained, every foot of ground gained must be vigilantly safeguarded for it can be easily lost and only with strenuous effort regained.

The Israelites will roam over the inhospitable Sinai landscape for some forty years. Don't take this too literally, as forty in biblical parlance is what we would call a round number, like when a child hears for the umpteenth time, "If I've told you once, I've told you a hundred times . . ." It simply means that we've been down this road many times before. When they finally do reach Canaan, the Promised Land, it's not going to prove to be "a land flowing with milk and honey" (Exodus 33:3a) touted in the travel brochures. Never in their history will they really be there. They'll always in some sense be on the road.

And so it is for all of us. At birth, we set out on the journey of a full lifetime, hoping at its close to find ourselves in the never-ending Promised Land of God. Some years ago, my Jesuit spiritual director, a man of great insight, true wisdom, and a million-dollar laugh, would chide me, "You never want to be on the way. You always want to be *there.*" He was right. I've always been highly in favor of cutting to the chase and eliminating all that bothersome twaddle in the middle. Alas, this is not to be. We are a pilgrim people—always have been—always will be.

Following Jesus' years in our midst, we speak of being suspended between the *already* and the *not yet*. It's this suspended part we really hate, but we're stuck with it, and we come to believe through the Exodus story and others that it might actually do us some good—like cottage cheese (not specifically mentioned as a form of penance in the Bible).

What Do You Mean There's No Air Conditioning?

The Israelites definitely didn't think it was good for them. A whinier lot you'd be hard-pressed to find. Scarcely has the thud of Egyptian horses' hooves subsided before they're pulling at Moses' sleeve (figuratively speaking) like bratty kids in a supermarket. Selective memory sets in, and suddenly Egypt looks like paradise lost. Forgetful of God's recent deliverance, the scene turns into, "Yeah, but what has he done for us lately?" Moses is not amused. God is more forbearing. The scenario plays out like this:

> The whole congregation of the Israelites complained against Moses and Aaron in the wilderness. The Israelites said to them, "If only we had died by the hand of the LORD in the land of Egypt, when we sat by the fleshpots and ate our fill of bread; for you have brought us out into this wilderness to kill this whole assembly with hunger." Then the LORD said to Moses, "I am going to rain bread from heaven for you, and each day the people shall go out and gather enough for that day" (Exodus 16:2–4a).

The bread from heaven is called "manna." Centuries later, bread from heaven will take on a far more exalted connotation in Jesus' eucharistic Bread of Life discourse (John 6:31ff). For now, however, it's enough to recognize the patience God demonstrates with his people when their faith leaves something to be desired. Thank God for God!

Who . . . and What Is God?

As we move along, collecting additional attributes of God as we go, the light may begin to dawn that the fierce God said to command the pages of the First Testament is a figment of our imagination. God is God, the one constant. The second Person of the Trinity "became flesh and lived among us" (John 1:14a) with the arrival of Jesus, but the first Person remains the same God we're gradually discerning in the Hebrew Scriptures.

If God didn't change, who did? We did, and we do, and we unceasingly will. Little by little, generation by generation, century by century, we're coming to appreciate with greater clarity who God really is.

If, as we assert, we are to live in a covenanted relationship with our God, the shift in this relationship should come as no surprise. It happens all the time with our other interpersonal relationships, and we find it not only acceptable but highly desirable. It signals a healthy and growing connection with one another. We constantly learn new things about those who have been close to us for years. They retain the capacity to surprise us, to challenge us, to prompt us to view them from a fresh perspective.

Other factors enter into the unfolding vision of the nature of God. There is a tendency, when considering something new, to build on what is already well known. There's a certain logic to this. Yet again shedding our more informed contemporary perspective, we revert to the awareness that our ancestors in the faith were surrounded by polytheistic societies whose gods were blessed or cursed with any number of dispositions, most of them distinctly unpleasant. The Israelites could be forgiven for assuming, at least initially, that their own God would exhibit similar characteristics. Over time, their experience with this God would forcefully demonstrate the contrast. Allowing for the accepted outlook on the matter at the time and allowing time for this outlook to expand and grow helps put obsolete lines of thought into perspective.

Less Desert, More Dessert

A favorite theme of spiritual writers is the desert experience, and almost invariably, touching on this theme reminds them of the prototype, the Exodus trudge through the Sinai. The gospel writers will prod this memory when they speak of Jesus' desert experience (Matthew 4:1–11, Mark 1:12, Luke 4:1–13), a time of temptation, deprivation, and searching for a God who seems suddenly out of reach.

Nearly everyone can recall one or more desert periods in their spiritual lives when prayer (if it could be managed at all) seemed an exercise in futility—words dry as dust directed toward a God who had apparently moved and left no forwarding address. Saint John of the Cross called such times the "dark night of the soul." Good analogy, but desert is better for it really does appear that we're standing alone in a literally God-forsaken wilderness, and no matter how earsplitting our cries, there is no answer.

Opportunities for spiritual development abound during what we believe to be the least likely of times. Looking back later, we realize this is true. But let's face it; we hate deserts. We much prefer dessert, the sweetness of God's palpable presence. We're not that different from the Israelites who, confronted with a very real desert sure to present very real hardships, wanted nothing so much as to scurry back to Egypt. Life in Egypt hadn't exactly been Club Med, but better the devil you know than the one you don't.

In the end, however, after much cajoling on the part of Moses, they plunged ahead. It wasn't easy during those desert years. It wasn't easy after they arrived in Canaan. It was never easy, but it was worth the struggle. In our lives as in theirs, being covenanted to this God is not a bowl of cherries, but neither is it all pits, and in the end, it is well worth the struggle.

Mounting Expectations

The essence of the Exodus saga is contained in the events at Mount Sinai. Everything leads up to this, and most of what follows is anticlimactic. The Israelite tribes will carry two inestimable assets away from Sinai that they didn't possess upon arrival: a religion and the Law. First, the Law—the Mosaic Law.

Notice the capital "L." This is a clue that what we have here is not a simple statute or decree, but rather an entire body of edicts and ordinances which from this point forward govern every part of Israelite life. The heart of the Law is the Decalogue, or Ten Laws (Commandments), but these are far from the total. Exodus 20:1–17 lists the Decalogue, but keep reading. There's more in chapters 21–23 and much more in the next book of the Torah, Leviticus.

What's more, there's quite another roster in the Book of Deuteronomy (which means Second Law). The slate of ten found in Deuteronomy 5:6–21 differs from that recorded in Exodus, suggesting separate sources are at work again. Numbering is uncertain as well, although the usual practice is to view the first three commandments as pertaining to the obligations of people to God and the remaining seven as concerning the responsibility of people to one another.

For all that they have been rightly honored from that day to this, the precepts in the latter group were not exactly news on the day Moses received them. They had been around a long time, some recorded in the famous law code of the Babylonian king, Hammurabi, as much as five hundred years earlier. Simply put, these seven principles are basic rules governing the behavior of any people who attempt to live in community.

This in no way diminishes their significance to the Judeo-Christian ethic, but it does suggest that even the most revered set of norms in our tradition must be looked at anew from time to time and brought into accord with contemporary culture. Jesus must have thought so as a good part of his most famous sermon did just that. Matthew tells us all about it in the Sermon on the Mount, a lengthy discourse that consumes three chapters (5–7). Putting his audience at ease at the outset, Jesus assures them he has not come to abolish the Law, but to fulfill it (Matthew 5:17). He is then heard to repeat a kind of formula several times, "You have heard that it was said, . . . but I say to you . . ." (Matthew 5:21–22, 27–28, 33–34, 38–39, 43–44), relating directly or indirectly to one of the Ten Laws or elements of the broader Mosaic Law.

It's as if he were saying: "That was then; this is now. When Moses received these commandments over a thousand years ago, humankind was like a small child of whom only the bare essentials could be expected. Humanity has grown up to some degree over the years, so today, from those who would follow me, more will be expected." It seems reasonable to infer that from us, two thousand years later, *much* more might be expected.

Same Commandments, Different World

Shifting all ten commandments into the present day would require an entire book in itself. However, using one as an example could prove instructive as to how to approach the others.

"You shall not murder" (Exodus 20:13, Deuteronomy 5:17). Although this translation is the choice in the *NRSV* and the *NEB* and may well reflect the more precise definition, the *NAB* and the *NJB* stay with the traditional "kill." Either way, the commandment underscores unequivocally the value of human life. Some of the life issues we face today were part of Israelite experience as well: murder, war, capital punishment. That we are still striving to come to grips with our ethical obligations in these areas implies that the answers are neither quick nor easy.

Add to this the additional burden of life issues Moses' generation never could have envisioned, and the Respect Life month, which Catholics observe every October, begins to look like an excellent idea. So complex are the questions involved in such areas as euthanasia, in vitro fertilization, cloning, stem cell research, and ordinary versus extraordinary treatment procedures for the seriously ill, that staff ethicists are now standard in many health care facilities. These trained professionals are on hand to assist families and medical staffs in making difficult, even heart-wrenching decisions regarding the medical care of someone they care for professionally or personally.

If you don't think times have changed since Hammurabi and Moses committed those few words to stone, consider that ours is the first generation in human history challenged to redefine death. Until quite recently, it was a relatively straightforward matter: no pulse, no respiration, no life. Now, pulse and respiration can be continued for some time. They may need to be, i.e., to allow the harvesting of organs for transplant (another life/ethics issue). So what presently constitutes death? Is it when there is no longer brain activity? How do we determine when bodily function definitively ceases?

Physical hazards are not all that endanger life. Psychologists have shown us that abuse of all kinds, from bodily torture to emotional battering, stands to compromise both the quality and the duration of human life. Something as innocent as a thoughtless remark may have long-term consequences in someone's life. There's probably no question but that we kill with our tongues far more often than we kill with weapons, and one can be as lethal as the other. The adage "Sticks and stones may break my bones, but names can never harm me" is one time-honored proverb that should be honored no more. In truth, it's precisely the other way around. Bones generally heal in time; hurtful things said to us may linger always.

The implications for us in the four short words of this commandment may well be inexhaustible inasmuch as barely a week passes without some new medical or scientific procedure surfacing, bringing with it a host of new ethical quandaries. One of the attendant dilemmas accompanying scientific advances is the lack of time available to process their ramifications. Whereas previous generations enjoyed the luxury of years in which to explore the ethical and moral implications of a new notion, we often seem to have weeks, even days to accomplish an impossible task. This will be an ongoing source of frustration for ethicists as the scientific community presents them with an expanding array of issues never foreseen by Moses' Sinai Law. In the end, however, all of them come down to the value of human life and the love we show for it.

English is a language with deficiencies like any other, and one of those is its lack of terminology describing various forms of love. We love everything from pizza to parents (not necessarily in that order). The love called for in working through life situations is not "Valentine's Day in the sixth grade" love, but rather "You're my brother/sister, made in the image of God. Like my own, your life has great value, so I want your life given the respect and dignity of a child of God, the respect and dignity I would want for myself."

Alfred McBride speaks to this in *The Ten Commandments: Sounds of Love from Sinai* (St. Anthony Messenger Press, 1990):

> So long as love is experienced and practiced, life has a chance. This is the basic message of the Fifth Commandment. If this value were absorbed into our inner lives, it would crowd out the destructive impulses that beget anti-life behavior. This liberating value of the Fifth Commandment would free us from war, murder, genocide, terrorism, abortion, and all the other forms of mayhem humans inflict on one another.
>
> Love is the closest experience we have to the act of creation. Love does not murder life. Love wants to produce, sustain, and care for it. Some speak of love as a seamless garment that wraps its creative protectiveness around life from conception to death.

We've really not begun to probe the repercussions of this one injunction from the Decalogue, let alone the other nine. Conceivably, these few observations have demonstrated that the commandments are living entities and, as such, they should constantly be works in progress, reshaping themselves to an ever changing world.

Gimme That Old-Time Religion

Prior to the Sinai experience, the Israelite belief in and relationship to God could not properly be designated a religion. The seeds of faith were present, if not always sprouting into sturdy seedlings. So there's one question answered before you had a chance to raise it: Which came first, faith or religion? Faith must precede religion, for faithless religion is no religion at all. In *Great Religions of the World* (Saint Mary's Press, 1986), Loretta Pastva, S.N.D., defines faith and religion so articulately I wouldn't dream of trying to top her:

> Religious faith is the deeply personal relationship that each of us experiences with what is sacred in life.

> Religion is the sum total of all our attempts to celebrate our faith publicly through worship, to reflect on the story of our faith, and to live out the values of that faith as a community.

Worship—Story—Community. These are the foundational elements of religion—*any* religion. One religion may emphasize or denigrate one element more than another, but they're all there in some fashion.

By its very nature, faith requires expression. Can you imagine saying nothing, doing nothing about the most electrifying moments in your life—your graduation(s), your wedding, the birth of a child, a major career advancement? You *could* say or do nothing and be just as much a graduate, a spouse, a parent, an achiever, but where would be the fun in that? These are "shout it from the rooftop" events. Festive celebration is in order. As I customarily tell the graduating seniors in my classroom, I could shake their hands at the end of the final class period, wish them a nice life, close the door behind them, and they'd be just as graduated. There would, however, linger an indefinable air of unfinished business. There is a felt need to commemorate the occasion and, in doing so, to gather all those who mean the most to them to participate as well. In other words, the occasion calls for assembling the community.

This is what happens (or should happen) when faith-filled people congregate to share and memorialize this faith as a group—a group, by the way, frequently dubbed a congregation. Such a shared experience becomes a rite or formalized practice. For Catholic Christians, the eucharistic liturgy and the sacraments are rites of primary import. The manner in which a rite is conducted is known as a ritual. Rites and rituals are common to all religions broadly, and they come in a fascinating diversity of forms, hallowing a broad spectrum of convictions.

For the Israelites, it all began at Sinai. When Moses descended from his rendezvous with God, he didn't sling the tablets of the Law into a backpack and give the order to move out. Those chunks of rock had become the most sacred tangible objects the people possessed and necessitated reverent care and safekeeping. So the Ark of the Covenant came to be constructed. *Ark* is a rather old-fashioned name for any chest or repository. This one, however, was very special—just how special is detailed in Exodus 25:10–22.

A sort of domino effect comes into play here as one thing leads to another. The tablets made the ark a necessity. The Ark, in turn, required some type of appropriate housing. Permanent structures were not an option in the midst of the protracted camp-out in the desert. Tents were the order of the day there, so a tent it was—the Tent of Meeting, also called the Dwelling Tent. Exodus 25–27 recounts in laborious detail the specifications for this abode of God (singular), not above the firmament but right down in the dust and heat of an earthly wilderness.

Sacred objects and sacred spaces demand unusual care. Wisdom would suggest setting aside a particular person or persons whose sole duties would be to safeguard these holy items and serve the God whom they represented. Exodus 28–30 detail the institution of the Israelite priesthood with Moses' brother, Aaron, as high priest. As you read through these chapters, you'll find considerable rite and ritual. Keep in mind that the writing of this book took place many years after the events described, making it reasonable to suppose that a good bit of what was by then a "done deal" found its way into the text.

Catholics will also find quite a lot that seems surprisingly familiar: an elaborate repository containing that which is held most holy, a lampstand, which burns before this receptacle (Exodus 25:31–40), priesthood, vestments (Exodus 28), anointing oil (Exodus 30:22–33), incense (Exodus 30:34–38). If the roots of Judaism lie in that barren soil, so do our own. Bias of any kind toward our ancestors in faith is tantamount to animosity toward our grandparents. The Christian, including regrettably Catholic, record in this regard is less than praise-worthy.

On the Road Again

Moses and company finally hit the road again at the opening of the Book of Numbers (after a whole lot of minute details and legal particulars laid out in the remainder of Exodus and *all* of the Book of Leviticus). They have been redefined by the Law which will govern every aspect of life from this time forward and the religion which will bring their emerging faith into ritualized shared observance.

They're on their way, but most of them will not arrive. The generation that wiped the dust of Egypt from its sandals and set out will not be the generation that ultimately sets sandal in Canaan, not even Moses. The final chapter of the Torah, Deuteronomy 34, chronicles Moses' death and burial on Mount Nebo, a site where Pope John Paul II paused to pray during his visit in 2000.

Again and again in Scripture, we will read of godly souls who, like Moses, strove through most of their lifetimes to attain a worthy goal and never lived to see it. From our vantage point, we can easily see the merit in their endeavors and what that has meant and continues to mean to those who succeeded them. In the end, the pilgrimage teaches far more than the Promised Land.

From Freedom Back to Slavery

Hit the Fast Forward button and advance roughly seven centuries. When the videotape clears, you'll be looking at a thoroughly different picture. The twelve tribes of Israel have been settled in the Promised Land, Canaan, for a period nearly twice as long as all of American history. By this time, they should have matured substantially in their understanding of God and their relationship to him, right? Of course, right. But these are human beings remarkably (or distressingly) similar to you and me, so snags are inescapable.

Like all of us fallible folks, the Israelites have a spotty history when it comes to living up to expectations, never mind living up to a covenant relationship with the living God. As is generally the case with solemn agreements, this one was a lot easier to make than to live on a daily basis. "All the words that the LORD has spoken we will do," (Exodus 24:3b) tripped off the collective tongue effortlessly. Living out this commitment from morning to night, day in and day out, was quite another matter.

This is why it's called commitment. It says, "This is what I took on; this is what I signed up for, so this is what I'll do whether or not I much feel like doing it." Commitment is hard work. Ask any married person. Ask any ordained or professed religious. Ask any contracted professional.

If you really want to learn about commitment, ask a member of what Tom Brokaw called "The Greatest Generation," men and women who were still in their teens or barely out of them when they enlisted in their nation's armed forces "for the duration." They didn't know how long that would be or what would be asked of them. Service to the commitment they had made took most to places they had only read about in school or couldn't find on a map; it took some to years of hardship in prison camps; it took others to long convalescence from horrific wounds that too often cost arms, legs, eyes, and ears. This commitment took some to graves, marked and unmarked, and others to God only knows where— they've never been found.

Honoring a commitment isn't for wimps and weaklings. It's tough, and it changes a person. Those fresh-faced young people who left for Europe, the Pacific, and later Korea and Vietnam were markedly different people upon their return.

It won't be necessary to dwell on all the particulars of Israel's dereliction in the commitment department. The most flagrant violation of the covenant will do nicely, and this was idolatry. The First Commandment laid down the law on idolatry in a way that could not easily be misinterpreted. "I am the LORD your God, who brought you out of the land of Egypt, out of the house of slavery; you shall have no other gods before me" (Exodus 20:2).

Yet, almost from the day their restless feet came to rest in the Land of Canaan, the worship of false gods became a problem. In considering why this happened, it helps to remember that Canaan was not an unpopulated territory, waiting patiently for the Israelites to arrive. It already had a substantial population of Canaanites, not to mention odd lots of Hittites, Amorites, Perizzites, Hivites, Jebusites, and several more who probably don't figure into your family tree.

With all those assorted people came all those assorted gods, and the Israelites found them enticing from time to time, quite a bit of the time actually. Joshua, Moses' successor, delivered a short pep talk shortly before departing the planet:

> "Now therefore revere the LORD, and serve him in sincerity and in faithfulness; put away the gods that your ancestors served beyond the River [Euphrates] and in Egypt, and serve the LORD. Now if you are unwilling to serve the LORD, choose this day whom you will serve, whether the gods your ancestors served in the region beyond the River or the gods of the Amorites in whose

land you are living; but as for me and my household, we will serve the LORD" (Joshua 24:14–15).

The people responded with a long-winded version of: "Us? Turn to other gods? Pish-tush! Never happen."

Protests to the contrary, it did happen, early and often. The fabled wisdom of the great King Solomon, over two hundred years after Joshua, was not sufficient to save even him from the scourge of idolatry:

> For when Solomon was old, his wives turned away his heart after other gods; and his heart was not true to the LORD his God, as was the heart of his father David. For Solomon followed Astarte the goddess of the Sidonians, and Milcom the abomination of the Ammonites. . . . Solomon built a high place for Chemosh the abomination of Moab, and for Molech the abomination of the Ammonites, on the mountain east of Jerusalem. He did the same for all his foreign wives, who offered incense and sacrificed to their gods (1 Kings 11:4–8).

And Solomon had WIVES! "Among his wives were seven hundred princesses and three hundred concubines" (1 Kings 11:3a). The size of the marital fold was one measure of the prestige of the ruler in Solomon's era. Marriage customs have both altered and altared since then, again suggesting the advisability of allowing the past the courtesy of acceptance while seeking more admissible criteria for our own day.

All those wives! All those gods! While we might be tempted to cut the beleaguered king a little slack, God had no such inclination: "Since this has been your mind and you have not kept my covenant and my statutes that I have commanded you, I will surely tear the kingdom from you and give it to your servant" (1 Kings 11:11b). At length God relented just enough to spare a single tribal unit for posterity.

Two points:

- God meant what he said in the First Commandment.
- The Israelites never get much better at holding up their end of the deal.

It doesn't take a zoom lens to see enormous consequences littering the road ahead.

Why Me, Lord?

Chalk this up on your list of attributes of God: patience, l-o-n-g suffering. For those who have no doubt that God busily scribbles in his little black book, hoping against hope that we'll do something that will irrevocably seal our doom, this has to be the most remarkable good news (which is what *gospel* means). While at the same time perhaps questioning the wisdom of his brainchild, free will, God gave the Israelites (and gives us) every chance to use it well. He wanted them and wants us to succeed. The only way we can fail is if it is our choice, a choice God will ratify with the kind of anguish only a parent can truly grasp.

More than three centuries pass, and with a few notable exceptions, things have not greatly improved at the turn of the sixth century B.C.E. Whether they realize it or not, the Israelites are nearing Last Chance Gulch, and they really need a heroic figure on a white horse to ride in and save the day.

Enter Jeremiah, minus the horse. It's Jeremiah to the rescue, but his is a thankless task inasmuch as the Israelites fairly forcefully refuse to be rescued. Poor Jeremiah finds little profit in being a prophet. Recruited over his own strong reservations (Jeremiah 1:6), this son of a priestly family almost immediately finds himself railing against Israelite infidelity in respect to the Covenant (Jeremiah 2:1–3:5). This tirade is merely for openers; there's much more to come over the course of Jeremiah's long, unhappy career.

The prophet's mission boils down to two often repeated messages, neither of them welcomed by those to whom they were addressed:

- You're wrong.
- You've got to change.

Before condemning Israelite deafness, consider how warmly we tend to greet bearers of similar tidings even when, like Jeremiah, they come to try to save us from ourselves. Take into account as well that Jeremiah does not as a rule address his words to individuals, but to the nation. What questions does this raise respecting our own role in and responsibility for the virtues and vices of today's institutions?

Jeremiah's road was a lonely one. Increasingly he sensed the desperation of Judah's situation. This tiny southern kingdom was all that remained of the Israelite nation after the fall of the northern kingdom some hundred and fifty years earlier. The menace of Babylon, the super-power of the age, hung over it like dragon's breath, and the only weapon in Judah's arsenal was its covenant with God, which it persisted in ignoring. As Cardinal Carlo Maria Martini states in *A Prophetic Voice in the City: Meditations on the Prophet Jeremiah* (Liturgical Press, 1997): "If the covenant means happiness, then the loss of this covenant is equal to unhappiness." Unhappiness in the form of a formidable Babylonian army was camped under Jerusalem's imposing walls.

Jeremiah kept trying, by turns coaxing, threatening, reasoning, reminding, wheedling, roaring—all to no avail. It's as if the national mute button was in operation. Parents and teachers easily relate to this phenomenon: "I feel as if I'm talking to a wall here!" Martini continues: "Jeremiah is a very modern figure because he is the prophet of apostolic solitude, a prophet who speaks in a society that does not listen, just like our modern society." To whom do we fail to listen? If these voices were heard, what might they have to say? What difference might they make in the unfolding of the future?

A cataclysmic seismic shift loomed dead ahead for Judah, one not reflecting the will of God but the obstinate refusal of the people to admit they'd taken a wrong turn down a dead end road . . . to turn around and set out yet again in the direction of their God. Louder than the frantic voice of Jeremiah were the siege engines of mighty Babylon. Jerusalem proved unequal to the barrage, and the reverberations from its fall echo throughout the remainder of biblical history.

Back to Babylon

Well over a thousand years after their forefather, Abraham picked up his sizable brood and moved from a region near Babylon around the Fertile Crescent to Canaan. His even more sizable brood of offspring reluctantly make the same journey in reverse in 587 B.C.E. After all those years, after all that plodding through Sinai, struggling to settle down, building a kingdom (complete with magnificent Temple), after all that, it's back to square one—back to Babylon, and in disgrace no less (2 Kings 25, 2 Chronicles 36:11–21, Jeremiah 39:1–14).

They've lost it all, or so they think. Jerusalem, indeed all of Judah, is a wasteland. The city walls lie in ruins, and when last they saw Jerusalem, fires still smoldered and smoke still rose. Zedekiah, the last of the kings descended from the revered David (see chapter 6), has been led away, blinded and chained, his heirs left dead behind him. Solomon's resplendent Temple has been stripped of its glory, its structure demolished, and its treasures carted off as spoils of war.

During the frenzied pandemonium of the conflict's final days, the Ark of the Covenant, too, is lost, its disappearance remaining a mystery to this day. 2 Maccabees 2:4–8 claims that Jeremiah himself hid the Ark, together with the Dwelling Tent, in a cave. Other rumors of its whereabouts come from points as distant as Ethiopia. The majority of scholars, nonetheless, believe the Ark to have been carted off to Babylon. If the Temple and the Ark were no more, did this mean that God had departed? Were the Israelites his people no more? Was the neglected covenant at last rescinded? So it must have seemed:

> By the rivers of Babylon—there we sat down and there we wept when we remembered Zion [Mount Zion in Jerusalem]. On the willows there we hung up our harps. For there our captors asked us for songs, and our tormentors asked for mirth, saying, "Sing us one of the songs of Zion!" How could we sing the LORD's song in a foreign land? If I forget you, O Jerusalem, let my right hand wither. Let my tongue cling to the roof of my mouth, if I do not remember you, if I do not set Jerusalem above my highest joy (Psalm 137:1–6).

Ezekiel on Self-Improvement

Among the attributes of God noted earlier were his unwavering fidelity to *his* side of the Covenant and his steadfast patience with the people to whom he was committed. Few episodes of biblical history reveal these characteristics more clearly than the Exile. The Israelites (now, due to their Judean origins, gradually becoming known as Jews) have bottomed out. Their state of mind is so low they can check under rocks without lifting them, a posture not unfamiliar to the majority of humankind at one time or another. If John of the Cross weren't still tens of generations away, they could have borrowed his "dark night of the soul" idiom.

As so often happens, the answer to their monosyllabic prayers (What? Why? How? HELP!) was right in their midst—the priest/prophet Ezekiel.

In this singular man, we find yet more evidence of the right person being in the right place at the right time with the right gifts, and using those gifts for the good of all. In its introduction to the Book of Ezekiel, *The New Oxford Annotated Bible* (Oxford University Press, 1991) reads:

> As a prophet to the exiles, Ezekiel assured his hearers of the abiding presence of God among them. He constantly emphasized the Lord's role in the events of the day, so that Israel and the nations "will know that I am the Lord" (a refrain that occurs many times throughout the book). He underscored the integrity of the individual and each one's personal responsibility to God (chapter 18). To a helpless and hopeless people he brought hope of restoration to homeland and temple by their just and holy God. In Ezekiel we have an unparalleled synthesis of the terrestrial and celestial in Israel's religion, truly fitting for one whose ministry marks the transition from pre-exilic Israelite religion to post-exilic Judaism.

Ezekiel is one of those transitional figures who stands with one foot planted firmly at the outermost edge of an era which is closing and one on the brink of a new age just ahead. For this reason, he is at times dubbed the "Father of Modern Judaism." Just as the Israelites were not the same at the end of the Exodus trek as they were setting out on the journey, so their descendants will be markedly different people when they ultimately return from the Exile after about half a century than they were trudging off to Babylon. Much of the credit goes to Ezekiel.

Like Jeremiah, Ezekiel had pulled out every trick in his prophetic repertoire to get the Judahites to hear and heed his message long before the Babylonians under Nebuchadnezzar huffed and puffed and blew their house down. Like Jeremiah, Ezekiel met with little success. Unlike Jeremiah, when catastrophe befell the nation, Ezekiel did not remain behind but accompanied the Israelites on their long march to the east.

Once there, Ezekiel abandoned his previous fiery oratory. The time for that was past. The deed was done, and, courtesy of voices like Jeremiah and Ezekiel, the weary people knew they had no one to blame but themselves for the predicament in which they found themselves. Now another type of message was sorely needed, and it could be summed up in a single word: hope. A commanding presence with a ringing proclamation of faith and trust might get those drooping Israelite shoulders squared and lift those chins sunken in despair.

All Is Not Lost

It is said that we can live without almost anything, but we cannot endure long without hope. The belief that this, too (whatever it may be at the moment), will end, that someday, somehow, things will improve can get us through the worst of times. Viktor Frankl, noted Austrian psychiatrist and survivor of Nazi death camps, observes in *Man's Search for Meaning* (Washington Square Press, 1984), that those who had the best chance of emerging alive from the horrors of those camps were those who most clearly had reasons to live. The hope, however dim, of finding loved ones, returning home, resuming a trade in due time kept countless inmates alive.

When it comes down to it, the only quality we truly know hell to possess is hopelessness: total, freely chosen, unending separation from God. Never mind the traditional imagery. If this is all there is to hell, it's sufficient. Restoring hope to a person restores the person, and with God, there's always hope.

Commencing at chapter 33 and continuing intermittently for the remainder of the book, Ezekiel attempts to rebuild a broken people, telling them all is not lost. God has not abandoned them. The Exile will end. They will return home—but when they do, a land laid waste will greet their anxious eyes, and restoring it will be a monumental task (chapter 36).

> Therefore thus says the Lord GOD: Now I will restore the fortunes of Jacob, and have mercy on the whole house of Israel; and I will be jealous for my holy name. They shall forget their shame, and all the treachery they have practiced against me, when they live securely in their land with no one to make them afraid, when I have brought them back from the peoples and gathered them from their enemies' lands, and through them have displayed my holiness in the sight of many nations. Then they shall know that I am the LORD their God because I sent them

into exile among the nations, and then gathered them into their own land. I will leave none of them behind; and I will never again hide my face from them, when I pour out my spirit upon the house of Israel, says the Lord GOD" (Ezekiel 39:25–29).

Improvise!

Those who are convinced that religious practices rarely change have read little religious history. Change is not only inescapable; it can be life giving, even life saving.

Stranded in Babylon, bereft of the Temple, which centered them as a community, God's people required another model for communal worship. Although it is by no means certain, many authorities attribute the rise of the synagogue to the period of the Exile. Vastly different in form from sacrificial temple worship, synagogue services, which could be held just about anywhere, revolved around prayer and readings from the biblical books, especially the Torah. Reeducation in that area was long overdue, and the time spent in a foreign land was ideal for a refresher course.

Although the Hebrew Scriptures had been gradually finding their way into written form since the tenth century B.C.E. when Solomon occupied the throne, much remained to be done. Adversity spurs action while prosperity permits procrastination. Especially is this true when there looms the possibility of extinction. We've read the end of the story; we know how the Exile turned out. The Israelites weren't blessed with this kind of foreknowledge any more than we are when faced with our own "exiles." If this was going to be the end for them as a people, they wanted to leave some record of who they were and what they'd done. A few hurried words scrawled on a cell or barracks wall accomplished much the same thing in places like Auschwitz and Buchenwald.

So when, in 538 B.C.E., the Persian king Cyrus became the new king of the Mesopotamian hill, having wiped up the sands with the once great Babylon, one of his first edicts sent the expatriates home (Ezra 1:1–4). Not everybody went. Many of those who had constructed rather nice lives for themselves in Babylon elected to remain. Most, however, hitched up their tunics and began slogging their way back around the Fertile Crescent.

Geography plays a surprisingly prominent role in biblical narratives, but it really shouldn't be a surprise at all. If religions are conditioned by the worldview of the people who espouse them, history is conditioned by the world in which the people live. Some of the biblical stories—Eden, for example—would read very differently had the Israelites lived in the Amazon rain forest or in the glacial north.

One way to reap the rewards of Scripture reading is to learn as much as possible about the geographical lay of the land. It's really no different from reading about the War between the States, where it helps to know whether Georgia was part of the Union or the Confederacy, or the settling of the American West, where the Great Plains made daily life a formidable task.

According to writer Thomas Wolfe, "You can't go home again." Actually, you can, but don't expect it to be unchanged, and whatever you do, don't expect it to resemble even remotely what you've turned it into in your dreams during your absence. All this notwithstanding, the returnees must have been stunned when they got their first glimpse of Jerusalem and the surrounding countryside. Ravaged and ruined, it had been left to lie forlorn and neglected except by the few left by the Babylonians to tend it.

Any expectation of a happy homecoming was instantly dashed. Years of exhausting work lay ahead, and at no point would life return to its preexilic form. As is usually the case, this was both an asset and a liability—an asset in that the Judahites had learned hard lessons while in captivity and had no desire to repeat the blunders of the past; a liability in that they had lost all of their material advantage, not the least of which was the Temple.

Leaders who are up to the task once again come to the fore, gifted with the necessary skill and knowledge. Every time I see this occur in the biblical narrative, I sense an obligation to vigilance since I never know when even my limited abilities may have an important part to play. The tales of these particular leaders, Ezra the priest and Nehemiah the layman, are set out in the books bearing their names.

The Memory Lingers On

The Exile was over—sort of. Life-altering experiences never completely end because (1) life is never quite the same thereafter, and (2) the memory lingers on.

Wars once begun never end no matter how many treaties are signed. Not only do they alter the course of the participating nations; they transform the lives of every person who took part, even indirectly. Once the first bullet or arrow flies, nothing is ever entirely the same.

Whether the event in question involves the entire nation in armed conflict or one person in a personal tragedy, it is so traumatic that it is remembered always, and not merely by those who actually experienced it. Generations, even centuries later, remembrance sets off an emotional response.

The author of the Book of Revelation counted on that, referencing Babylon six times (Revelation 14:8; 16:19; 17:5; 18:2, 10, 21). By the time he wrote late in the first century C.E., once mighty Babylon was a heap of sandy rubble, certainly no threat to early Christians or anybody else. The superpower by then was imperial Rome, and it is to Rome that John refers.

Then, why not simply say this? Apocalyptic literature, the genre in which Revelation is written, is highly symbolic in style. Nearly everything serves as a stand-in for something else. This writer is acutely aware of the fact that, by substituting Babylon for Rome, he will initiate a tide of emotional reaction laying just below the surface in the people's residual memory.

Extraordinary occurrences etch themselves in history. If asked about the Exodus, few people would inquire which one. Today, Pearl Harbor, Holocaust, and Cold War all conjure up spontaneous reactions. A modern writer might induce the same sort of latent fervor through use of the term Auschwitz.

In any case, we see through the highs of Israelite experience (the Exodus) and its dregs (the Exile) metaphors for our own lives. Life's ups and downs are destined to be with us always apparently. While we don't find this the most comforting thought, it brings a good deal of consolation to learn through Israel's history that God is there through it all. Judging by their memoirs, we also stand an excellent chance of emerging from both highs and lows in a new and improved version.

Some would say this is not too high a price to pay.

CHAPTER FIVE

Three Central Characters

I f asked to name their favorite biblical personages, most people head the list with Jesus (good choice!) and follow with a few others who, in all probability, are familiar from the gospels or, at the very least, the Christian Scriptures. The appearance of a personality from the First Testament would be enough of a rarity as to occasion surprise. There are sufficient legitimate reasons for this phenomenon to get us off the guilt hook:

- As Catholics, we're just getting to know the great figures who people the pages of the Hebrew Scriptures. Once more, we have Vatican II to thank for making sure we hear a reading from this section of the Bible virtually every weekend.
- Realization dawns early in reading the Hebrew canon that there are a lot of people coming and going, and converting one entire wall into a giant flow chart is about the only way to keep track of them all.
- While there are, to be sure, a certain number of Sarahs and Davids and Rachels and Samuels, these are quickly over-whelmed by a preponderance of Amminadabs, Eliakims, Zerubbabels, and Shealtiels—none of whom are exactly commonplace, even in the polyglot American culture. We can't remember them, let alone pronounce them. And spell them? Forget it.

- Often, whole platoons of such appalling appellations come at us in mind-numbing rosters and genealogies, making us long for the days when our literary aspirations were a simple matter of finishing *War and Peace.*

Whatever the rationale, it shouldn't be regarded as terminal. We can and should come to know and appreciate our ancestral heritage. Our role model might well be the Orthodox branch of Christianity, which has long seen the value of celebrating this longer perspective of salvation history by honoring saints from the First Testament.

The Israelite Version of Central Casting

The Hebrew Scriptures really do have the potential to become a never-to-be-equaled maxi-series, and it may register better in modern media-saturated minds to view it this way. From this perspective, it is apparent from the outset that the vast majority of the throng are extras who can be safely ignored. A sizable number of others are walk-ons, appearing briefly and exiting the set. These, too, can be disregarded. (Aren't you feeling better already?) Some have cameo roles that, while essential to the scene, are not its central focus. Now we're getting to the supporting parts to which we should pay some attention. Clusters of lesser-known kings and bands of minor prophets can be included here. But so can such figures as Delilah and Bathsheba, without whom the stories of Samson and David wouldn't make much sense.

Ultimately, of course, we arrive at the leading men and women: Sarah, Isaac, Rebekah, Jacob, Rachel, Joseph, Miriam, Joshua, Ruth, Samuel, Solomon, Isaac, Jeremiah, and Ezekiel, among others. These are characters of consequence whom we neglect at our peril. But even they pale by comparison with the unparalleled stars of the show: Abraham, Moses, and David.

If the others will keep for another day, these towering figures will not. Ignorance of these three, who they were and what they did, fairly well dooms any further effort to plumb the Hebrew Scriptures. And what may be of even greater import to Christians is that it fairly well dooms our efforts to understand Jesus as well, because his words, deeds, and mission are associated with every one of these men. Matthew's gospel sets the tone with its opening line: "An account of the genealogy of Jesus the Messiah, the son of David, the son of Abraham" (Matthew 1:1). Where's Moses? As will be detailed in chapter 7, Matthew will take great pains to portray Jesus as the new Moses throughout his writings.

Matthew is not alone. Early in John's account: "Philip found Nathanael and said to him, 'We have found him about whom Moses in the law and also the prophets wrote, Jesus son of Joseph from Nazareth' " (John 1:45). " 'Your ancestor Abraham rejoiced that he would see my day; he saw it and was glad.' Then the Jews said to him, 'You are not yet fifty years old, and have you seen Abraham?' Jesus said to them, 'Very truly, I tell you, before Abraham was, I am' " (John 8:56–58). These few examples can do little more than begin to forge the chain linking Jesus to each of these icons of the Hebrew/Israelite/Jewish tradition.

Who were these men, and why were they held in such high esteem? For openers, one was a foundational figure, one a prophet and liberator, one a king. Beheld from almost any angle, they couldn't be more different and serve as vivid reminders of the uniqueness of each individual. They are the three central characters on the skeletal structure we're constructing:

Abraham   — c. 1850 B.C.E.
Moses   — c. 1250 B.C.E.
David   — 1000 B.C.E.

Verifiable dates for Abraham and Moses are unavailable at this time—the further back in time we travel, the more difficult precise dating becomes. "Circa" (c.) indicates an approximation, an educated guess based on what is known at present. David's reign we can nail. While we may find the absence of exact dates exasperating, it is not, in defense of our antecedents, unexpected. Until relatively recently, players in the human comedy were not as time obsessed as we nanosecond types seem to be. Then, too, an assortment of calendars was in use throughout the biblical world, each with its own system of counting years. Supersonic transports and instantaneous communication have made a common calendar indispensable.

In sketching each of these men in turn, we not only will learn something about them, but will see why what they did so long ago remains relevant to our faith today and locks a few more pieces in place on this persistent puzzle: What are we doing here?

Abraham: Father of Faith

As alluded to in chapter 3, Abraham (Abram) makes his entrance onto the biblical stage in Act I, Scene 1. The Book of Genesis tells us enough about him to make it seem we know quite a lot about this man, but in actuality we don't. First, there's the matter of dating which so often plagues us. Positioning Abraham at roughly the middle of the nineteenth century B.C.E. isn't merely a blind stab, but neither is it pinpoint accuracy. Scholars have arrived at this time period based on what Genesis tells us about his lifestyle, which resembles what is known about life during the early second millennium B.C.E. If later evidence makes it necessary to reassess this judgment, it wouldn't threaten the foundation of faith.

Then, there's the question of finding the historical person within the body of legend and lore that has grown up around him. If you think this is a snap, explore the many volumes published in recent years centering on the quest for the historical Jesus. Ironically, a substantial amount of faith becomes essential in studying the "Father of Faith" since we are a long way from knowing everything we'd like to about this fascinating figure. This lack has not caused the three great monotheistic religions of the Near East (Judaism, Christianity, and Islam) to falter in accepting Abraham as their patriarch.

The Journey to God Begins

Abram called "Ur of the Chaldeans [Babylonians]" (Genesis 11:31b) home. Ur was a Sumerian (not Samaritan) city. Strangely, we hear nothing of Sumer in the Bible. This is surprising inasmuch as Sumer on the Persian Gulf was one of the most advanced of early urban civilizations. If the Fertile Crescent is imagined as a giant rainbow arching across the lands of the First Testament, it has pots of gold at both ends, Egypt in the west and Sumer in the east. If you're typical, you could probably write a respectable paper on the glories of ancient Egypt while remaining absolutely stumped in composing a single sentence about Sumer.

Sumer may be in need of better public relations because we really do owe the Sumerians a tremendous amount. Their clever idea of inscribing soft clay tablets and then baking them (cuneiform writing) is responsible for preserving untold numbers of documents until the present day. And, in this present day, we still make good use of the Sumerian system of mathematical systems based on sixes and tens. If Abram was Sumerian, chances are he was no backwoods boy (bad metaphor; there was a decided dearth of woods in those parts).

Leaving Ur for Haran (Genesis 11:31), Abram literally took the first step in a journey toward God that would continue until the end of time. Had he realized the significance of that moment, he might have been paralyzed into inaction. This was the ripple effect multiplied to infinity. On a lesser scale, it happens to us all on a regular basis. Our words and deeds, or the lack of them, start a chain reaction of which we are completely unaware. Words that remain etched in my memory may have long since faded from the recollection of those who uttered them. We, in turn, may have unconsciously influenced others in ways we never intended and couldn't have imagined.

This was brought home to me quite clearly when I heard myself parodied by students during a homecoming assembly and thought, "*This is what they recall from my class?*" (Sigh) Any action we take is a risk, but inaction can be far worse. In setting out, Abram was trying; sometimes he was more trying than others. He faltered and failed. Palming his wife Sarah off as his sister to save his hide in Egypt was a poor plan (Genesis 12:10–20), compounded by the fact that he did it twice! (Genesis 20)

God Finds Abraham

Not all religions can point to a single person as their founder. Jesus is, of course, the founder of Christianity, as Muhammad is of Islam. But is Abraham the founder of Judaism? Not really, although he is undeniably the patriarchal or father figure. Abraham does not initiate the encounter—God does (Genesis 12:1–3). Throughout the narrative, Abraham responds to God's direction. "So Abram went, as the LORD had told him" (Genesis 12:4a).

We find nothing especially extraordinary about this; it seems sensible to obey an order from God. A little more twenty-first-century American skin shedding is needed here. We tend to forget that all we have gleaned about God during the roughly four millennia separating us from Abraham was totally unknown to him. Like all societies of his time, his was polytheistic, awash in a sea of deities, each of whom had a distinct function. The notion of one all-purpose God was unheard of and would have been considered outlandish.

Although it is not recorded in the Genesis account, Abraham had to have asked (on behalf of us all): "Who are you?" That he would heed the call of this mysterious being and head north, then west toward Canaan, earns him for the first time the title "Father of Faith"—not Father of *the* Faith, just plain Faith. Abraham put his trust in an unknown god at a time when gods were not reputed to be especially friendly.

More than his own fate rested on Abraham's decision. He was the patriarch, and his family was a far cry from today's nuclear group comprised of Ma, Pa, and the kids. It involved a large extended family, similar in many ways to the family structure, which still exists in eastern Mediterranean countries. Abraham made decisions for them all and was responsible for them all. While acknowledging that the clan was undoubtedly seminomadic, the fact remains that this proposed expedition involved considerably more than a weekend outing. The family's livelihood was at stake; their very lives were at stake. There's a lot riding on this decision to obey the call of an unknown god.

When I attempt to walk a mile in Abraham's sandals, I wonder if I would have been so trusting with so much in jeopardy. I'd probably have insisted on some assurance that the venture would succeed, that this god would live up to my expectations. Like most people, I suppose, I long for certainty. However, if my desire were granted, there would be no need for faith and, as we have already seen, God gives every indication of preferring us to come to him freely and to believe even when we just don't get it.

William J. O'Malley, S.J., nails it nicely in *Meeting the Living God* (Paulist Press, 1998) when he says:

One's answer to the God Question is an act of *faith*, an *opinion*. It is neither "a blind leap in the dark" (which would be sheer idiocy) nor a belief based on evidence so clear and distinct that one can have no occasion to doubt it (which is impossible). An act of faith, like any opinion based on a great deal of evidence (Which career? Should we marry? Can we afford a child?) is a *calculated risk*. In all those free choices . . . including the choice for or against the existence and relevance of God . . . the more calculation, the less the risk. But there is always a risk you might be wrong.

An enormous amount of "calculation" has been done by minds great and small in the nearly forty centuries since Abraham, and the result has been a steady amassing of "evidence." Yet it is still not "so clear and distinct that one can have no occasion to doubt it." This will never come to pass. We and all those who follow us on the journey toward God will constantly require faith.

Again Abraham Stands Firm

It may appear that Abraham's life was full, but appearances can be deceiving. There was a black hole at its core, the lack of a firstborn son. This was a role of extreme importance in patriarchal clans. To the first-born son went much power and prestige, plus a goodly share of the worldly goods amassed by the father. So coveted was this position that some would go to nearly any length to acquire it. Read what Abraham's crafty grandson did to snatch the title and its rights from his older twin in Genesis 25:27–34. Upon Jesus' birth, he is immediately acknowledged as a firstborn son (Luke 2:7a), albeit his mother's.

> *SHORT ASIDE:* The designation "first son" has been used by some as evidence that Jesus had brothers and makes a prime example of how not to interpret the Bible. The reference is to his position in the family. Whether an only son or one of ten, Jesus was the firstborn son.

Little wonder Abraham was dejected. When he gripes that the steward (manager) of his household will wind up inheriting everything,

God tells him that that won't happen, that he will have as many descendants as the stars in the sky. "And he believed the LORD; and the LORD reckoned it to him as righteousness" (Genesis 15:2–7). For the second time, Abraham earned the title "Father of Faith."

Not such a leap of faith, you say? Babies are born on a fairly regular basis? Not to Abraham and Sarah, and by this time they weren't exactly middle-aged. There was a son, Ishmael, born to Abraham by Sarah's slave, Hagar. This was a perfectly acceptable practice. Sexual mores have gone through a host of modifications in the course of salvation history and, as you've no doubt noticed, continue to do so, leaving us to sort through what is meant by those who implore us to "return" to biblical family values.

When Abraham receives three unusual visitors, Sarah is disinclined to believe their promise that she herself will bear a son within the year (Genesis 18:12–15). She finds the prospect laughable. While acknowledging that the exaggerated ages of primeval Genesis should not be read at face value, we can be confident that Sarah was well past the time when age-defying moisture creams would have done much good. So when her son is in fact born, he is named Isaac, meaning "laughter." There must have been a great deal of that—laughter, rejoicing, celebration on a grand scale. After all those years, after the last hope had long since died, here he was, the Son of the Promise. How he must have been cherished (and no doubt spoiled). The future of the family depended on him. Everything depended on him, and then. . . .

Oh, Please, Lord! Anything But This!

As quickly as this unprecedented joy arose, it threatened to end. "He [God] said, 'Take your son, your only son Isaac, whom you love, and go to the land of Moriah, and offer him there as a burnt offering [holocaust] on one of the mountains that I shall show you' " (Genesis 22:2). What emotions must have coursed through Abraham—bewilderment, shock, grief, rage! How could this unfamiliar God who had proven so trustworthy thus far ask something like this? Only God knew what it would cost Abraham to obey.

Imagine this mournful journey: Isaac high-spirited at the prospect of an outing with his father; Abraham dragging his feet and trying to maintain a cheerful attitude before the unsuspecting boy. Of course, Isaac is saved at the last possible moment (although he may have been in therapy for the rest of his life), and Abraham earns his third star as Father of Faith.

Did this incident actually take place as described? We don't know. God as depicted here bears a much closer resemblance to the many gods Abraham had once worshipped. He was quite familiar with sacrifices to deities—but not to this God! No, *not* to this God. When idolatry reared its ugly head, as it would many times in Israelite history, this story was ready and waiting to be retold. It illustrates vividly that this God does not require human sacrifice—other types of sacrifices, yes, as the crops and creatures offered at shrines where the Ark of the Covenant reposed and at Solomon's Temple centuries later would testify, but people, no.

As Father Abraham clutched his beloved son to his chest, he probably wasn't thinking about this. He was thinking how precious Isaac's life was, and in this parental act, we see a bit more clearly how precious all our lives are and what faith really means.

> Now faith is the assurance of things hoped for, the conviction of things not seen. Indeed, by faith our ancestors received approval. By faith we understand that the worlds were prepared by the word of God, so that what is seen was made from things that are not visible" (Hebrews 11:1–3).

> By faith Abraham obeyed when he was called to set out for a place that he was to receive as an inheritance; and he set out, not knowing where he was going (Hebrews 11:8).

> By faith he received power of procreation, even though he was too old—and Sarah herself was barren—because he considered him faithful who had promised (Hebrews 11:11).

> By faith Abraham, when put to the test, offered up Isaac. He who had received the promises was ready to offer up his only son, of whom he had been told, "It is through Isaac that descendants shall be named for you" (Hebrews 11:17–18).

> Abraham, Father of Faith!

Moses, the Man for All Reasons

We've already had a considerable conversation about Moses in his capacity as liberator and leader of the Exodus. Still, we should spend a little more time with him here. In truth, it's almost impossible to say too much about this man, so large does he loom on Israel's stage. Of the three biblical giants characterized in this chapter, Moses stands tallest, center stage in the glare of spotlights which never entirely dim due to his ongoing influence over Israelite/Jewish belief and practice. For centuries, the revered Torah was also known as the Books of Moses in the belief that he in some sense authored them. This assumption is largely disregarded today, both because we know the Torah did not gain its final written form until long after Moses' day, and because the final episode chronicles Moses' death (Deuteronomy 34), which is something of a tour de force for an autobiographical writer.

It is Moses who at last effects the release of the Israelites from Egypt. It is Moses who leads the prolonged Exodus. It is Moses who speaks to God on Sinai and brings back the Law, which will ever after bear his name. It is Moses who acts as mediator between God and his wayward people. It is Moses who, as spokesman for God, is the great prophet. Had hats been fashionable, Moses would have had a closetful for he wore many.

None of this has ever been lost on those who revere him. Moses' place in salvation history remained or remains unchallenged, depending on your perspective. Christians use the past tense, seeing in Jesus the fulfillment of Moses' own words, "The LORD your God will raise up for you a prophet like me from among your own people; you shall heed such a prophet" (Deuteronomy 18:15). The writer of Matthew's gospel was mindful of the need his Jewish audience had to discern this and takes great pains to portray Jesus as the new Moses. Present-day Jews use the present tense, seeing in Moses an exemplar without equal.

We may not believe ourselves up to the task of being Moses but then neither did Moses. Life experience is cumulative, snowballing along almost without our notice. It has been said that life is what happens while you're making other plans. Nonetheless, the knowledge, wisdom, skills, and adventures we gradually collect can reappear in the strangest ways later in life. We should be careful about deleting items from our resumé; we may have need of them one day. Moses is a choice case in point.

Born to Hebrew slaves in Egypt and slated for slaughter, Moses is rescued by an unlikely savior, the pharaoh's daughter, who, in a peculiar plot twist, returns him to his birth family to raise (Exodus 2:1–10). "When the child grew up, she brought him to Pharaoh's daughter, and she took him as her son. She named him Moses, 'because,' she said, 'I drew him out of the water' " (Exodus 2:10). Curiously, this greatest of Hebrews is ever after known only by his Egyptian name. The names of great pharaohs such as Thutmoses stem from the same root.

Moses' upbringing was offbeat to say the least, but it was this very quality that proved invaluable to him later when his life flew off in a direction he never anticipated (as our own so often do). Having been raised with one foot in his own Hebrew culture and one in the Egyptian court, Moses was uniquely qualified to relate to each as the need arose. He was an insider who understood the sufferings of the Hebrew people, an empathy that would get him into hot water when he killed an Egyptian for beating a Hebrew (Exodus 2:11–15).

He was an insider with a working knowledge of the intricacies of Pharaoh's court, an ability that would stand him in good stead when he needed such access. Moses didn't see himself as the man for the job when, in fact, he was the *only* man for the job. It's the old "can't see the forest for the trees" thing. God requests; Moses demurs. God becomes more insistent; Moses becomes more reticent. God is patient; Moses goes, and grows. My, how Moses grows!

David, the Bible's Hinge Man

Having examined the pivotal roles played by Abraham, the father figure, and Moses, the nearly everything figure, we come now to David, the hinge figure. This is not what he's remembered for, of course, but David's life span does fit rather neatly into the historical progression, including as it does the year 1000 B.C.E., more or less at the halfway mark between the time of Abraham and the time of Jesus. This is one of the most useful dates on our skeletal outline, making it easier to see where other incidents and individuals fall on the time line.

This, however, is incidental. What we have in David is the great king, the architect of the nation. David, together with his son and successor Solomon, gave Israel its place, however briefly, in the sun. Powerful empires, kingdoms, civilizations of all kinds, tend to hold up one period in their history as a golden age, the time when, to borrow a hackneyed phrase, they were all that they could be. This wistful nostalgia commonly surfaces when the power in question is either in decline or has long since faded away. For Israel it would ever be the glory days of David and Solomon—especially David. As is to be expected, selective memory is at work here. All was not wine and roses—or milk and honey. Regardless, this period became the standard against which all others came to be measured, and David stood squarely in the center of most of it.

David: The Early Years

When David first appears on the biblical map, he is merely the youngest of a batch of boys fathered by Jesse, and the dot on the map from which he springs is a village just south of Jerusalem known as Bethlehem. The prophet Samuel has been sent to anoint one of Jesse's sons king. Israel's first king, Saul, wasn't working out. A replacement would be needed when Saul's unhappy reign came at last to a sad end (two conflicting versions: 2 Samuel 1 and 1 Chronicles 10).

Saul himself had been anointed by Samuel over the prophet's strenuous protests. When approached by Israel's tribal elders to select a king for them, Samuel was adamant in his aversion to the idea and graphic in his recital of what they could expect, none of it positive (1 Samuel 8:10–18). Rulers of old were almost invariably absolute monarchs, sole masters of their realms and answerable to no one. Life for his subjects was as good or as bad as he wished or allowed it to be. Of course, Israel already had a king, its God, who was not given to such power trips. So, as the clincher in his closing argument, Samuel bellows: "And in that day you will cry out because of your king, whom you have chosen for yourselves; but the LORD will not answer you in that day" (1 Samuel 8:18).

Why not? Is God finally weary of this tedious process of "people building"? Returning to the characteristics of God, this thought must be scrapped as inconsistent with the endlessly patient God who never fractures the Covenant. Something else must be at work here. As usual, it's us, humanity, being entirely too human yet again. "The LORD will not answer" because the people will have set a chain of events in motion that cannot be undone. Choices have consequences. When many of Samuel's dire predictions come to pass, not for this generation but for many yet to come, God cannot negate this freely made decision, put history on rewind, and start again with Samuel. The admission that this was a bad idea sometimes comes too late.

Then, having a strong distaste for having nobody to blame but ourselves, we ornery humans have the effrontery to blame God, or worse, to say that the mischief unleashed by our misuse of *our* free will is *God's* will. This would be a propitious time to pause to render heartfelt thanks for God's patience, then and now.

Another of our less than admirable traits surfaces when Samuel at length stops for breath, believing, I'm sure, there was no possible way his audience could have failed to buy his argument. Wrong! The elders continued to chorus their insistence that they be given a king just like the other kids . . . er, nations. If humanity is maturing, it looks to be a painfully slow process.

The voice of reason having failed, Samuel anoints Saul first king of Israel. There's no real need to detail Saul's checkered career in these pages except to say that for some years Saul's waning fortunes and David's waxing ones were tightly intertwined and are recounted at length in 1 Samuel 13–31. Notwithstanding David's early anointing, he will not take the throne until after Saul's death, ending years of David's fending off Saul's murderous moods, years in which David continued to honor Saul as king and assure him he intended no harm. All this and one of the most beautiful, if unlikely, friendships in any piece of literature, that between David and Saul's son, Jonathan, can be found in the chapters noted above.

David: The Great King

David is again anointed king, first of Judah (2 Samuel 2:1–7), then of all Israel (2 Samuel 5:1–5). Both events took place in Hebron, the site of the Tomb of the Patriarchs, traditional place of entombment for Abraham, Sarah, Isaac, Rebekah, and other memorable figures from

Israel's beginnings. (Today, the tomb abuts an Islamic mosque where a deranged gunman opened fire on Muslims at prayer in recent years.)

If Jerusalem would seem a more logical choice, it was eliminated from consideration because, quite simply, it wasn't part of Israel. Strategically situated atop hills, such as Mount Moriah and Mount Zion, Jerusalem (previously called Jebus) was relatively easy to defend and almost invulnerable to attack. After dwelling in Canaan some two hundred years, the Israelites still did not hold the city. David made rectifying this situation his first order of business (2 Samuel 5:6–12). Now the nation had a capital, and David moved his numerous wives, concubines, and children into the city. Israel was taking on the trappings of a nation.

Also brought to Jerusalem was the Ark of the Covenant which had been the centerpiece of one shrine or another since the end of the Exodus (2 Samuel 6).

Its arrival in Jerusalem was met with great celebration, and no one entered into the spirit of the jubilation with greater enthusiasm than David. "David danced before the LORD with all his might" (2 Samuel 6:14a). One of his wives, Saul's daughter Michal, was disgusted by his performance (2 Samuel 6:16), but David never saw honoring God as beneath his dignity. Nor did he, like so many other overblown egos occupying thrones, see God as beneath him. David's genuine humility may well be his most endearing character trait, one which will serve him well on less admirable occasions.

While enjoying the perks of sovereignty in a regal residence, David is troubled that the Ark has no permanent abode and broaches his court prophet Nathan about the construction of a temple. Nathan concurs but returns next morning saying, "Rub out and figure over" (free translation). During the night Nathan has had a dream whose ramifications will echo down the centuries.

The Promise to David

With this, we arrive at the first runner-up in the competition for most pivotal central events in the Hebrew Scriptures. So if you're reading this in bed and you're beginning to nod, save this section for tomorrow because you'll definitely want to remember it. The tale is told in 2 Samuel 7:5–16:

Go and tell my servant David: Thus says the LORD: Are you the one to build me a house to live in? I have not lived in a house since the day I brought up the people of Israel from Egypt to this day, but I have been moving about in a tent and a tabernacle [ark]. . . . Moreover the LORD declares to you that the LORD will make you a house. When your days are fulfilled and you lie down with your ancestors, I will raise up your offspring after you, who shall come forth from your body, and I will establish his kingdom. He shall build a house for my name, and I will establish the throne of his kingdom forever. . . . Your house and your kingdom shall be made sure forever before me; your throne shall be established forever.

Take note of the play on words that survives even in translation. David's intent is to build a house for God. By this he means a stone and mortar structure, a temple befitting the Ark it would house. Having gotten along quite nicely without such a building for some time, God has David defer this project to his successor, implying that there is more important business to which David should direct his attention. Instead of David building a house for God, God will build a house for David. By this God does not mean an edifice but a dynasty, a line of kings who will be of David's lineage and occupy David's throne.

Now notice how long this "house" of David is destined to endure: forever! Repeated three times for emphasis! David's subjects and the generations which followed them believed this implicitly. Like the covenant with God that made them the Chosen People, the promise to David was inviolable, one certainty in a most uncertain world.

The Davidic line did seem solidly entrenched for more than four centuries as one after another, David's progeny and their progeny ruled from his throne. David was followed by his son Solomon, who was in turn followed by his son Rehoboam, and so on down the generations. Nowhere in the promise to David is there the slightest assurance that all of David's heirs would be of his caliber—and few were!

There were a few shining lights:

• Solomon who did erect the Temple along with countless other structures in a building frenzy across the land;

- Hezekiah whose court prophet was Isaiah but who had the very bad fortune to father Manasseh, possibly the worst of them all (2 Kings 18–21); and
- Josiah who was compared to David and who strove mightily to rid Judah of idolatry (2 Kings 22–23:30).

Good or bad, able or inept, they came and went until nearly all of Judah went to Babylon for a half-century of exile. Zedekiah, unremarkable for his courage, saw his sons slain before he was himself blinded and led into captivity (2 Kings 25:1–7). That sorry chapter ended the Davidic line and its promise of forever. Or so it seemed to the depressed expatriates who viewed the demise of the throne of David as more than sufficient evidence that God had at last given up and abandoned them.

Appearances, however, can be deceiving, and promises may come to fruition in ways never anticipated. Over six centuries later, a writer would create a memorable document whose intended audience was composed of the offspring of those same deportees. We call this document the gospel of Matthew. Its opening sentence reads: "An account of the genealogy of Jesus the Messiah, the son of David, the son of Abraham." Jesus, born like David in Bethlehem, would preach earnestly about "the Kingdom" in this gospel, a realm that would begin here on earth, then transcend all temporal boundaries to embrace life unencumbered by the confines of time and space. David's line would most assuredly last forever, but in a guise no one could ever have imagined. God, we find, is unpredictable, and it is unwise to try to confine him to the manageable safety of a box of our own making.

The Anointed One

Imagination was not in short supply. During the course of Israelite history, a substantial amount of speculation was focused on a somewhat indistinct savior figure who was to come. The Hebrew title given this unknown deliverer was *Messiah* (in Greek, *Christos*). In either language, the designation translates to "anointed" or "the anointed one."

Earlier, we saw Samuel set off with a flask of perfumed olive oil in hand (today we call this chrism) to anoint first Saul, then David, Israel's king. Priests from the time of Aaron were anointed, as well as were some prophets. The anointing rite set a person apart, consecrating him to a hallowed vocation. The tradition lives on as each year diocesan bishops preside during Lent at a Chrism Mass during which the holy oils to be used by the parishes of the diocese during the coming year are blessed and distributed. Baptisms, confirmations, ordinations, and serious illnesses will be sanctified by them.

The author of Matthew's gospel goes to considerable lengths to establish Jesus as the Christ, a title, not a surname. His is the only one of the four canonical gospels to so much as mention the magi, or wise men, and he does so for good reason. This engaging tale is sure to fascinate his Jewish readers who will "get" each and every nuance we miss. Chapter 2 of the Matthean account has just about everything: exotic figures from faraway lands, an evil protagonist, danger, suspense, even a chase scene (sort of). The chapter is made up of three cleverly linked stories which, taken alone or together, serve to underscore Matthew's constant drumbeat: Jesus, son of Abraham, son of David, the new Moses.

First, we hear that "wise men from the East came to Jerusalem." This is it. Matthew is circumspect in his identification of these enigmatic travelers, and Matthew is the only evangelist to mention them at all. Notice that nothing is said about their mode of transportation, i.e., camels, let alone number and/or names of those in the group. Early Christian centuries tended to opt for a rather large number, but Renaissance artists elected to portray one visitor per gift, leaving us with a seemingly indelible impression of three. Contrary to the traditional carol, they were in all likelihood magi instead of kings, members of a Persian scholarly class of learned men who delved into, among other things, astronomy, which would have made them very interested in changes in the night sky.

However intriguing, this part of the story will keep for another day. Our focus here is the gifts they bring. While gold might remain on a modern holiday wish list, frankincense and myrrh would make a poor showing. None of the three offerings seems terribly appropriate for a young child. Another tap on the reader's shoulder here: Matthew's tale of the arrival of the magi is not concurrent with Luke's story of the arrival of the shepherds. The Church has wisely celebrated the Matthean event on Epiphany, traditionally January 6, ending the Twelve Days of Christmas (Shakespeare's *Twelfth Night*). Since Vatican II, Epiphany, known in a number of cultures as Little Christmas, has bounced around the early January calendar somewhat, but the idea is the same. "On entering the house, they saw the *child* . . ." (Matthew 2:11a).

But gifts! What about the gifts? Gold was a gift for a king. Frankincense was used, as incense still is, by priests. Myrrh was, among other things, a burial spice, used in some instances on slain prophets. If Jesus was offered gifts symbolic of the three anointed offices, he must in himself embody them all. He must be the Messiah. What's more, he must be more than the Jewish Messiah inasmuch as the gift bearers are Gentiles (non-Jews).

You may be rolling your eyes at this point and muttering, "Could this be more obscure?" Living as we do far removed from the time period and the culture, the message is hazy at best, but for Matthew's readers it was clear as crystal.

Why, then, was there such reluctance to confirm Jesus in this role? With the Roman boot firmly planted on Judea, Samaria, and Galilee by the dawn of the first century C.E., messianic hopes were running particularly high. While there were several quite different notions about the nature of the Messiah in circulation, the most prevalent was a strong warrior-savior who would rally the Jews into a fighting force, throw the Romans out, and restore the glory days of Israel. In the minds of many Jews, what was needed was another David.

Matthew, then, goes to considerable lengths to establish the connection between David and Jesus. All in all, there are seventeen mentions of David in Matthew's gospel as opposed to two in John's. For Matthew, it is essential to stress that both are members of the tribe of Judah, born in Bethlehem. The Davidic line continues in Jesus as does the promise, but both will manifest themselves in ways unimagined. The waiting Jewish people had a hard, sometimes impossible, time making that sharp right turn in their imagination. Personally, I find this entirely understandable. More than once, my prayer regarding a certain situation in my life has gone something like this: "All right, God, listen up. Here's the problem. Here's the solution. Here's your part. Now let's get busy." So set am I on my predetermined solution that I gaze fixedly straight ahead watching for it to appear on the horizon, never noticing that God is creeping around by my right ear with something much better that never occurred to me. Sometimes, it all but requires a whack between the eyes with a two by four to get me to adjust my focus to accommodate greater clarity.

The New Moses

The story of the magi's visit segues into the vicious attack on Bethlehem's youngest sons, instigated by the power-mad and paranoid king, Herod the Great. The fact that he orders all those "in and around Bethlehem who were two years old or under" killed (Matthew 2:16b) is still another indication that Jesus did not experience these events as an infant. Warned in advance, Jesus' family flees with him to Egypt, thereby escaping the clutches of a threatened ruler who seeks to secure his throne through infanticide. If you had been steeped in the Torah since birth, it's highly probable that a parallel episode would spring immediately to mind: Moses being saved from Pharaoh (Exodus 1:15–2:10) in, by sheer coincidence, Egypt.

Once Herod is no more and it's safe to return, Jesus leaves Egypt en route to the Promised Land, and a new Exodus has begun. Here the promised land, like the promise to David, will take on a totally unexpected form, ultimately expanding to a dimension no one could have foretold.

Matthew continues to develop his *new Moses* motif in chapters 5–7, his Sermon on the Mount. Luke's gospel contains a corresponding incident, but in his version it's the Sermon on the Plain (Luke 6:17–49). Each writer has a sound reason for positioning Jesus as he does. For Matthew, it's crucial that his audience immediately recall Moses on Sinai. This new Moses has not "come to abolish the law or the prophets . . . but to fulfill" (Matthew 5:17). But when he broadens and deepens the interpretation of the Decalogue, he does so, not as a prophet, but as God. "You have heard that it was said to those of ancient times. . . . But I say to you . . ." (Matthew 5:21–22). Like the promise to David and the Exodus journey, this new Moses represents something far beyond the original concept.

Broad Ancestral Shoulders

Jesus in his human nature was a product of his predecessors—as are we all. Matthew and Luke illustrate in their respective genealogies (Matthew 1:1–17, Luke 3:23–37) that Jesus' family tree was peopled by a great many more men and women than Abraham, Moses, and David (and Moses was not a blood relative). Even these biblical lineages are far from complete. But because Jesus' ties to these three were so pronounced and so often underscored in all four gospels, the letters of Paul, and other writings of the Christian Scriptures, we've spent an inordinate amount of time on them here, and still only scratched the surface.

It may now be easier to see why insight into the roles and legacies of these three extraordinary men is indispensable in coming to an awareness of who Jesus himself really is and what this might mean in our own lives.

CHAPTER SIX

Four Groups of Books

R ounding out our sketchy outline and much too brief visit to the First Testament, a concise guided tour to its general configuration and contents is in order. Bear in mind that the foremost incentive for delving into this topic is to accurately assess the material being presented in any given biblical book. The ability to do this lends definition to the God portrayed within its pages. Ronald D. Witherup, S.S., points the way in *The Bible Companion: A Handbook for Beginners* (Crossroad Publishing, 1998):

> Several different ways exist to subdivide the OT [Old Testament]. The Jews traditionally thought of their Hebrew Bible (the Christian OT) as having three sections:
>
> - Torah (Law)
> - Nebi'im (Prophets)
> - Kethubim (Writings)
>
> This threefold division appears even in the NT [New Testament] in which one passage speaks of "the law of Moses, the prophets, and the psalms" (Luke 24:44). . . .
>
> Christians, however, developed a different system of understanding the divisions of the OT. Reflecting a more messianic outlook, Christians divided it into four sections:
>
> - Pentateuch (Law)   • Prophets
> - Historical Books   • Writings

We have already committed considerable space to the Torah/ Pentateuch and a certain amount to the Historical Books so, although we shall revisit them to some extent in this chapter, most of our attention will center on the Prophets and the Writings.

The Towering Torah

Just as the gospels stand head and shoulders above any other Christian literature, the five books of Moses, the Torah (Genesis, Exodus, Leviticus, Numbers, and Deuteronomy), tower over all other Hebraic writings. Over the many centuries of Jewish history, it has not been uncommon for particular sects to recognize only these books as scriptural. Roland E. Murphy, O.Carm., one of the general editors of *The New Jerome Biblical Commentary* (Prentice Hall, 1990, 1968), sums up their significance:

> The marvel of the Pentateuch is that it is so many things at once: Torah, or the will of God for Israel; promise, or an adumbration [divine manifestation] of the future of the people of God; cult, or the way to worship the Holy One; a story of human rebellion and divine redemption; a call to attend to the origins of the Judeo-Christian tradition.

The reverence in which the Torah is held to this day is readily apparent at every synagogue service. Holding pride of place, preferably along the structure's east wall, the Torah scrolls customarily repose in an ark when not in use. The scrolls themselves are handwritten on parchment by scribes in much the same manner as they were long before Jesus' day. As columns of Hebrew text flow right to left from the hand of a skillful copyist, care is taken not to touch the word of God once it has been committed to writing.

Anna Marie Erst, S.H.C.J., discusses the veneration of Torah scrolls in *Discovering Our Jewish Roots* (Paulist Press, 1996):

> Each end of the scroll is attached to a wooden pole or stave and then wound on the poles. Around the scroll is a band of cloth to prevent it from unwinding when not in use. Since it is the most precious possession of the Jews, the Torah is lovingly decorated. A mantle of rich cloth with ornate stitching covers it. A metal shield and the pointer used in reading the scroll are hung from the poles. Crowns are placed over the tops of the poles. Some

crowns have little bells attached that tinkle when the Torah is moved. Because the script on the parchment could be damaged if a reader placed a hand on it while reading, a pointer [*yad*] is used. The Torah is "undressed" when brought to the reading table and then "dressed" after the completion of the reading(s).

Upon returning from attendance at a synagogue service, high school students in my senior religious studies class would unfailingly comment on the respect accorded God's word as recorded in the Torah. In recent years, Catholic practice has begun to confer comparable deference to liturgical books of the gospels. Still, we have a long way to go before equaling our religious forebears in this respect.

The tragedy of *Kristallnacht*, the horrific "Night of Broken Glass" perpetrated by Nazi agents on November 9–10, 1938, is heightened for me by the destruction, primarily by arson, of 275 synagogues across Germany and Austria. In a paroxysm of fire and shattered windows, Jewish houses of worship and their contents, including revered Torah scrolls, were profaned and obliterated.

David H. Buffum, American consul in Leipzig at the time, wrote: "Three synagogues in Leipzig were fired simultaneously by incendiary bombs and all sacred objects and records desecrated or destroyed, in most instances hurled through the windows and burned in the streets" (*Night of Pogroms*, U.S. Holocaust Memorial Council, Washington, DC, 1998). How many beloved Torah scrolls were ground beneath the heels of jack boots that night may never be known, but the thought of how such a sight would have affected the hearts of Jewish onlookers is painful to contemplate. The thought that many of those who executed such acts claimed to be Christian, even Catholic, is more painful still.

The Historical Books: Still Not Histories

The Pentateuch is, in at least one sense, comfortingly predictable. It's comprised of five books. When we wade into the Historical Books, things get a lot more complicated. Just a reminder at the outset: the fact that these works are historical does not mean they are histories. Suspend your usual expectations regarding historical treatises. For the most part, they don't apply here. Today's commonly expected niceties such as precise dates, documented people and places, accurate geography, cannot be relied upon in these pages. As a matter of fact, some books in this category are not historical at all; they're fiction. Don't hyperventilate. Remember, God speaks to us in a host of ways. The realization that some of them are not factual doesn't make them less true.

Nonetheless, the obvious distinctions to be found among these books make this the most difficult of the four groupings to nail down. Some of these works have been touched on earlier. The full list as it customarily appears looks like this:

Joshua	Ezra
Judges	Nehemiah
Ruth	Tobit
1 and 2 Samuel	Judith
1 and 2 Kings	Esther
1 and 2 Chronicles	1 and 2 Maccabees

The Hebrew Bible—39 Books (Or Maybe 46 Books)

The Historical Books are found in the order listed above immediately following the Torah/Pentateuch in most Bibles—*most* inasmuch as Tobit, Judith, and Maccabees are among the apocryphal or "deuterocanonical" books found in Bibles using the Septuagint canon for the Hebrew Scriptures. The which?

In its initial form, the Hebrew Scriptures contained thirty-nine books. By the third to second centuries B.C.E., there were about as many Jews living outside the Promised Land as in it. Scattered across the Mediterranean world, many had little familiarity with the Hebrew language. The "universal" language was Greek. Much like English today, Greek provided common ground for those who had economic or political dealings beyond their own borders.

Jewish scholars in the highly sophisticated city of Alexandria in Egypt (supposedly some seventy in number; hence, the name "Septuagint") created a Greek translation of their sacred writings. In doing so, they included seven books not embodied in the earlier version.

Upon the advent of Christianity, it became necessary to choose which version would become the First Testament of the combined

Scriptures. The Septuagint almost universally won the toss until the Protestant Reformation of the sixteenth century. Reformers by their very nature tend to revert to what they perceive as the rudimentary form, believing it to be the unadulterated tradition. This has led to long-standing descriptions of Bibles as being either Catholic or Protestant when, in fact, their Second Testaments are identical, and the contrast lies in the First. Much contemporary Scripture scholarship is interdenominational. As a result, several modern English translations contain all forty-six books but place the controversial seven in a separate section called the "Apocrypha" or "Deuterocanonical Books."

The March of Time

From Joshua through Nehemiah, the books are reasonably chronological. This doesn't mean that they cover every single year of every single century. Far from it! They highlight those events and characters which bear most directly on the ever-developing saga of God and the people, downplaying or even omitting other happenings, which might have been front and center on the world stage.

The exception in this set is the Book of Ruth, which reads more like a tender love story than a historical study. It is a treat to read (you probably already know one passage from it—try Ruth 1:16–17), and it has a very real purpose among the heavier works. As Witherup notes, "It [Ruth] has two primary functions: (1) to indicate the universality of God's salvation, and (2) to set up the ancestral lineage of King David, Israel's greatest ruler."

1 and 2 Chronicles are to the Historical Books what the Book of Deuteronomy is to the Torah, a repeat from a different perspective of material already covered in the preceding books. It can be quite instructive to compare the viewpoints manifested in Samuel and Kings with those in Chronicles. Differences, even contradictions, need not always be reconciled. They are often better pondered.

The Fiction Section

The Books of Tobit and Judith are distinctive on at least three counts. Both are fictional; both are among the apocryphal or deuterocanonical works; and both were written relatively late, c. second century B.C.E. Geographical and historical inaccuracies and inconsistencies serve to verify the literary genre. Their lack of historical standing makes them no less useful. As we found in the Genesis myths, God can and does reveal great truths in nonfactual formats. Such formats can often serve to present these truths more vividly.

For so short a book, Tobit contributes a surprising amount to our growing understanding of God. *The New Jerome Bible Handbook* maintains: "The message of the book, illustrated through ordinary faithful lives, is that God is indeed both just and free. Suffering is not a punishment but a test. God does, in the long run, reward the just and punish the wicked. The believer is called upon to trust God and to mirror in daily life the justice, mercy, and freedom of God."

Two interconnected strands make up the book. In a sense, both are love stories involving Tobit's son, Tobias. Undertaking an arduous journey on behalf of the father he loves, Tobias chances upon Sarah who has been more unlucky in love than possibly any other biblical character (Tobit 3). Tobias overlooks her alarming marital history and marries her. His romantically poetic address to her should have sold her on him if nothing else did (Tobit 8:4–8). That passage is finding increasing favor as the first reading at Catholic wedding liturgies. Ron Witherup recaps the intent of the Book of Tobit as, "Maintain your identity, keep close to your traditions, remain faithful to God, and all will turn out well."

Judith is the gory tale of the fearsome general Holofernes who very literally loses his head over the gutsy Judith who doesn't let her celebrated piety get in the way of saving the day. This is a real page turner although there aren't many pages to turn (both of these books are short), and like most adventures of its type, it is fiction. "[T]he first sentence of the book contains a blooper," says Mary Reed Newland in *A Popular Guide through the Old Testament* (Saint Mary's Press, 1999). "Nebuchadnezzar, the author says, is the king of Assyria when everyone knows that he was king of Babylon. It is so obviously wrong that we know that the author is teaching a lesson, not a history, in the manner of folk and hero legends. Judith may not have been a historical person, but she was a model of faith and courage, and that was what the Jews of that time needed."

One of the lessons here is that God will come to the aid of his people, especially in times of oppression, not infrequently through the most unlikely of instruments—even a woman! Before you cry, "Gender discrimination," bear in mind that it was Holofernes who was the victim of sexual harassment in the workplace.

Esther Saves Yet Another Day

Every year, during the month of Adar (February or March on the modern calendar), Jews celebrate a non-Mosaic festival, Purim, a joyous commemoration of Queen Esther, another woman of intelligence and courage who put herself on the line to save her people.

The story in its original form may date from the period immediately following the Exile, although it was surely edited and augmented as late as the second century B.C.E. Whereas the version we possess in our Bibles is largely fanciful, it is possible that the story is based on collective memories, a fragmented oral tradition, and Esther—and her uncle Mordecai may have had counterparts in history. Some of the confusion stems from the addition in the Septuagint of passages not found in the older Hebrew canon. This may have been done to add a more religious flavor to the book as the name of God does not appear anywhere in the older version.

Esther, you see, is not the consort of a Davidic king or any other king having to do with Israel. Esther is the Jewish queen of a Persian king, a king whose evil advisor has taken it into his head to exterminate all the Jews in the area. Long story short: Esther saves her people; the villainous henchman swings. All of this is observed in the manner of an old-time melodrama annually at Purim. Children dress up as Esther and other characters. The story is dramatized, and at the mention of the scoundrel's name, everyone stamps their feet, twirls their noise-makers, and generally creates as loud a din as possible.

Great fun, but serious, too, as one of the Purim prayers attests:

Grant us, O Lord, the vision to see and the courage to do Your will. Imbue our hearts with the fidelity of Mordecai and the devotion of Esther, that we may never swerve from the path of duty and loyalty to our heritage. Endow us with patience and strength, with purity of heart and unity of purpose, that we may continue to proclaim Your law of love and truth to the people of the earth, until all have learned that they are one, the children of the Eternal God. Amen.

GOD FOR GROWNUPS

"Hammering" History Home

The final pair of books included under the general heading "Historical" is 1 and 2 Maccabees, the story of a second-century B.C.E. revolt by Judeans against a particularly nasty regional ruler of Syrian-Greek heritage, named Antiochus Epiphanes. Greek power over the narrow land bridge that was Judea had resulted from the fourth-century B.C.E. conquest of the Persian Empire by Alexander the Great. (You remember the Persians—they assumed the role of superpower from the Babylonians who in turn had vanquished the Assyrians. All of these, with the possible exception of the Persians, had seemingly taken special pleasure in making life miserable for the inhabitants of Israel and Judah. Next up after the Greeks—the Romans. Same story.)

Following his untimely death, Alexander's empire was divvied up among his generals. Judah, which rarely got a break in these matters, fell under the aegis of Antiochus Epiphanes. Under his "protection," Judaism was in danger of being eradicated altogether. Jewish practices were banned. The Temple, not Solomon's but a second lesser version erected after the Exile, was confiscated and desecrated with pagan images (1 Maccabees 1). Desperate times call, as they say, for desperate measures. A priest named Mattathias and his five sons took to the hills where they assembled a kind of guerrilla force of like-minded countrymen (1 Maccabees 2). After Mattathias' death, his son Judas assumed leadership. On him was bestowed the nickname Maccabeus, "the hammer," possibly because of the ferocity of the fighting.

When the battle was won and the Temple recaptured, the next order of business was to purify and rededicate the house of God. Part of this duty was to reignite the eternal flame, which burned perpetually before the Holy of Holies. According to legend, only one vial of the requisite holy oil could be found, sufficient only for a single day. But when the lamp was lit, it continued to burn for eight days, providing sufficient time for the preparation of additional oil. This extraordinary happening is observed annually during the Jewish month of Kislev (December) as Hanukkah, the Festival of Dedication or Lights. The special Hanukkah menorah is set with eight candles, one for each of the eight days the oil held out. A ninth candle is included from which to light the others.

124

Having secured Jerusalem, the sons of Mattathias formed a ruling dynasty of their own, the Hasmoneans, with Simon installed as high priest. Thus began a brief period of self-determination for Judah before the tromping of Roman legions was heard to the northwest.

Interesting to Catholics is the long-held custom of looking to the Books of Maccabees for biblical evidence supporting the doctrine of purgatory. Once, when Judas and his men were collecting the bodies of their fallen comrades, it was noticed that many wore amulets sacred to pagan idols:

> He [Judas] also took up a collection, man by man, to the amount of two thousand drachmas of silver, and sent it to Jerusalem to provide for a sin offering. In doing this he acted very well and honorably, taking account of the resurrection. For if he were not expecting that those who had fallen would rise again, it would have been superfluous and foolish to pray for the dead. But if he was looking to the splendid reward that is laid up for those who fall asleep in godliness, it was a holy and pious thought. Therefore he made atonement for the dead, so that they might be delivered from their sin (2 Maccabees 12:43–45).

You may have trouble using this passage as a proof text, however, as the Books of Maccabees, too, are apocryphal.

Of greater import than the purgatory issue, perhaps, is the remarkably developed theology of afterlife. The notion of resurrection is prominently featured. While this may not have been the prevailing view (it wasn't even at the time of Jesus—see Acts 23:6–9), it had at least surfaced.

With Maccabees covering events as close to the birth of Jesus as a hundred thirty years, the grouping of books with a historical flavor draws to a close. The next chapter of Judah's foreign domination, the arrival of the Romans in 63 B.C.E., is not chronicled in the Hebrew Scriptures. Chapter 7 will have more to say about their influence.

Prophets, Not Fortune-Tellers

The prophetic writings consume considerable space in the Hebrew Bible—eighteen books in all. Within the collection as a whole, there are smaller sets, i.e., major and minor prophets, or writing and nonwriting prophets. The biblical books obviously deal with writing prophets; their names are right there in the titles. But, just so you know, there were a good many prophets who, so far as we know, never wrote a word. Some of them are quite prominent: Samuel, Nathan (who delivered the promise to David), Elijah, Elisha, and so on. We shall spend such time as we have, however, with the writing prophets.

Before launching into this discussion, it's usually advisable to define the role of "prophet" as it often becomes skewed. Prophets are synonymous in some people's minds with foretellers of the future. This aspect is not entirely absent, but it is not pivotal. Our English word derives from the Greek *prophetes*, meaning "to speak for." In Hebrew, the word is *nabi*, "one who is called." The quintessence of the biblical prophetic role is one who is called to speak for God.

Yes, the future frequently finds a place in prophetic utterances but more often than not, it is within a time line of past-present-future: This is where we've been; this is where we are now; this is where we will be— if we don't return to God; . . . if we don't change our ways; . . . if we don't listen; . . . if we don't live up to our covenant obligations, etc. It's less an ability to use a crystal ball than an ability to put two and two together. If these existing conditions do not change, the end result will inevitably be. . . . Parents and teachers are adept at this. (Granted, they ordinarily do not speak for God, although it never hurts if the youngsters being reprimanded believe this to be the case.) If a heavy smoker seeks treatment for breathing problems and a persistent cough, the physician need not be a soothsayer to know what the patient's future holds should he refuse to alter his lifestyle.

If prophets essentially spoke for God, it should also be kept in mind that they spoke to a specific audience in a specific time and place for reasons appropriate to all those factors. A prophetic voice to the Israelites in the eighth century B.C.E. was not addressing Americans in the twenty-first century C.E. That the messages delivered by those long-ago voices still find resonance with modern ears, minds, and hearts is one reason we believe biblical writings to be inspired. But to take those words out of context and make them predict contemporary events is just plain wrong.

Hopping down off that soap box, I am now ready to provide you with a list of the Bible's prophetic books by categories:

Major Prophets:

Isaiah
Jeremiah
Ezekiel

Minor Prophets (not because their words were of less import but merely because there were fewer of them; the books are arranged according to length):

Hosea	Jonah	Zephaniah
Joel	Micah	Haggai
Amos	Nahum	Zechariah
Obadiah	Habakkuk	Malachi

Related Writings (not properly prophetic but related to the prophetic books):

Lamentations
Baruch
Daniel

Can You Say Pseudonymous?

Quite a few books in both testaments bear the name of a single individual. We are inclined to take these at face value, assuming that the person whose name appears on the document is, indeed, its author. Come to find out, this assumption can lead one seriously astray. Through the long centuries of biblical writing, pseudonymous writing was not only prevalent but entirely acceptable. To write pseudonymously is simply to write under another person's name.

Why would anyone do that? Two rationales are most common. First, a writer may believe that attributing work to himself will assure limited readership and even less credibility, so a name with greater authority is assigned. Second, there may be a sincere conviction that this is what a deceased figure would have to say on a given subject were he still around to write about it, so the later writer speaks on behalf of the earlier. Today, we would sputter and fume about such a practice, but at the time these books were composed, it was perfectly admissible.

The Book of Isaiah makes an ideal case study. Isaiah is one of the longest of the prophetic books, and it's positioned first among them. In the course of its sixty-six chapters, we encounter not one author but three. Chapters 1–39 are the work of the original or First Isaiah and encompass events from the eighth century B.C.E. Second Isaiah, or Deutero-Isaiah, chapters 40–55, speaks of the Babylonian Exile, and so must derive from the sixth century B.C.E. The final section, chapters 56–66, is the product of Third Isaiah, or Trito-Isaiah, who has returned from the Exile and laments his ruined homeland while looking ahead to its restoration.

In addition to obvious historical differences, such elements as writing style, vocabulary, familiarity with the language, and geographical acquaintance are among the most widespread clues to pseudonymous writing. It seems only reasonable then to refrain from taking too literal a stance regarding any name heading a biblical book. Just as we've seen with myths and stories, pseudonymous writings are no less credible for taking an unexpected form. God speaks through a legion of voices and, in truth, we know very few of them by name.

The Spotlight's on the Messiah in Isaiah

It may come as something of a surprise that the term *messiah* never appears anywhere in the Hebrew Bible, turning up only in the Christian gospels, Acts of the Apostles, and one quick allusion by Paul in his Letter to the Romans. The word *anointed,* on the other hand, is used liberally throughout the First Testament and sparingly in the Second. Regardless, the messianic concept is prevalent in Isaiah (all three authors). For this reason, readings from this prophet are selected for the Sundays of Advent during the A and B cycles of liturgical passages, as are the Christmas readings in all three cycles. The best known of these is taken from the original Isaiah (11:1–10), a portion of which reads: "A shoot shall come out from the stump of Jesse [David's father], and a branch shall grow out of his roots." Another, from Third Isaiah, was appropriated by Jesus as part of the "inaugural address" Luke has him deliver at the outset of his public life (Luke 4:16–19): "The spirit of the Lord GOD is upon me, because the LORD has anointed me; he has sent me to bring good news to the oppressed, to bind up the brokenhearted, to proclaim liberty to the captives, and release to the prisoners; to proclaim the year of the LORD's favor" (Isaiah 61:1–2a).

Also to be found in Isaiah are the mysterious suffering servant texts from Second Isaiah (Isaiah 52:13–53:12) which form the first reading every Good Friday. Although the parallels with Jesus' experience are unmistakable, scholars continue to struggle with the impasse of whom the author was describing.

Lawrence Boadt, C.S.P., concludes in *Scripture from Scratch* (St. Anthony Messenger Press, 1298, 1998):

> The Book of Isaiah came into being through the work of several authors and editors reflecting on the original inspired manuscript of Isaiah of Jerusalem. Whatever the details of this process, the Church believes that the Holy Spirit guided each new insight that was eventually incorporated into the final work.
>
> Revelation is rarely if ever a one-time moment of insight, but the community of faith's slow growth toward understanding God's ways. This understanding is then written down, sometimes piece by piece, and then joined, sometimes with a long period of gradual development and many editorial hands, as in the case of the three Isaiahs.
>
> The New Testament cites Isaiah more than any other book of the Old Testament as the prophetic preparation for Jesus Christ. In its present form, the Book of Isaiah has greater power than almost any other book of the Bible because it testifies to the enduring will of God to save in every age.

Jeremiah and Ezekiel Bracket the Exile

Overshadowing Isaiah in length, and many would say in importance, is the sad saga of Jeremiah for whom prophecy was not the most restful of vocations. His sufferings come from without and within. In chapter 20, after being lashed and placed in stocks, Jeremiah feels angry, hurt, tricked, and betrayed by the God he tries so hard to serve. He threatens to quit, saying he will not so much as mention God's name (Jeremiah 20:9). But he knows he cannot keep himself from pleading with the people to change, no matter what it may cost him.

Jeremiah teaches many lessons to his own time and to ours, none more poignant than that serving God is not always agreeable and, contrary to some contemporary sermonizers, does not automatically or even usually pave the way to riches and ease. Jeremiah was as human as they come and not above speaking candidly with God. His cry has found an echo in many a mouth, including perhaps our own. In the end, it is his faith that saves him, if not his people. Jeremiah never gives up on God and, of course, God (though it doesn't always seem that way) never gives up on Jeremiah.

While Jeremiah grew hoarse entreating his countrymen to change their ways and avoid the Exile, Ezekiel was in effect waiting in the wings to take over the prophetic chores once the people were relegated to Babylon.

READER TAKE HEED: Entering the Book of Ezekiel can be a bewildering experience, full of fantastic visions, i.e., the dry bones (Ezekiel 37:1–14), and strange symbolism. Here we encounter for the first time, but certainly not the last, a literary genre known as apocalyptic writing. So much of another book, Daniel, is devoted to this style that it is questionable whether it should be ranked with the prophets at all. Apocalyptic passages are also found in the writings of some of the minor prophets, such as Zechariah. Still, the most exceptional illustration of this type of literature is found in the Book of Revelation, so a more penetrating look will be reserved to chapter 10.

Prophecy in a "Minor" Key

The minor prophets should not be seen as less meaningful, merely less lengthy. They can be not only instructive to read but great fun. Take, for example, Amos (my personal favorite in case you were expecting true objectivity here). Amos, who by his own admission is not a career prophet, is a Judahite sent to upbraid residents of the northern kingdom of Israel in the eighth century B.C.E. We all know how much we appreciate having someone from the outside start pointing out our shortcomings . . . even if he's right (actually, that makes it worse). So it would behoove Amos to make a low-key, discreet entrance, right? Addressing himself to the wives of the most powerful men in Israel's capital city, Samaria, he opens with: "Hear this word, you cows of Bashan who are on Mount Samaria, who oppress the poor, who crush the needy. . . . The time is surely coming upon you, when they shall take you away with hooks, even the last of you with fishhooks" (Amos 4:1–2). My, that was diplomatic!

Mark the comments about the poor and needy, though (see Amos 8:4–14). It is in large part through the words of the prophets that what we consider today the Judeo-Christian social justice ethic begins to form. If you keep a running scorecard on the conditions most frequently railed against by the prophets, you'll find social justice issues right up there with idolatry and failure to live out the Covenant.

This, too, demonstrates moral development. Initially, such concerns surfaced little if at all. It wasn't due to callousness; it was due to a lack of belief in an afterlife. If you don't believe you're going anywhere else, naturally you'll want to stay here as long as possible. Thus, long life was viewed as the greatest of all possible blessings, and quite possibly accounts for the exaggerated life spans found in Genesis: "Thus all the days of Methuselah were nine hundred sixty-nine years; and he died" (Genesis 5:27). Well, I should think!

If you hope to stick around a good long while, there are a couple of other assets which would make that long road smoother—health and wealth. If you were possessed of these, you were blessed by God; if not, w-e-l-l. . . . At the very least, one need feel no remorse for the poor and the afflicted. They must have brought it on themselves or, if it couldn't possibly have been their fault, they must be suffering for the sins of their forebears.

By the time we start hearing from the writing prophets, c. eighth century B.C.E., thoughts about afterlife had changed substantially and, with them, ideas of social responsibility. The obligation to care for others had been right there in the Law all along, but understanding was growing. Nonetheless, blasting old ideas out of people's thinking takes considerable doing.

Centuries later, when Jesus encountered the man born blind, "His disciples asked him, 'Rabbi, who sinned, this man or his parents, that he was born blind?" (John 9:2) You can almost hear Jesus sighing from here. Even today, when tragedy strikes, Jesus' followers say things like, "What did I do to deserve this?" or "Why would God do this to me?"

God *didn't* do it. More often than not, we're suffering the consequences of someone else's misuse of free will, which, as remarked earlier,
sets a domino effect into motion that cannot be undone. God may permit
events to unfold, but God cannot be their cause. It would be inconsistent
with the nature of God as we have come to perceive it.

Prophets sometimes lived out their messages more forcefully than
they could ever write them. Hosea comes to the fore in this respect.
Hosea marries Gomer. Gomer is a "working girl." Hosea basically says,
"Let me take you away from all this," and Gomer is fine with it for awhile
but eventually grows restless and is unfaithful to Hosea. Hosea the
faithful and Gomer the faithless represent God, ever faithful to Israel and
the Covenant between them, and Israel, ever unfaithful pursuing other
gods and forgetful of Covenant obligations.

Micah is the last of the four eminent prophets from the great
prophetic century, the eighth century B.C.E, the others being Isaiah,
Hosea, and Amos. Micah, too, is disturbed by social injustices (see
chapter 2). The best reason for mentioning Micah, however, is that it
affords us an opportunity to cite one of the loveliest bits of phraseology
found anywhere in scripture: "He has told you, O mortal, what is good;
and what does the LORD require of you but to do justice, and to love
kindness, and to walk humbly with your God?" (Micah 6:8) This single
verse would be adequate for an entire retreat.

The last of the minor prophets we'll look at is Jonah, dubbed by one
commentator as the Bible's comic book. This rings true to me as I never
can read this short story (which is what it really is, rather than a
prophetic utterance) without laughing. The lesson that God is a universal
God, desirous of the salvation of all humankind, is apparent from the
outset as Jonah is commissioned to travel to the city of Nineveh. He
carries the message that God (whom they know not at all) is unhappy
with their behavior.

Nineveh, you see, was the capital of the odious Assyrians. Marching
in there with orders of any kind would be tantamount to arriving at the
Reichstag in 1940 and telling Hitler that his conduct was unbecoming.
Jonah considers his options and decides on a Mediterranean cruise
instead. Well, you know the fish story that ensues. Ultimately, Jonah
winds up in Nineveh where, wonder of wonders, the Assyrians actually

listen and go into sackcloth and ashes mode—the *in* style for mourning and repentance—which annoys Jonah to no end (he's something of a grump by nature, it seems). He has no interest in seeing a merciful God spare a sorry lot of Assyrians.

When Jonah sits down to wait it out, God allows a bush to grow above him for shade, but even this withers. Now Jonah is truly ticked off, and we get the story's lesson from no less a personage than God: "You are concerned about the bush, for which you did not labor and which you did not grow; it came into being in a night and perished in a night. And should I not be concerned about Nineveh, that great city, in which there are more than a hundred and twenty thousand persons who do not know their right hand from their left, and also many animals?" (Jonah 4:10–11)

The collected works of the minor prophets are filled with such gems which are all too rarely mined. Treat yourself and see what an unexpected God springs from these pages: the just God of Amos, the faithful God of Hosea, the kindly God of Micah, the merciful God of Jonah (who also sports a wry sense of humor).

Writings or Wisdom Literature?

Everything that fails to fit neatly or awkwardly into one of the other three groupings winds up by default in the last. While some Christian writers designate these books as Wisdom literature, the Jews have always wisely termed them the Writings. Some works in this section do follow the literary form of Wisdom literature, but not all. In fact, this section lays before the reader a virtual smorgasbord of literature that includes poetry, song lyrics, a great debate, and folk wisdom.

Whereas the books of the first three divisions bear a certain relationship to one another, these books could scarcely be more different. Yes, the connecting thread of Covenant continues. And yes, we learn still more about the nature of the God we worship and what a relationship with that God entails. In fact, these books teach us profound lessons about what we are doing here, the Second Big (B-I-G) Question.

Matching Wits with God

First up to the plate in this new game is Job, and whoever made this determination should be congratulated. He would have been hard pressed to find a more engaging read. If all you know about Job is that certain people are said to have the patience of . . . , you have a real treat in store for you.

Certain aspects of this book are a bit fuzzy. There are no allusions to historical events, so it's unclear when it was written, although probably after the Exile. Job 1:1a has the title character living in the "land of Uz," a locale unknown as yet but supposed to have been Edom, somewhere to the east, which makes Job something other than Israelite. Did Job really exist, or is he an allegorical figure who represents each of us? In the final analysis, it doesn't much matter because the focal point of the book is not a person at all, but rather the question of why the innocent suffer.

One of the most serious enigmas facing humanity, it is a direct outgrowth of the earlier supposition that suffering is the result of our own or our ancestors' wrongdoing. If, as the Hebrew/Israelite/Jewish grasp of God advanced, this theory began to be discarded, then the question had to be addressed all over again: Why do the virtuous suffer?

Nowhere is it better examined than in *When Bad Things Happen to Good People* (Avon Books, 1981), Rabbi Harold S. Kushner's story of his own experience with personal tragedy and his "need to put into words some of the most important things I have come to believe and know." His point of reference is Job.

If what was said earlier about the confirmation of God's blessing being found in long life, health, and wealth, Job was the most sanctified of men. Well on his way to a long life, Job had both health and wealth in overflowing abundance (Job 1:1–5). All is lost in the twinkling of an eye as the result of a celestial wager between God and Satan (the name means "adversary").

God brags about Job's many virtues (1:8). Satan cynically retorts that it's fairly easy to be loyal and upstanding when everything's going your way. What would happen if it weren't? (1:9–11) God agrees to test him, and the unfortunate Job is about to see his entire world collapse (1:12). Cattle rustlers make off with his herds; lightning strikes his flocks; thieves carry off his camels; and the house falls in on his children (1:13–19). So much for wealth! Job's faithfulness is immovable, and he says only: "Naked I came from my mother's womb, and naked shall I return there; the LORD gave, and the LORD has taken away; blessed be the name of the LORD" (1:21).

This good man's troubles do not end there. Next, he is covered with "loathsome sores . . . from the sole of his foot to the crown of his head" (2:7b). So much for health! In the end, he finds himself sitting "among the ashes" trying to figure out which direction that eighteen-wheeler came from.

Three friends arrive to commiserate with Job, and at this point the book truly opens up. The bulk of the remaining text is devoted to dialogue or debate between Job and his friends over the grounds for the dire straits in which he unexpectedly—and undeservedly—finds himself (3:1–37). Finally, God speaks in one of the most magnificent oratorical responses found anywhere in Scripture (38–41). If you read nothing else in this book, spend some time with these four incomparable chapters.

The Book of Job has a Hollywood ending. God returns to Job everything he had before the bottom fell out of his life—and doubled. The corroboration of his blessed status is found in the book's final verses: "After this Job lived one hundred and forty years, and saw his children, and his children's children, four generations. And Job died, old and full of days" (42:16–17). It seems almost anticlimactic.

Sing to the Lord!

If Job is a hard act to follow, the only sensible course is to turn to the exalted Psalter, Israel's songbook. In Hebrew, the book's title is *Tehillim*, meaning "cultic songs of praise" (cultic in the sense of being used in formal religious rites rather than the more pejorative sense of current usage). It is certainly true that psalms of praise constitute a major portion of the total. There are, however, a number of other classifications: royal psalms, both national and personal psalms of lamentation, psalms of thanksgiving and of blessing and cursing, processional and pilgrim psalms, and more—150 in all, constituting one of the Bible's most protracted volumes.

Actually, the Psalter as we have it today may date from the latter half of the third century B.C.E. and is comprised of five (a reminder of the Torah) shorter collections: 1–41, 42–72, 73–89, 90–106, 107–150. Within these are found several near duplications. Compare Psalm 14 with Psalm 53.

The name most often associated with the psalms is David. Close to half of the psalms are ascribed to him, which is a tribute to the esteem in which the beloved king was held for his musical ability, as well as his statesmanship. David's skill with the lyre is recorded in 1 Samuel 16:14–23. Nonetheless, David couldn't possibly have composed all or even most of the psalms credited to him as many postdate him. Attaching his name to them is not so much pseudonymous as simply an effort to honor him.

The psalms in our Bibles constitute an assortment of song lyrics. They form a kind of hymnal for the second Temple period following the Babylonian Exile. Such psalms as 24, 111, and 118 are certainly cultic. Others, i.e., 42–43 and 115, are antiphonal, inviting the assembly to respond to the leader and clearly illustrating the source of this liturgical usage among some Christian traditions, certainly Catholics, in responsorial psalms.

If you'd like to commit an entire psalm to memory, the two terse verses of Psalm 117 may be right up your alley. Avoid Psalm 119 at all costs. It's the Psalter's longest by far. Should you decide to go for it for the sheer challenge, one aid to memorization is built right in; Psalm 119 is an acrostic. Its 176 verses are broken down into sets of eight, each alphabetically headed by one of the twenty-two Hebrew letters. Of course, this is not much help if you don't know Hebrew, even less when the Hebrew is translated to English, thereby destroying the pattern. Psalm 119 can also be subtitled the Psalm of the Law as synonyms for Law or Torah appear in every verse: law, decrees, precepts, statutes, commandments, ordinances, word, etc.

Consonant with the majority of literary forms appearing in the Bible, psalms are routinely found in the cultures of the Near East. A large library of cuneiform tablets found in the ruins of Ugarit, a much older Semitic city north of Israel, yielded a multitude of psalms, some of which could be the preliminary versions of those later collected in biblical form.

Neither is the Psalter the sole source of this literary genre in Scripture. The Canticle of Moses (Exodus 15:1b–18) and the Song of Deborah (Judges 5:2–31) are the oldest known Hebrew poetry, likely dating from the thirteenth or twelfth centuries B.C.E. In the Christian canon, Luke uses canticles to great effect, placing them in the mouths of Mary (1:46–55), Zechariah (1:68–79), angels (2:14), and Simeon (2:29–32).

The psalms of the Hebrew Bible were carried over into newly emerging Christianity almost immediately. The earliest direct quotation is Paul's in his Letter to the Romans, where he cites Psalm 117 (15:11). The gospel of Mark also contains a line from Psalm 118 (11:9).

The greatest tribute to the Psalter may well be found in Catholicism's official daily prayer, the Liturgy of the Hours, once known as the Divine Office. Modeled after the prayer hours of the Jews, this order of prayer for every time of day is required for members of some religious orders and other clergy, advocated by others, and popular since Vatican II among the laity as well. The psalms form the backbone of this ancient form of prayer, and during the course of its four-week cycle, nearly all 150 are recited or sung. For as Justin Martyr observed in his second-century C.E. description of a Sunday liturgy (one of the earliest extant): "The Scriptures are read, and Psalms are sung."

The psalms easily burrow into human hearts because they seem to arise from human hearts. By turns glad, mad, and sad, the psalms run the gamut of emotions and reveal a people very much at home with their God and who speak to him on the most familiar terms about situations we know and experience today. Jesus died with Psalm 22 on his lips (Matthew 27:46b). It's safe to say many of his followers have done the same. The psalms are Israel's prayerbook—and ours.

The Wisdom of . . . Solomon?

Three works found among the Writings are credited to Solomon, and he may well be the inspiration behind them, but he is certainly not their author inasmuch as he was long dead before any of them attained their final form. Two of the three, Proverbs and Wisdom, can lay legitimate claim to being Wisdom literature. In this genre, Wisdom is personified; that is, given the traits of a human. Sometimes called Lady Wisdom, the attendant pronouns are therefore uniformly feminine.

Consider first the Book of Proverbs, the first nine chapters of which are unquestionably Wisdom literature. Beginning at chapter 10, the book shifts into proper proverb mode and commences to pepper the reader with a rapid-fire succession of short, pithy sayings. Proverbs are by nature folk wisdom and are universal in nature. Every culture, every clan, every family has them ("As my grandmother used to say . . .").

Each succeeding generation passes them along, largely because they contain a tremendous amount of practical . . . well . . . wisdom. They speak of life as we all know it, and the insights of those who preceded us can tell us much about where the rubber hits the road. When mouthing yet again one of my own family's adages, I find myself wondering exactly how many generations have repeated these words, probably verbatim.

Next, take a look at the Book of Wisdom. I know it doesn't follow in biblical succession, but it is kith and kin to Proverbs. Here we have a prime example of Wisdom literature. Here we also have the most highly developed theology of afterlife found in the Hebrew Scriptures. Credit this to its very late date. In terms of composition, the Book of Wisdom is the last biblical book written, dated somewhere during the first century B.C.E., some say as little as three decades prior to Jesus' birth. It is also one of the apocryphal writings. Immortality and the reward of the righteous are prominent themes here, particularly in chapters 1–5. Wisdom 3:1–11 is frequently heard in Catholic funeral liturgies. The concluding portion of the book is of interest for an entirely different reason, providing a lengthy commentary on Israel's central event, the Exodus (11:2–19:22).

The third book associated with Solomon is a contrast to the other two. Oh my, is it ever a contrast! For starters, it goes by any one of three names: the Canticle of Canticles, the Song of Solomon, and more commonly these days, the Song of Songs. A love story by any other name would still raise eyebrows to new heights. Solomon may have seemed a logical signature to attach since history cast him in the role of the perfect Romeo (long before the Shakespearean version). It wasn't much of a stretch, what with Solomon's proclivity for marriage. "Among his wives were seven hundred princesses and three hundred concubines" (1 Kings 11:3a).

Whether Solomon's resume had anything to do with inspiring this book or not (probably not), the finished product is the Bible's most erotic composition. (There will now be a short pause as this volume hits the floor, and everybody runs to read the Song of Songs—it's not very long.) Over time, many have hastened to assure readers that the meaning is allegorical, pertaining to the depths of covenant love to be found between God and his people. This is a perfectly valid interpretation and the book's poetry is beautiful when read this way. Nonetheless, the literal validation of human sexuality finding its highest form of expression in a fervent love relationship between a man and a woman is inescapable and every bit as beautiful and authentic.

An Optimist Disguised as a Pessimist

Next on the docket: the Book of Ecclesiastes. Do not make this your choice for a rainy Monday at the end of an exhausting workday. It will not lift your spirits. The book's title is a Latinized version of the Hebrew *Qoheleth* who is the Teacher spoken of in the text. "Vanity of vanities, says the Teacher, vanity of vanities! All is vanity. What do people gain from all the toil at which they toil under the sun? A generation goes, and a generation comes, but the earth remains forever" (Ecclesiastes 1:2–4). It goes downhill from there.

When all is said and done (and it takes a while), writing Qoheleth off as a poor candidate for Optimist Club membership does him a terrible disservice. Upon closer examination, it becomes evident that this is a serious student of the human condition who asks hard, but justifiable questions. What is worth devoting your life to, and what isn't? What endures after everything else has become faded or jaded?

For Qoheleth, it comes down to God. Life is not in vain as long as God guides the course of the world. His view constitutes more what can be expected in this world than the next. Probably written in the third century B.C.E, Qoheleth may not have had a terribly well-developed sense of afterlife. When you look at what he rejects as so much "vanity and a chasing after wind" (Ecclesiastes 2:26b), you find the book has a surprisingly contemporary outlook. We could do worse than to spend some time poring over Qoheleth.

The most famous passage in Ecclesiastes is "For everything there is a season, and a time for every matter under heaven: . . ." (3:1–8). It even became a pop ballad a while back, entitled "Turn, Turn, Turn." Biblical wisdom can turn up in the most unexpected places.

Last, But Not Close to Least

The final title from the Writings and the last book to be explored in the Hebrew canon is the Book of Sirach, also known as the Wisdom of Ben

Sira or, earlier, Ecclesasticus, which is disconcertingly close to Ecclesiastes. Another late arrival, possibly dating from the second century B.C.E, Sirach is the concluding entry in the list of apocryphal books incorporated by the Septuagint.

If ever you're seeking practical advice on anything from correct speech to choosing friends, Sirach can assist you . . . at length. This is by far the longest of the Writings with its fifty-one chapters brimming with pragmatic guidance. The suggestions, recommendations, and warnings are reminiscent of the Book of Proverbs and, in a sense, of all Wisdom literature.

In an attempt to assist people with plain old day-by-day living, wisdom books lean heavily on what is sensible. Among signs I have seen posted on office walls are "Life is so daily" and "Everything takes longer than I thought it would." We're not the first to come to these conclusions.

And Finally . . .

We learn a lot about human nature in the course of reading the dissimilar biblical Writings. But what do we learn of God? What divine characteristics emerge from these pages to add to our expanding concept of the mind behind it all? If Job contrasts the sheer power of God with God's love for the righteous and concern for their welfare, the Book of Wisdom takes a longer view of life and features God as the liberator of the Exodus.

The Psalter puts us in the driver's seat and gives us a wealth of channels through which to praise, thank, atone, or petition God either collectively or individually. The Song of Songs reveals God in a spousal relationship with his people and his people in spousal relationships with one another.

And all of the Writings have much to say about who we are expected to be. If we see ourselves as created in the numinous rather than physical image of God (Genesis 1:26a), then all the qualities these books encourage in us reflect the God whose creation we are: faithful, joyous, honorable, pure of heart, loving. . . . The list goes on and on. If this is the so-called harsh, unyielding God of the Old Testament, I think I can live with that.

CHAPTER SEVEN

Jesus According to Mark, Matthew, and Luke

Having explored, however inadequately, the themes, events, characters, and books that help to shape the concepts of God held by our Hebrew/Israelite/Jewish forebears in faith, we turn now to the one person who anchors it all for Christians: Jesus, the Christ. This entails a shift to the Second Testament of the Bible, the Christian Scriptures.

The framework we have constructed to help navigate the Hebrew Scriptures is useless here as there is but one central character: Jesus, first, last, and everywhere in between. No book of the Christian canon could exist without him. He is the centrifugal force that pulls everything together. Jesus may well be the most universally recognized name in human history. Even those whose sense of Christianity is peripheral often believe they know Jesus rather well. Those who center their lives on him are convinced of it.

Still, who is Jesus really, and what does he mean in our lives? I have been posing this two-pronged question to everyone from high school seniors to a wide demographic mix of adults for years. For me, this inquiry is the crux of Christianity. Like the hub of a great wheel, all other considerations radiate out like spokes from this axial issue. It was asked by Jesus' disciples and others during his lifetime, by bewildered survivors after his death, and by every serious seeker from that time to this. Doubtless, it will be pondered until the end of time. The Christian concept of God is inextricably bound up in it.

John W. Donohue, associate editor of *America* magazine, spoke to this topic in a column he wrote for the magazine:

> More than thirty years ago, Mary Crozier, who was then the TV critic for *The Tablet* in London, recalled that she had not been brought up in any church and had not read the New Testament until at age nineteen she read Matthew and John in the original Greek for an Oxford exam. "How extraordinary, strange, and haunting a story I found this coming to me with all the freshness of another language. . . . Anybody thus reading this story for the first time must answer the question: is it true, or is it not true? If it be true, then Christ lives, and if he lives, then I must become a Christian."

I almost envy her encounter with the Jesus story as a young adult. She carried with her no baggage of preconceived ideas or, worse, over-familiarity. Cradle Catholics may actually be at a disadvantage when contemplating serious Bible study as adults. Dutifully warming a pew Sunday after Sunday through the years, we have heard weekly snippets from this gospel or that to the point that we may no longer really hear them. Once we hear intoned, "There was a man who had two sons . . ." (Luke 15:11ff.), our mental Rolodex calls up the card "Prodigal (or Lost) Son," and we feel free to mentally bird walk down all kinds of paths entirely foreign to the matter at hand.

Jesus was right (as he tended to be) when he warned: "Then pay attention to how you listen; for to those who have, more will be given; and from those who do not have, even what they seem to have will be taken away" (Luke 8:18). In this chapter, we shall make an effort to pay attention to how we listen and, in the process, perhaps hear a little more or hear a bit differently.

Challenging as it may be, I encourage you to at least attempt to read the gospels as though you were totally unacquainted with their contents. For if we are only going through the motions of listening, isn't there a danger we are also only going through the motions of believing? Mary Crozier's forthright conclusion bears consideration from us all. Is what we read in the gospels true or not? If it is, Jesus is alive, and I have no option but to fall in behind him, to become an authentic Christian.

Faith, particularly the type of adult faith described in the opening chapters, is not part of the human genome. It is not inherited like hair texture and eye color. Granted, faith is a gift from God, but if it is not nurtured, it is apt to atrophy, just shrivel up and die. We sigh and muse about how much easier those first-century disciples had it. But really they didn't. The operative query for all those, first to presumably last, who come in contact with Jesus and who take this encounter seriously remains: Who is Jesus really, and what (if anything) does this mean in my life? You won't have all the answers after reading these two chapters (nobody ever has all the answers; this is what makes the faith journey such a daring and exciting venture), but chances are you'll have a lot more questions. This is as it should be. Answers are good; questions are better.

Jesus: The "Real" Story

Life would be so much easier for Christian scholars had Jesus simply dropped his completed autobiography into the waiting hands of his apostles at the time of his ascension.

> *ANOTHER POINT TO PONDER:* Scientists assert that had Jesus' ascension taken place exactly as it is described in the Bible, he would not yet be out of our solar system. H-m-m-m! Does this suggest that we should jettison this belief? Not at all! But it certainly implies that we need to view it from another angle.

But no such luck. Not only did we not get a finished "Life and Times of Jesus, the Christ," but there was no "Handy Dandy Guide to Discipleship" or "The Definitive Catalogue of Sins, Numerically Ranked." We got what we've had from the beginning: a continuously developing idea of the nature of God, the capacity for rational thought, and free will. Used in combination, this triad helps more than anything else with our ongoing inquiry: What are we doing here?

Prevailing dating of Jesus' death, resurrection, and ascension places them in the year 30 C.E. The earliest gospel, Mark's, is commonly slotted between 65 and 70 C.E. This leaves a gap of thirty-five to forty years between the end of Jesus' public life and the first organized written account of it. So firmly is the quintessential nature of the gospels ingrained in us that we forget how many of Jesus' first followers lived and died without ever laying eyes on one. The three best-known figures recorded in the Acts of the Apostles—James, Peter, and Paul—had all suffered martyrs' deaths before Mark's gospel came to be.

The Evolution of the Jesus Story

What happened during those three or four decades? How was the Jesus story preserved? By now, you can probably guess—oral tradition. People talked, no doubt at length, about this extraordinary person, wrestling with the same question posed at the opening of this chapter. If you had been privy to these conversations, to which events do you think they would have pointed? Wouldn't the puzzling quandaries surrounding Jesus' death and resurrection have commanded the lion's share of attention? Almost certainly! And because they did, many authorities posit that the gospels were almost composed backward. Proportionately, far more ink is devoted to these elements of Jesus' life than to any other. This is so true for Mark's gospel that it has been dubbed a passion narrative with a prologue.

As is often the case with illustrious figures, those aspects of their lives that drew the most attention during their lifetimes remain pivotal after their deaths. Only later is attention drawn to other areas, such as their parentage and childhood. While he could easily have had other reasons, the absence of any mention of Jesus' early life in Mark's gospel is worth noting.

In all probability, the first written record of Jesus took the form of collections of his sayings and deeds. This practice has continued into modern times. During the Cultural Revolution of Mao Tse-tung in China, loyal Maoists were almost never found without their little red books, containing the words of Chairman Mao. The "Analects" preserve the words of Confucius. Jesus' own utterances are not infrequently positioned differently in the various gospels, leading scholars to believe they were appropriated from collections of this sort. Do any survive? If they do, they have yet to be found. Only the evidence of them remains. The set of sayings known as "Q" (from the German *quelle*, simply meaning "source") has gained the most acceptance, is manifested in Matthew and Luke's work, and will be referenced again later.

Seeing Mark, Matthew, and Luke "With One Eye"

Before we proceed much further, it is necessary to clarify why it is that three of the four canonical gospels are being lumped into a single chapter while the fourth receives a chapter all its own. It can be explained in a single word, and the word is *synoptic*. Mark, Matthew, and Luke are nearly universally termed the "synoptic gospels." A derivative of the Greek *synoptikos*, meaning to see "with one eye," these three accounts (not biographies) of Jesus are often studied together because they hold so much of their material in common.

John's gospel, on the other hand, stems from separate sources entirely, sharing very little with the other three. As we shall shortly see, the link connecting the synoptics is the gospel of Mark. When reading from the synoptics, it can be enlightening to take advantage of the cross references provided in most Bibles to see what Matthew and Luke do with earlier Markan material.

Another eye opener is to read one of the gospels in its entirety in a single sitting or, at most, two or three prolonged sessions. Here's a tip: choose Mark. Not only is it the shortest of the four, it's the prototype, virtually inventing the literary form known as gospel. This experience is almost guaranteed to bring the narrative to life in ways impossible when hearing Sunday readings. Facets of the book will all but leap from the page:

- what kind of writer the author is (characterize him as you would any secular literary figure you encountered in that long ago "lit" course);
- what sort of audience he seems to be addressing; Jewish? Gentile?;
- what the dominant themes of the book are (what this author really wants you to get);
- how Jesus is characterized (if this were the only gospel we possessed, how would we perceive Jesus?);
- who the "stars" of this gospel are (in addition to Jesus who is the star of every gospel).

For the purpose of this reading, utilize no study materials, commentaries, footnotes, cross-references, atlases, concordances, or biblical dictionaries. Just read. You may find a Jesus unlike any you've ever encountered.

The same thing happens in our other close relationships when we unexpectedly are made aware of an aspect of a person's character or personality of which we were previously completely ignorant. Surprise, we're told, is one sign of a healthy, growing connection. Jesus, you may find, has an infinite capacity to awaken surprise in us, surprise that leads to wonder, wonder that ends in awe.

The Gospel Truth

What is a gospel? Simply put, a gospel is an organized account of Jesus—what he did, what he said, what it meant. No gospel accounts for every period, let alone every year, of Jesus' life. Each presents Jesus from a specific perspective, rather like a prism. The unalloyed "white" that is Jesus is filtered through the planes that are the four evangelists and emerges in a wide range of different, yet not incompatible, colors.

This coloring is shaded by a number of determinants:

- who the author is and what his own background and experience are,
- when and where the document was written,
- who it was written for,
- what sources were available to the author
- how talented any given writer is.

The finished gospel has a very human author (or authors) but, as is true of all biblical writings, is also considered inspired. Clearly seeing the hand of the human does not hide the hand of God.

To see more clearly how four works dealing with the same subject can be so similar and at the same time so dissimilar, try writing a letter. Pretend that you are a devout contemporary Christian writing to someone of your acquaintance who is not. If you emulate the customary model of such correspondence, you will select the content of your epistle using two databases, yours (the sender's) and the recipient's. First, you will cull from the many words and deeds of Jesus those which, were there no others, serve unequivocally to convince you that this Galilean artisan (his trade surely encompassed more than carpentry) is worthy of your trust, your love, your faithful allegiance—in other words, what sold you. You speak from your own standpoint—whose else can you use? And you write more or less conversationally (see Luke 1:1–4), personally, and convincingly, using direct scriptural citations sparingly if at all.

You will do all this with an eye firmly fixed on the recipient. It may be of some assistance to have a real person in mind. From what you know of this individual's life experience, personal philosophy, likes and dislikes, what can you sift from the body of information at your disposal that would be most apt to draw a response from this person?

In essence, this is the process the evangelists used in unfolding the Jesus event for their very specific audiences. Once you have completed your letter, keep it at your elbow as you read the gospels. Chances are, you'll discover an affinity between your own missive and that of one of the gospel writers. This occurred often when students read such communiqués aloud in class. It startled them when I'd say they sounded markedly like Mark, etc.

After trying your own hand at such an assignment, it becomes far easier to see that we should expect to find the fine hand of the human author displayed, sometimes overtly, sometimes covertly. It also brings a new realization that the audience for whom the book was written played a primary part in determining what was written. Analogies are always inexact, so before hands commence waving in the air, let me assure you that I am fully cognizant that the gospels are not letters. Regardless, the process really is comparable.

"Mark"ing the Birth of the Gospels

If Jesus' words and actions managed to be preserved for three to four decades through the time-honored modes of oral tradition and sketchy writings, what necessitated Mark's unconventional new format? Few there are who, upon awakening some bright summer morning, announce, "I think I'll write a book." Something triggers the process. To see what might have launched Mark on his literary career, let's take a look at his world. (Remember the notion that worldview is a major determinant of religion?)

By the year 65 C.E, Jesus' disciples were scattered throughout the Mediterranean world, due in part to their dispersion following the death of Stephen and the ensuing persecution (Acts 6–8:4). A leading figure in this earliest persecution ordeal was a Jewish Pharisee named Saul. We'll hear from this worthy personality again under the name of Paul.

During these opening chapters in the history of Christianity, it should be noted that the Jewish disciples of Jesus didn't see themselves as Christian at all, but instead as followers of the "Way" (Acts 9:2; 18:26; 19:9, 23; 22:4; 24:14, 22). If Jesus was, as they believed, the fulfillment of the Hebrew Scriptures, the Messiah, then the implications for the belief and practice of their ancient faith had entered a new phase. They remained Jews but in an electrifying new way.

This manner of referring to a system of religious belief as a "Way" is rather common across a broad spectrum. In one of the classical Chinese religions, Taoism (pronounced as if the *T* were a *D*), Tao may be translated "Way." In this tradition's most familiar sacred writing, *Tao Te Ching*, the allusion is to the "Way of Nature."

After Paul got knocked on his ear while en route to Damascus (told three times for emphasis in Acts 9:1–19; 22:3–16; 26:2–18), convincing him that he ought to change his "way," he crisscrossed the land of the eastern Mediterranean, almost invariably taking his message first to the local synagogue (Acts 17:1–2, 10–11, 16–17; 18:1–4; 19:8–9). Foothold after foothold became established, and Paul continued his resolute journeys by land and sea until, ultimately, he arrived in Rome (c. 60 C.E.) not of his own volition (Acts 27–28).

At the time, Rome was ruled by the mercurial emperor Nero—and this may have been true in more ways than one. That Nero was mad is almost a given; that his madness might have been induced in part by mercury (the same substance that gave rise to the term "mad as a hatter" much later in England) is at this point speculation.

It is said that Nero fiddled while Rome burned (doubtful, since fiddles were in short supply during this era!). Be this as it may, a cata-strophic fire swept the city on the Tiber in the year 64 C.E. Fingers pointed suspiciously, if surreptitiously, at the emperor who had made no secret of his dream to turn Rome into a shining tribute to his august self, much as the narcissistic Ramses II had done a thousand years before in Egypt. This could not happen until less desirable sections of the city were razed. Fire accomplished that nicely, but Caesar would be foolish to admit to the arson. A scapegoat was needed, and who better than that annoying little group even the Jews disliked? It was a bad time to be

Christian in Rome. Many died, including, tradition tells us, those twin pillars whose statues now flank St. Peter's Square at the Vatican, Peter and Paul.

Mark's gospel is thought to have originated no earlier than 65 C.E. because the fire of 64 saw the dawn of the Christian troubles. Peter and Paul must have fallen victim to the bloodshed somewhere between 64 and 67 C.E., though no exact dates are available. One Dionysius of Corinth claimed that the two "were martyred at the same time." Imagine the loss to the young communities they founded, some of them weak and unstable, sustained by personal or written counsel from unquestioned authorities such as these.

Peter and Paul were not the only leaders lost, and not all were falling victim to Nero's volatility. By the 60s, the eyewitness generation from Jesus' day was disappearing simply by attrition. Even if Nero had stuck to a career in music, the result would have been much the same. Those who had been looked to for direction for decades were disappearing as much from age as from mauling. Those far-flung communities they had tried to hold together would now be dangerously isolated, leaving the quintessential body of belief vulnerable to splintering. Something needed to be done to confront both situations. A truly orderly account of Jesus' words and deeds could be immensely helpful. Naturally, no one can say with certainty that these were the thoughts coursing through the mind of Mark as he began to write, but it's highly probable they played a part.

Who Was Mark?

One more time: authorship in the Bible is seldom as straightforward as it appears. Nowhere is this more apparent than in the gospels. Who was Mark? Finding a reliable answer to this question is not helped along by the fact that Mark (Marcus) was the most common given name for Roman males during the first century C.E. Maybe it would be less taxing to begin with who Mark is not. He is not one of the Twelve, that inner circle among Jesus' disciples. His name appears nowhere on the various rosters of the Twelve—or Eleven after the defection of Judas (Matthew 10:2–4; Mark 3:16–19; Luke 6:12–16; Acts 1:13).

This favored clique doesn't get a very good press from Mark either, something he might be more reticent to do were he one of their number.

This raises the possibility that he was not an eyewitness or, if he was, who knows for how long, where, and when. If it is uncertain that he was an eyewitness, then the question of the need for secondary sources surfaces. What can we surmise about this writer, which may give us some insight into why he wrote what he wrote?

After weighing the evidence, the scale tips toward the John Mark alluded to in Acts 12:12. The name *John* is Hebraic while *Mark* is a Hellenized (Greek) form of the Roman. Bearing a name from each culture was a fairly common practice. This particular John Mark accompanied Paul and Barnabas on a relief mission (Acts 12:25) and, later, on their missionary journey, an experience that apparently ended badly.

Since they were related (Colossians 4:10), Barnabas suggested taking the young man with them on their next expedition, but Mark's performance the first time out must have left a lot to be desired as Paul emphatically declined (Acts 15:36–39). If it's the same Mark, the two later wound up being fellow prisoners (Philemon 24). The relationship between the two must have warmed as Paul later asked Timothy to "Get Mark and bring him with you, for he is useful in my ministry" (2 Timothy 4:11b). Whatever their relationship, the two were on familiar terms, making Paul a probable secondary source.

An even better one might be Peter. An extremely old tradition connects them. The second-century patristic writer, Papias of Hierapolis, cites an even earlier record:

> When Mark became Peter's interpreter, he wrote down accurately, although not in order, all that he remembered of what the Lord had said or done. For he had not heard or followed the Lord, but later, as I said, [heard and followed] Peter, who used to adapt his teaching to the needs [of the moment] without making any sort of arrangement of the Lord's oracles. Consequently, Mark made no mistake in thus writing down certain things as he remembered them for he was careful not to omit or falsify anything of what he had heard.

The author of the earliest gospel never identifies himself, nor does he bring himself into the manuscript in any way with the possible exception of 14:51–52: "A certain young man was following him [Jesus], wearing nothing but a linen cloth. They caught hold of him, but he left the linen cloth and ran off naked." Because the episode is not intrinsic to the plot and because it appears in no other gospel, it has led some to believe the anonymous youth was Mark who, ashamed of his cowardice, used this as a method of confession and atonement. We'll never know.

The detailed discussion of the authorship of this gospel is intended to illustrate that authorship of the gospels is nowhere near as uncomplicated as it initially looks and, as can be ascertained in the case of Mark, we do not possess all the pieces to the puzzle yet. Probing the authorship of the other gospels may by necessity be more concise in these pages, but it remains axiomatic that the more we know about who did the writing, the better we will grasp the writing itself. This truism holds for time and place, also.

The When and the Where

Turbulent events nearly always find their way into the literature of their time. If you were trying to date a book written at some indeterminate point in the first half of the twentieth century, and there wasn't so much as a passing reference to the Great Depression or World War II, you'd be reasonably safe consigning authorship to the 1920s or before. As noted, it is believed that Mark did not write prior to Nero's persecution as there was no need. It is also supposed that the book could not have been written later than 70 C.E., the year the Romans destroyed Jerusalem and its Temple. Almost certainly, some at least indirect reference to this cataclysmic event for Jews would have found its way into Mark's writing had he known about it.

Rome has long been the accepted locale for this gospel. If Mark was as closely associated with Peter as is thought, it would only be reasonable to place Mark in the city where Peter and Paul met their ends. The dominant themes of this gospel blend with the Roman scene under Nero. The gospel's rise in Rome would also help explain its rapid dissemination. The ancient adage "All roads lead to Rome" should have been supplemented by: "All roads also lead away from Rome." Whatever traveled the matchless system of roadways connecting even the remotest regions of the Roman Empire arrived at its destination expeditiously. Mark's new gospel was being used for the writing of Matthew and Luke's within two decades of its inception.

Mark's Target Audience

Although there were surely converts from Rome's Jewish community among Mark's newly Christian readers, they were clearly not the majority. Mark takes great pains to explain Jewish customs, which would not have been necessary if his readers were already familiar with them. Ritual purification of hands is spelled out in 7:3–4; Passover observance in 14:12; and the day of preparation for the Sabbath in 15:42. He carefully translates Aramaic terminology: 3:17; 5:41; 7:11, 34; 10:46; 14:36; 15:22, 34. He goes into considerable geographical detail as well, indicating that his readers are largely non-Palestinian.

Conclusion? Mark's audience is principally composed of Christian converts from paganism who have never set foot in the biblical world of the eastern Mediterranean.

Mark, the Media Writer

Once my students have read Mark's gospel in its entirety, I ask them to critique his style. It is absorbing to see how perceptive, and accurate, their conclusions can be, based solely on their own reading of the text. Most say that Mark would make a great modern media writer because he gets right to the point and doesn't seem much concerned about flowery language. True. Commentators have dubbed Mark the no-frills gospel. His Greek vocabulary is not extensive, and his syntax can only be described as basic.

Yet, there's an excitement and energy to this gospel that carries its reader along at a great pace. This quality has earned it the title, the action gospel. As one writer wisecracked, "If Jesus ever sat down, Mark does not record it." (I wish I could remember who wrote that in order to express my thanks for a superb line, which I have used extensively over the years.) If you take my advice and read Mark in a single sitting, you're likely to come away feeling a little breathless, hemmed in by demanding crowds and assailed by droves of demons. Mark may not be hung up on style, but he's a fabulous storyteller. Even if he weren't, he'd still take home the trophy for creating a completely new form of literature.

What Mark Wants His Readers to "Get"

The dominance of the Passion is undeniable in Mark and furnishes still another justification for a Roman locale. The motif of Jesus' suffering is linked to the idea of discipleship. Newly baptized Christians, seeing their colleagues carted off to imprisonment, or worse, for nothing more offensive than their faith in Jesus, had to be asking if they'd made the right decision. Mark reminds them that it is the nature of a disciple to follow the master. And where did this master go but to the cross?

His disciples should not expect anything less. Should they not wind up literally dangling from a cross (an all-too-real possibility), they would at the very least be required to metaphorically carry one as they encountered the hardships of life. The good news (gospel) is that the story doesn't end at the cross but at the empty tomb. Looking ahead to the Third B-I-G Question, all of the gospels send the same message: for Christians, death is never the last word. The last word is life.

The first half of the Markan account takes place in Galilee and features a mystifying literary technique known as the messianic secret (1:33–34; 3:12; 5:43; 7:36; 8:26). In some of these instances, Jesus charges demons not to reveal his identity. In others, he asks those who have just witnessed preternatural healing to tell no one. Fat chance! Even without the resources of *The National Inquirer*, such astounding news would have been bouncing off every tongue in the area before nightfall.

Human beings haven't changed that much! Take one of the best known instances, Mark 5:35–43, the restoration to life of the synagogue leader's daughter. Raising the dead is quite likely to raise the roof. What is Mark trying to pull off? Well, nobody's entirely sure. The most prevalent view is that Mark is attempting to prevent Jesus from being seen as simply another itinerant wonder worker, that he's striving to pull people's gaze past the incident and focus it on Jesus. Although Mark's action scenarios accent Jesus' deeds more than his words, in the final analysis, it's who Jesus is that counts.

Jesus in Mark

If the gospel according to Mark were our only gospel, our perception of Jesus would coincide with the Markan themes and his unique way of committing them to writing. As a result, we would meet an extraordinarily human Jesus with whom we might feel quite comfortable. It seems he can't stick his nose out the door without someone wanting something, so this is a Jesus who gets tired, who tries to get a few moments to himself. As one student astutely observed, Mark's gospel shows life's wear and tear on Jesus.

More than in any other gospel, however, in Mark we encounter Jesus the healer and the Jesus whom demons obey. So he may be typically human but, through the fatigue and sweat, an element of the divine is clearly discernible. Mark begins to sketch a portrait of Jesus; others will give it color and definition.

The Story According to Matthew—aka Levi

By now, you should be approaching biblical authorship with a certain degree of quiet resignation, so you won't be taken unawares when I say: here we go again. This time the name under the historical microscope is Matthew, who comes with an attached gospel. As was true of Mark's gospel, Matthew's writing does not identify its author. But here's a bright spot: There seems never to have been any question but that the Matthew meant is the tax collector described in Matthew 9:9–13.

Before you get too comfortable, check out the same episode in Mark 2:13–14 and Luke 5:27–29 where the assessor in question is called Levi. While the reason for this is not entirely clear, all three synoptic writers are definitely talking about the same person. This much is known:

- Matthew and Levi are both semitic names, and Jews were not given two; if they had a second given name, it would have been Greek or Roman;
- the name Levi appears on no biblical listing of the Twelve;
- a name change is within the realm of possibility, following the tradition dating from the patriarchal age.

So it's safe to say this gospel has always been somehow associated with Matthew, the tax collector, who was one of the Twelve. But we're not out of the woods yet. Did he actually write it? W-e-l-l . . .

Matthew's work and Luke's as well are thought to be products of the 80s. Many zero in on the middle of the decade, but 80 to 90 C.E. provides a little wiggle room. Again, this is an estimate based on the best available evidence, and there are dissenting voices positioning either or both gospels later, but the 80s seem most likely. This would have afforded enough time for Mark's gospel to circulate on those Roman interstates— a major consideration as both writers rely heavily on Mark's prototype.

Fifty to sixty years after Jesus' time, an apostolic Matthew would be getting right up there, especially for an era where life expectancy was far shorter than our own. Is it even reasonable to credit the gospel to him? Should we, instead, credit something else to him? Bishop Papias, earlier cited in regard to Mark, pops up again with this comment from c. 130 C.E.: "Matthew collected the sayings [*logia*] in the Hebrew language, and each one translated (interpreted) them as best he could."

This sounds more like one of those collections of sayings, which has led some to believe it is this foundational material, rather than the completed gospel, which carries the most Matthean influence. There may have been an earlier version which scholars term proto-Matthew. Papias's allusion to Hebrew is puzzling as well, since this gospel, like all the books of the Christian canon, originated in Greek and contains plays on words only possible in Greek.

As if this didn't present enough possibilities, the question of why an eyewitness member of the inner circle would be dependent on an "outsider" (Mark) for so much of his text must be thrown into the mix. Even the Call of Matthew episode cited above is lifted from Mark. Remember that one of the proofs that Moses couldn't have been the sole writer of the Torah is contained in the verses describing his own death? Something like this comes into play here. Somebody (or bodies) other than or in addition to Matthew had to be involved in the composition of this gospel because he was quite simply too old.

What about a school of disciples? This is a distinct possibility. What if future scholarship should challenge any association between Jesus' apostle and the authorship of this book. Would it matter? Not really. Content is what counts, not the name on the cover . . . er . . . scroll.

Jewish Roots Go Deep

Inasmuch as Christianity is a direct outgrowth of Judaism, all of the gospels are to some extent Jewish. Of the four, Luke's is the least Jewish in tone and Matthew's far and away the most. As our imaginary letter at the opening of this chapter demonstrated, the content of a particular composition is determined in large part by those to whom it is directed.

In the case of Matthew's gospel, the audience is unequivocally Jewish. The style, the themes, even the Jesus portrait all have strongly Jewish overtones as we shall see. Where Mark carefully explained Jewish customs, Matthew does not. It seems only logical to suppose, then, that the gospel stemmed from a locale whose young Christian community was comprised primarily of converts from Judaism.

For many, the arrow points straight to Syrian Antioch on the northeastern shore of the Mediterranean, where Jesus' followers were first called Christians (Acts 11:26b). The vote is not unanimous, however, with other sites with similar demographics, such as the Phoenician (Lebanese today) cities of Tyre and Sidon, in the running as well.

If Mark commenced scratching away at his gospel propelled by the rapid attrition of the eyewitness generation, Matthew may have been impelled by an expectation that had failed to materialize, the return of Jesus. This nonevent had been troubling believers even before there were such things as gospels. Paul's First Letter to the Thessalonians, the Christian canon's earliest work dating from c. 51 C.E., makes it clear that Jesus' return was expected during Paul's lifetime (his perspective grows in later letters).

Thirty-odd years later, Christians were growing restless. There may have been an inclination for the freshly converted members of Matthew's community to yield to familial pressure to return to Judaism. Their expectations of God may have been terribly unrealistic, as are our own sometimes. "For my thoughts are not your thoughts, nor are your ways my ways, says the LORD" (Isaiah 55:8). Matthew's gospel is an earnest entreaty to see Jesus as the son of Abraham, son of David, new Moses, fulfillment of the Law and the prophets, Messiah—in summary, the fullness of truth. And truth once discovered may not in conscience be forsaken.

Matthew, the Catechist

Matthew's approach to gospel writing is demonstrably different from Mark's. For all that, however, Matthew appropriates nearly all of his predecessor's work, 600 out of 661 verses. Where Mark strings episodes together like beads on a string with little attention to smooth transition, Matthew structures his book with great care. His two-chapter prologue, our first experience with Jesus' human origins, is followed by five books within the gospel. And it is no accident that the Torah also is made up of five books.

Each book is neatly arranged into two parts, a narrative or story and a discourse or sermon. The reader is alerted to the close of each book by a repetition of a formula something like: "Now when Jesus had finished saying these things . . ." (7:28a; 11:1a; 13:53; 19:1a). At the end of the fifth and last, he emphasizes this by saying: "When Jesus had finished saying all these things . . ." (26:1a).

Having tidily wrapped up the essence of his work, Matthew concludes with two chapters, 26 and 27, on Jesus' arrest, suffering, and death, and one chapter on his resurrection, chapter 28. However the authorship of this gospel finally shakes out, the mind behind it might be characterized as "Matthew the methodical."

So superbly organized is this gospel that Catholicism has put it to good catechetical use for centuries. Everything a follower of Jesus needs to know is here and presented in so orderly a fashion that information is both easy to find and easy to absorb. Now I didn't say everything we might *want* to know is there; we'll never have access to all of that. But that which is essential to belief is so accessible that the author has all the earmarks of an educator, a rabbi (teacher).

From his sources, among them that collection of Jesus' words known as "Q," Matthew pulls together everything he can find that Jesus said on a particular topic and constructs sermons out of them. Does this mean that Jesus didn't actually deliver those sermons? Probably not verbatim. Tape recorders and transcribers had yet to arrive on the scene.

Lack of technology notwithstanding, Jesus in all likelihood said many of the things ascribed to him in Matthew's sermons any number of times. He walked from town to town, speaking to one group after another. So far as we know, there were no evangelical crusades in the area's Roman amphitheaters. Thus, the imperatives of his preaching must have been repeated again and again.

Prior to each sermon, Matthew chronicles events bearing on the sermon to come, but these are generally secondary to the sermon itself. If, as we said, Mark is far more interested in what Jesus did, Matthew is infinitely more concerned with what Jesus said. Although these sermons

can be found under different names, we'll settle here for those used by
The New Jerome Bible Handbook:

- Sermon on the Mount (chapters 5–7)
- Mission discourse (10:1–42)
- Parables of the kingdom (13:1–52)
- Community discourse (18:1–35)
- Eschatalogical discourse (24:1–25:46)

Of the five, the first and last are most widely recognized. You may not
think you know the fifth because its title is such a mouthful, but if you
grab your Bible and run your eye over it, you'll discover it's more familiar
than you think. Why the tongue twister of a name? Actually, this, too,
claims more widespread usage than you might think. Eschatology
involves theological discourse on the last things: death, judgment, the
survival and/or destination of the soul, etc. Fittingly, the last chapter of
this book will be devoted almost entirely to eschatology.

A "Q" about Matthew's Sources

Despite the preponderance of Markan information to be found in
Matthew, large portions have no tie to Mark whatever. Some of these are
commonly credited to our old friend "Q." The theoretical Q source
consists of approximately 220 verses the gospels of Matthew and Luke
have in common, which are not found in Mark. There are also passages
exclusive to Matthew, known as "M" material, whose derivation is for the
most part unknown. Chief among these are chapters 1 and 2 dealing
with Jesus' lineage, birth, and infancy. Matthew's account of these events is
so unlike Luke's that the two cannot be reconciled into a single story, and
these two gospels are the only ones offering anything at all on the subject.

What Matthew Wants His Readers to "Get"

Matthew's gospel sets out to ground Jesus firmly in his people's history.
Several examples have already been provided that hammer home the
links to Abraham, David, and Moses. You'll find more if you examine the
gospel thoroughly.

Another technique Matthew uses to gain the same effect is to strew
his pages with copious quotations from the Hebrew Scriptures. Many of

these are accompanied by a formula along this line: "All this took place to fulfill what had been spoken by the Lord through the prophet . . ." (1:23; 2:15, 18, 23; 4:15–16; 8:17; 12:18–21; 13:35; 21:5; 27:9–10). That Jesus is the fulfillment of all that went before him is one of Matthew's primary points. As Jesus launches into his celebrated Sermon on the Mount, he makes a disclaimer which is crucial to Matthew: "Do not think that I have come to abolish the law or the prophets; I have come not to abolish but to fulfill" (Matthew 5:17).

The kingdom also ranks high on Matthew's priority list; he brings the kingdom to the reader's attention twenty-one times. In this gospel, the kingdom of God is not just pie in the sky when you die; it is earnest effort right here, right now to make this earthly "kingdom" as nearly as possible a facsimile of the heavenly one. *The New Jerome Bible Handbook* describes it well:

> The kingdom of heaven is the great object of hope, prayer (6:10), and proclamation (3:2, 4:17) which unifies the entire Gospel, especially the five great discourses, and provides its eschatalogical goal. It contains God's promise of salvation to redeemed humanity, on earth as in heaven, in time and eternity, socially and politically as well as personally. It entails justice (6:33), peace (5:9), and joy (13:44).

A third important strand of Matthean theology embraces righteousness. This virtue requires a person to practice justice, to be fair and equitable, upright and honorable in one's dealings with God, with others, even with oneself. I offer this variety of equivalent terms as we may think first of self-righteousness, the unpleasant tendency to view one's own convictions as unassailable. Righteousness, on the other hand, by its very nature requires humility. In this gospel, Jesus first speaks of it to John the Baptizer at the time of his baptism (3:15). It figures prominently in the Sermon on the Mount (5:6, 10, 20; 6:1, 33).

With typical Matthean design, the primary themes flow into one another smoothly. Jesus, the fulfillment of two thousand years of faith history, invites the righteous to join him in fashioning a community on earth, which will strive to mirror the unending kingdom of heaven to come.

Jesus in Matthew

A paragraph on Matthew's Jesus portrait is almost redundant since, to a great extent, it has already been drawn in discussing his audience and themes. This Jesus is Jewish down to his sandal straps: son of Abraham, new Moses, and restorer of the Davidic promise. Yet, he is a great deal more than merely a Jewish messiah; he comes for Gentiles as well, seen in the arrival of the magi from the East and the acceptance of their gifts.

The universality of Jesus is the last thought Matthew leaves us with in his account of Jesus' final commission to the Eleven:

> "All authority in heaven and on earth has been given to me. Go therefore and make disciples of all nations, baptizing them in the name of the Father and of the Son and of the Holy Spirit, and teaching them to obey everything that I have commanded you. And remember, I am with you always, to the end of the age" (Matthew 28:18b–20).

Matthew paints Jesus as rabbi. Hebrew for teacher, the word was in use for centuries prior to acquiring any clerical significance. Jesus, the teacher, speaks at length five times in this gospel and more concisely on other occasions. Some form of the word *teach* is associated with him twenty-three times in Matthew.

Always and everywhere, Jesus remains the dutiful and righteous son of the Father who sent him.

And Then There Was Luke

A friend of mine who set rather high standards for her growing children had a list posted in her kitchen during the summer months, "Things to Do When You Have Nothing to Do." Heading the list was: "Learn Greek." Those five determined overachievers might have begun their daunting assignment here, for with Luke we have arrived at exquisite "Greek 101."

Quite probably the premiere writer of the Christian canon, Luke could easily have carved out a career teaching master classes in Greek. His elegance of style and careful craftsmanship carry over into translation, so if you're a language buff, this is the gospel for you. More on that shortly. First . . .

What Do We Know about Luke?

Again, not a lot, and not half as much as we'd like. If asked, most people could scare up at least one somewhat obscure item from his resume: he was a doctor. There's only one reference to this (Colossians 4:14) but no reason to doubt it. An age-old tradition has him artistically gifted, but there are no biblical references for this. From like-minded lore, we're also told that Luke never married and lived to the age of eighty-four, a ripe old age indeed.

This is all very interesting and may garner a slot on *Jeopardy,* but it doesn't do much to serve our purposes here. So what can we say?

Second-century patristic writings make Luke a native of Antioch in Syria, that seedbed of early Christianity. If Syrian, he was surely a Hellenized one who may have come to Christianity from that standpoint. As a Gentile, he would lack Matthew's easy intimacy with the Hebrew Scriptures, nor would he need it. He seemingly writes not from Antioch but from a Greek province known as Achaia for an audience with a background resembling his own.

There is no evidence that Luke figured prominently in the apostolic church. Like Mark, he was not one of the Twelve, thus not an eyewitness. Also like Mark, Luke has a history with Paul. In his second manuscript, the Acts of the Apostles, Luke describes a long-time relationship with Paul, beginning abruptly in 16:10–17 and continuing through 20:5–21:18 and 27:1–28:16. Too accomplished a writer to have committed a gaffe so obvious as a change from second to first person, Luke obviously intended these passages to be read from his own perspective. There is no reason either to consider them pseudonymous. Judging from indications in the text, Luke and Paul were together off and on from the journey to Philippi until the time of Paul's imprisonment in Rome (Philemon 23).

Diverse Sources Become a Single Gospel

Assuming the Pauline association to be authentic, we have one source for this gospel already established. It would have been a youthful Luke who sailed with Paul if he did not commit his books to writing until about the middle 80s C.E., over twenty years after Paul's execution. This makes Luke's gospel roughly concurrent with Matthew's and, together with Matthew's, it makes ample use of both Mark's earlier work and the Q source. Where Matthew contains a sizable amount of "M" material, Luke embodies a comparable quantity called "L," which is his and his alone. Of course, his Acts of the Apostles is entirely original. We'll look into this in chapter 10.

Going Through Luke Side by Side

CLUE: When reading Luke, if you come across one of anything, look for two.

Luke loves to parallel practically everything: characters, episodes, parables, even books (Acts strikingly parallels the gospel). It's one of his favorite literary devices, and he leads off with it, laying out two annunciation and birth narratives in his first two chapters. Within them is found the additional parallelism of the two principal characters, which in turn points to Luke's fondness for paralleling men and women. Let's delve deeper.

Luke addresses both of his books to one Theophilus, constituting the first parallel. Who this Theophilus was or whether he even existed remains a mystery. No prominent figure of the time has thus far surfaced as a logical candidate. Because the name means "friend of God," there has been speculation that it is a personna for anyone fitting this description.

Beginning with chapter 1:5, Luke embarks on the intertwined story he will weave around the announcements of the impending arrivals of John and Jesus and their actual births. John's annunciation story consumes 1:5–25 and is followed immediately by a corresponding tale of Jesus' approaching birth. In both cases, the pregnancies are unexpected to say the least (1:7, 34). In both, news of the impending births is delivered by the angel Gabriel— live and in living color. While angels in Matthew customarily appear in dreams, allowing for some semblance of a reality cushion, in Luke they're just suddenly there, fraying nerve ends to the point where their opening remark aims to ease the tension, "Do not be afraid" (1:13a, 30b). Great things are to be expected of both John (1:15–17) and Jesus (1:32–33).

Of perhaps greater curiosity are the analogous roles played by the central characters of the stories, not John and Jesus, but their parents, Zechariah and Mary. Near the opening verses of his gospel, Luke introduces his predisposition to place comparable male and female figures in equal juxtaposition. Zechariah is a Temple priest and Mary a Galilean village girl. Still, she is made to look in no way inferior. In fact, she acquits herself better than her more educated counterpart in one area. Instead of demanding proof from the angel as Zechariah does (and earns himself nine months worth of silence for his trouble), Mary quietly complies.

Luke favors both of his "stars" with a solo, an exquisite canticle composed almost entirely of lines borrowed from books of the Hebrew canon and woven together with marvelous effect by this exceptional writer. So beautiful are these lyrical elegies that Catholicism's *Liturgy of the Hours* prescribes them for daily recitation, Zechariah's canticle during Morning Prayer and Mary's during Evening.

What's the Story on the Christmas Story?

Luke 2:1–20 is one of the best loved of biblical readings. Families have been gathering to read it together on Christmas Eve for generations. I'm certainly not suggesting such a commendable practice be discontinued. I am suggesting comparisons between Luke's version of events and Matthew's (remembering that neither Mark nor John contribute anything to the debate).

Missing from Luke are Matthew's magi, their star, and their messianic gifts. No innocents are slaughtered, making the flight into Egypt unnecessary. Did Luke bypass these because he didn't know about them, because the messianic and Mosaic associations would be largely lost on his Gentile audience, because they didn't serve his purposes, or for some other reason? It's hard to say.

He does, however, have a set of characters all his own which could lead us to ask the same questions of Matthew. Jesus' visitors in Luke are at the far end of the social scale from the magi. They are Judean shepherds who find the infant in a shelter, probably a cave for animals, the only accommodations available to his weary parents who had made the trek from Nazareth to Bethlehem to be counted in a Roman census. Joseph, central to Matthew's story, relinquishes this role to Mary in Luke.

A few elements are shared: the virgin birth in Bethlehem during the reign of Herod the Great. The possible rationale behind the inclusion of some of these components can be found among Luke's many themes, which we'll examine shortly.

We would be remiss in leaving Luke's treatment of Jesus, the early years, if we failed to mention one more parallel event and two additional episodes. The event is the circumcision of the two boys. In accordance with ancient Mosaic Law (Leviticus 12:3), this visible sign of the Covenant is conferred on John and Jesus "on the eighth day" (1:59–63; 2:21). This ritual not only served as an initiation rite for the Chosen People, but officially bestowed a child's name—John's and Jesus' names were determined before the boys were born. Induction ceremonies remain popular in secular as well as religious circles. Christian baptism may well be the only custom observed across nearly the entire spectrum of Christian practice.

Two exclusively Lucan events from the infancy narratives seem to balance the two solely Matthean incidents (the slaughter of the innocents and the flight into Egypt). In their stead, Luke presents us with two Temple scenes. First, Jesus' parents present him to God as required under the Law for firstborn sons (Exodus 13:2, 12). They are met by two elderly, devout individuals, Simeon and Anna, another pair of gender parallels and another canticle, this one featuring snatches of Isaiah (2:22–40). Simeon's canticle, too, is preserved nightly in the Liturgy of the Hours' Night Prayer.

This charming interlude is followed by the only reference in any of the canonical gospels to Jesus' childhood beyond infancy, the story of Jesus in the Temple at the age of twelve (2:41–52). Verging on manhood, Jesus is seen here as a faithful young man from an observant family. Passover was one of the pilgrimage feasts, which required all who were able to assemble in Jerusalem for its celebration. Afterward, the roads would have been clogged with pilgrims returning home, making it easy for someone to disappear.

Jesus' remark, "Did you not know that I must be in my Father's house?" (2:49b), has been the subject of heated debate revolving around how much Jesus really grasped about either his dual nature or his role as an adult at that point. Human like ourselves, "Jesus increased in wisdom and in years, and in divine and human favor" (2:52). Divine like no one else, Jesus remains enigmatic, causing us to constantly grapple with the question: Who is Jesus really, and what does this mean in my life?

Reams of Themes

"Luke, the gospel of . . ." So many designations ensue from these four words that all we can hope to do here is introduce them. By doing only this, however, you will receive some glimmer of the riches to be found in, around, and behind Luke's well-chosen words.

The Gospel of Mercy, Forgiveness, and Great Pardons: Chapter 15 is Luke's lost and found department in which three parables of "the lost" are laid end to end, making it nearly impossible to miss the value of the missing object/person. The parable of the man with the lost sheep is twinned with that of the woman with the lost coin, then topped by a Lucan exclusive, the parable of the lost (prodigal) son.

Parables are intended via unexpected twists and turns to act as wake-up calls. They are less the bedtime stories we have been inclined to make of them than shots of ice water right in the face. For example, "Which one of you, having a hundred sheep and losing one of them, does not leave the ninety-nine in the wilderness and go after the one that is lost until he finds it?" (15:4) Answer? Nobody in his right mind! Why put 99 percent of your livelihood's inventory at risk on the off chance you'd stumble across the missing 1 percent? This one lonesome sheep would have to be terribly valuable. Point taken.

The irresponsible son, one of the Bible's best-known figures, usually gets star billing in the parable even if the forgiving father really should. One of the pivotal sentences is often glossed over, "[W]hile he was still far off, his father saw him and was filled with compassion; he ran and put his arms around him and kissed him" (15:20b). This is one of those instances in which the Bible teaches more by what it doesn't say than what it does. If the father saw the boy top the hill way down the road, he must have been straining his eyes down that same road doggedly day by week by, perhaps month, by maybe year.

Putting the parable in an allegorical context, the father is a stand-in for God, a God so ready, so willing to take us back when we stray, that he nearly knocks us off our feet when we want to come home. This beautiful family drama should be spelled out painstakingly to all those who believe themselves beyond God's forgiveness, who bear impossible burdens of guilt needlessly, often for decades.

Jesus charges his listeners in Matthew's Sermon on the Mount, "Be perfect, therefore, as your heavenly Father is perfect" (5:48). In Luke's Sermon on the Plain (Luke would not be likely to place Jesus above the people), Jesus bids them, "Be merciful, just as your Father is merciful" (6:36). For other illustrations of God's forgiveness in Luke, see the story of the sinful woman (7:36–50), Zacchaeus (19:1–10), and Jesus on the cross (23:34, 39–43).

The Gospel of the Poor: Think of those figures from Luke's infancy narrative: Zechariah (and his wife Elizabeth), Mary and Joseph, Simeon and Anna, and those dirty, smelly shepherds who weren't anything like their counterparts on our Christmas cards in their Calvin Klein robes. From the outset, Luke makes it clear that the poor and insignificant are, in reality, the noble elect. As the story unfolds, there are many more: public sinners (for the most part, members of the world's oldest profession), lepers, Roman soldiers, tax collectors—anyone and everyone whom today we would term *marginalized,* who lived on the fringes of society, neglected or rejected or both.

Luke has Jesus launch his public career in his hometown synagogue, reaching back into Isaiah to read, "The Spirit of the Lord is upon me, because he has anointed me to bring good news to the poor" (4:18a). And only Luke tells the moving parable of the rich man and Lazarus (16:19–31).

Conceivably most telling is another contrast between Matthew and Luke's treatments of Jesus' most notable sermon. Matthew's first beatitude reads: "Blessed are the poor in spirit, for theirs is the kingdom of heaven" (5:3). Luke's simply states: "Blessed are you who are poor, for yours is the kingdom of God" (6:20b). Notice first that Matthew speaks in the third person, but Luke's Jesus addresses those before him personally in the second person. Then, observe that there is no "in spirit" in Luke, only "you who are poor."

Recalling what was said earlier about the primitive theology regarding long life, health, and wealth as blessings and their opposites as misfortune brought on by one's own sins or those of one's ancestors, it's safe to say that the Lucan poor had been called a good many things in their time, none of them "blessed." Such a statement would have been by turns startling and comforting.

The Gospel of Women: Among those most marginalized by their society were women. It has been pointed out that Luke repeatedly places women and men in parallel and equal positions. Yet another instance of this is found in chapter 7, where the healing of the Roman centurion's slave (two rejected classes right there) in 7:2–10 is married to the raising to life of the widow's only son (7:11–17). In the same chapter, Jesus favors the sinful, but repentant, woman over the pious protests of his Pharisee host (7:36–50).

Having mentioned the Twelve, Luke hastens to list Mary Magdalene, Joanna, Susanna, "and many others who provided for them out of their resources" (8:1–3). The parable of the Good Samaritan (also found only in Luke, 10:29–37) bumps up against Jesus' friendship with Martha and Mary (10:38–42). The assistance rendered by Simon of Cyrene (23:26) is joined to the compassion shown by the Daughters of Jerusalem (23:27–31). Finally, women are the witnesses to Jesus' death, burial, empty tomb, and resurrection proclamation, front and center for these key events in typically Lucan fashion.

The Gospel of Prayer: In Luke, Jesus is found at prayer prior to every crucial step in his ministry:

- at his baptism (3:21),
- before naming the Twelve (6:12),
- preceding Peter's profession of faith (9:18),
- at the Transfiguration (9:28),
- preparing to teach the disciples to pray (11:1),
- in the Garden of Gethsemane (22:41).

Further, Jesus exhorts his followers to be people of prayer as well (6:28, 10:2, 11:1–13, 18:1–8, 21:36).

The Gospel of the Holy Spirit: The third Person of the triune God is prominently featured in both of Luke's books. The emphasis is so strong in his second work that Acts has been called the "Gospel of the Holy Spirit." This Spirit extends peace and messianic joy to those who recognize Jesus for who he is. This pervasive sense of joy, never to be confused with the capricious emotion of happiness, really constitutes still another theme, but suffice it to say that Luke's sense of awe and wonder suffuses his writing. No matter what afflictions befall us as Jesus' disciples, and no one gets through life without them, the sheer joy of having Jesus in our lives acts like an underground aquifer, flowing steadily on impervious to whatever upheavals torment the surface.

Other themes that interest Luke include universal salvation, especially since his audience is Gentile, and the renunciation required to follow Jesus. It is a measure of his skill that he juggles these many ideas adroitly, enabling his readers to follow his thought effortlessly.

Jesus in Luke

The Lucan Jesus may most closely approximate the image entertained in many minds. Reaching out to the disenfranchised, forgiving sinners, seeking those who stray, praying faithfully, Jesus comes across as kind and gentle, traits reinforced by Luke's habit of softening violence and strong language where he finds it in his sources or eliminating it altogether. Failure to heed Jesus' challenges and expectations, however, risks turning him into what William J. O'Malley, S.J., terms "the bearded lady." It risks a serious misreading of his message. This is the same Jesus who urges his disciples to leave "everything" (5:11) and to "sell your possessions, and give alms" (12:33a). There are repeated predictions that Jesus must suffer, such as 9:22, 13:33, and 17:25.

All three of the synoptics include in their Last Supper scene a reference to the unifying motif of the Covenant. The ongoing connection may not be as overt as we found it in much of the First Testament, but like the Mosaic Law and the Davidic promise, it finds its fulfillment in Jesus. As we might expect, Luke says it best: "This cup that is poured out for you is the new covenant in my blood" (22:20b). The Covenant remains a living commitment sealed in blood but now it is sealed in the most precious blood that will ever course through any human vein.

Mark's on-the-go, extremely human healer is also Matthew's reflective teacher steeped in the religious tradition of his people. Yet he is also Luke's compassionate, absolving lover of the outcast and the humble. Luke makes certain the Holy Spirit figures prominently into the divine equation as well. And so our images of God expand, our concepts broaden, and questions arise that we previously couldn't even have framed. The quest continues.

CHAPTER EIGHT

Jesus According to John

Before "beginning was," God spoke out,
and that Word was with God, that Word was God.
The Word was with God before beginning began.
Among them, all that began was begun.
Not a thing enlivened with "is" began without them,
for the "is" in all that is, is the life of God.
They are the light the darkness can't comprehend. . . .
The true light, the Word, was coming among us,
entering the world that they themselves had made.
The Word came into the world and we scoffed at him.
But the few who saw through surfaces, he gifted:
he invited them into the Family of God,
and all reborn in him are enlivened by God.
The Word fused with flesh and dwelled among us,
and the life of God enlivens us even now.

—John 1:1–14

As a rule, I can be counted on to set new land speed records fleeing a biblical paraphrase in any form. Paraphrases are somewhat free interpretations, and so by their very nature are inexact as opposed to translations which at least strive to be faithful to the text. A splendid exception to my rule is William J. O'Malley whose renditions of scriptural extracts in his books of prayer rarely fail to shed new, often intense, light on all too familiar passages. O'Malley's version of John's opening words, found in

More Daily Prayers for Busy People (Saint Mary's Press, 1999), soars even higher than John's own lofty prose. I elected to cite it at the outset of this chapter because it so plainly introduces the Jesus waiting for us in this gospel.

With John, we enter a whole new world, peopled in large part by figures not encountered in any of the three earlier gospels and centered by a Jesus unlike any portrayed by the synoptics. Of course, the fact that Luke accents Jesus' tender nature does not suggest that this side of his character is absent from the other gospels, merely that this particular gospel highlights it more than any other. The same can be said for all of the qualities demonstrated by Jesus.

The gospels paint verbal portraits of Jesus; they do not tell his life story. If you've ever had a professional photograph taken, you may have passed around copies of the various poses among your friends and family to see which they liked best. There may have been more consternation than resolution as those who love you selected totally different pictures, each adamantly insisting theirs was the one that really looked like you. We're perceived quite differently even by those who know us best. It was true of Jesus as well. That is borne out in each of the synoptic gospels, and oh my, is it ever borne out in John. Prepare for a wondrous ride as John's soaring portrayal carries you through a gospel so unusual it often seems entirely unrelated to the others.

This rapturous prologue sets the stage. Not for John are either shepherds or magi, stars or mangers. Pursuing Jesus' human origins does not serve John's purpose; establishing Jesus' eternal divinity does. Why? The fourth gospel is also the last to have been written, normally believed to stem from the last decade of the first century. By that time, believers who had come to Christianity from Judaism were undergoing expulsion from numerous synagogues. Hinted at by Matthew, the plight of practitioners of the Way had only worsened by the 90s. Forced to detach themselves, not only from synagogue worship but from the Law, which had always defined every aspect of life, these converts were thrown back on that same old question: Is this Jesus the person we thought him to be? Is devotion to him worth enduring such pain?

Late in the first century, a wide variety of people were asking questions about Jesus. Some thought him human but not divine; others, divine but not human; still others, both. John addresses them all by returning to home base. O'Malley aside, a more direct translation of John1:1 is, "In the beginning was the Word, and the Word was with God, and the Word was God." The personification seen in Wisdom literature appears again. This time, it's Word as in Word of God, God enfleshed, i.e., Jesus. Make that substitution and read the verse again, "In the beginning was Jesus, and Jesus was with God, and Jesus was God." Not much room for equivocation there. We've revisited the opening of Genesis: in the beginning, God! Not much doubt either about the nature of Jesus in the eyes of John . . . truly human . . . truly divine.

Sorting Through the Authorship Possibilities

In one respect, John's gospel is comparable to the synoptics; its authorship is unclear. When in doubt, return to the most reliable scholarship which, in matters biblical, is almost always *The Jerome Biblical Commentary* or, as here, its more accessible cousin, *The New Jerome Bible Handbook*.

> The Beloved Disciple is identified as the witness behind the Gospel tradition in John 23:24, but John 21:20–23 contains a reference to his death. So clearly he cannot be the one and only author, even though he may be responsible for much of the Gospel, which is the result of several stages of editing.
>
> "The other question is: which John was the Beloved Disciple? Bishop Irenaeus of Lyons (who died in 202) said the Gospel was written by the Beloved Disciple, named John, at Ephesus, toward the end of his life. But passages in the Gospel itself (chapter 21) suggest that the Beloved Disciple was not John, the son of Zebedee.
>
> "Although the Gospel could have been produced by one author or editor, what is important is that it came from the traditions of the community of believers known as the Johannine community."

If you're growing nostalgic for a simpler time when you took Mark, Matthew, Luke, and John at face value, keep repeating that it's what's in these books that matters in the end, not who wrote them. And in case you're wondering, the John of the gospel and three short letters is almost certainly not the John of Revelation. A relationship was thought to exist until a comparison of writing styles, vocabularies, etc., made it seem next to impossible.

Whoever the Beloved Disciple was, we can assume, as Ronald Witherup does, that he "was probably a real, historical figure who followed Jesus and whose authority lies behind the Gospel because he was important in the Johannine community." Whether some sort of link remains with the apostolic son of Zebedee or the Beloved Disciple is someone else entirely, he surely could not have composed the final draft of this work as it is usually dated somewhere in the last decade of the first century when most, if not all, of those who knew Jesus personally had died.

The Who and the Where of the Johannine Community

Roughly two-thirds of a century after Jesus' days on earth, assemblies of his followers were eclectic blends of Jews and Gentiles across the Near East. Nonetheless, the fourth gospel shows every sign (a word which will have particular significance in John) of directing its message to beleaguered and confused converts from Judaism. Asia Minor is a safe bet for its origin. Whether the arrow still points to Ephesus as its locale is less certain.

Sandra M. Schneiders, I.H.M. whose work on this gospel is widely respected, speaks to the situation in which the Johannine community found itself in the closing years of the first century (*Written That You May Believe*, Crossroad Publishing, 1999):

> It was written during the time when Jewish authorities were attempting to consolidate Judaism in terms of belief and practice following the destruction of the Jerusalem temple in 70 C.E. Christianity, which had developed up to this time as an accepted Jewish sect among many such sects, increasingly came to be regarded as heretical because of its belief that in Jesus the awaited Messiah had come and also because Christianity, as it began to attribute divinity to Jesus, seemed a threat to the monotheism that is the heart of Jewish faith. . . . These Christians, living at the end of the first century, faced an agonizing choice between surrendering their membership in Judaism, the religious

community of the chosen people, and abandoning their new faith in Jesus of Nazareth as the Christ and the Son of God (see 20:31). . . . It is difficult for a Christian who has never been a Jew to realize the magnitude of this choice. . . . To voluntarily cut oneself off from the community of Israel, from synagogue worship and observance of the law, from rabbinic leadership and table fellowship with God's people was a radical severance from one's past, one's corporate identity, one's whole historical understanding of the truth of revelation and its divine institution in Israel.

Pulling together the varied threads woven through the words of the cited scholars, it becomes increasingly obvious that this gospel will accentuate those words and deeds of Jesus which bear most strongly on the situation in which the community finds itself, circumstances not of their own making or liking. And where will John find the material again? We return again to sources. The writer may well have been acquainted with one or more of the synoptics, and some of his tradition bears a certain similarity to theirs. But for the most part, John's gospel is formed from other source material. There is evidence of his use of a sayings collection other than Q, of a recorded assortment of Jesus' wondrous deeds known as the Signs Source (such remarkable acts are never called miracles, but always signs in this gospel), and of a separate tradition regarding Jesus' suffering, death, and resurrection.

Soaring and Diving with the A"peel"ing John

Even as John's beautiful words have the capacity to lift his readers to heights only dreamed of in our mundane world, they can just as easily plunge readers into unimagined depths of meaning. In writing about this gospel, I've been known to describe it as a diving expedition that submerges its readers "in a wonderful world of colorful characters, picturesque phrasing, and tantalizing themes quite unlike any other biblical writings." Or it may be compared to a layer cake, where far more lies beneath the surface than on it. If cake doesn't suit your lo-cal diet, liken a reading of John to peeling an onion, itself multilayered but possessing the ability upon occasion to reduce you to tears.

Whichever simile you choose, let it serve as a reminder that there is always more to John than meets the eye, and he most assuredly provides an intriguing contrast to what we have come to expect from Mark, Matthew, and Luke.

In John, for instance, Jesus rarely expresses himself in parables. There are only two, the good shepherd (10:1–18) and the vine and the branches (15:1–10). Here his language is thoughtful, often producing misunderstandings which are customarily cleared up later in the text, i.e., 4:31–34. Contrary to Luke's notion of a one-year public life which moves Jesus steadily forward on a single journey to Jerusalem, John speaks of three distinct Passover celebrations, implying a ministry of two to three years during the course of which he moves back and forth to Jerusalem several times. If in Mark the Twelve come across as a little dense (which could be sour grapes on Mark's part), they are more than redeemed in John, where they grasp Jesus' identity from the outset although they do not play a major role as a group.

The cast of the fourth gospel is also singular. Animating the pages of John are all kinds of folks who appear in none of the synoptics. Some have proper names; others do not, surmising that John intended us to see ourselves. So keep your program handy because here come Nicodemus, the Samaritan woman, the man born blind, and Lazarus (not the one in Luke's parable).

Little about this gospel corresponds to its synoptic counterparts, so our treatment of it will take a fresh approach as well. John's style, themes, and Jesus portrait are so intertwined that, instead of considering them independently, they'll be allowed to flow from the illustrative passages we'll examine. In academic biblical study, this is known as exegesis, examining a given portion of a scriptural work to see what its author intended the original audience to glean from it. Determining how the same section can reasonably speak to a twenty-first-century audience is a area of study called hermeneutics. As this terminology turns up rather regularly in biblical discourse, it may be handy to keep on file behind your left ear.

Gospel Light

There has been speculation that the author of this gospel was somehow connected to the world of the stage. So skillfully constructed are the individual scenes that they can be lifted almost literally off the page and performed as short dramas. If there's any truth to that, then my guess is that John was a lighting technician because nearly the entire gospel is a struggle pitting light against darkness. The motif is introduced in John's poetic prologue: "There was a man sent from God, whose name was John. He came as a witness to testify to the light, so that all might believe through him. He himself was not the light, but he came to testify to the light. The true light, which enlightens everyone, was coming into the world" (1:6–9). And this is precisely the way John's Jesus describes himself a little further on, "I am the light of the world. Whoever follows me will never walk in darkness but will have the light of life" (8:12b). Another clue to Jesus' identity is found in those two monosyllabic words, "I am." Put them where you can find them as we'll be returning to them shortly. Additional light reading lies in 11:7–10: "Then after this he said to the disciples, 'Let us to go to Judea again.' The disciples said to him, 'Rabbi, the Jews were just now trying to stone you, and are you going there again?' Jesus answered, 'Are there not twelve hours of daylight? Those who walk during the day do not stumble, because they see the light of this world. But those who walk at night stumble, because the light is not in them.' "

The conflict between light and darkness is joined here by one of John's favorite literary devices, misunderstanding. In scenes such as this, Jesus seems not to have heard the question and replies from left field somewhere. Other incidents are just plain mix-ups which provide a platform from which Jesus may make plain exactly what was meant. A sterling example follows the passage just cited: "After saying this, he told them, 'Our friend Lazarus has fallen asleep, but I am going there to awaken him.' The disciples said to him, 'Lord, if he has fallen asleep, he will be all right.' Jesus, however, had been speaking about his death, but they thought that he was referring merely to sleep. Then Jesus told them plainly, 'Lazarus is dead' " (11:12–14).

Nearing the end of his public life, Jesus is distressed and forewarns his disciples, "The light is with you for a little longer. Walk while you have the light, so that the darkness may not overtake you. If you walk in the darkness, you do not know where you are going. While you have the light, believe in the light, so that you may become children of light"

(12:35b–36). The straightforward prose of Mark holds no appeal for John and would be disastrously unsuited to the Jesus of the fourth gospel.

Keep an eye open as you read John for indirect references to this play of light against darkness. When Jesus encounters the Samaritan woman at the well, "it was about noon" (4:6b). It may well have been, but this is John so there must be another layer of meaning. At noon, the sun is directly overhead; it is the moment of maximum daylight. In this case, it spotlights Jesus, the light of the world. When Judas exits the upper room on the night of the Last Supper, John cryptically remarks, "And it was night" (13:30b). Judas, closely exposed to the light on a daily basis, has chosen to plunge back into the darkness. Nicodemus, whom we will spend some time with presently, requires nearly all of the book to come into the light. We meet him three times (3:1–21, 7:50–52, 19:38–42), but only in the last does it seem that he has finally come into the light.

In chapter 9, one of the most elegantly drawn literary gems to be found in literature, this study in contrasts reaches its climax with characters moving both directions. The Pharisees, whom society would see as "enlightened", are in fact sliding toward darkness while a man whom most would consider unlikely to see the light rises toward it steadily.

When we examine our lives in relation to "What are we doing here?" John's light versus darkness pattern gives comfort to our weary souls. For all that John's Jesus is a commanding figure who fills his followers with awe and who asks a great deal of them, he is as patient as the Hebrew Yahweh. Imperfect humans don't always get it right the first time . . . or the second, for that matter. Sometimes they just plain don't get it. They may take two steps toward the light and one back into darkness. But direction is more important than speed, and the light is there, if not before our mortal eyes, illuminating the eternal life to come (another of John's major points). That one literary leitmotif clarifies so much about the relationship of God and humanity that we could stop right now and have plenty to ponder. But we won't do that, for we have only just begun to plumb the depths of this extraordinary gospel.

Why Does John's Jesus Speak the Way He Does?

The nobility of John's Jesus arises primarily from the constant insistence this gospel provides that Jesus and the Father are one. Unity of Father and Son is stressed again and again. The late Johannine authority, Raymond E. Brown, S.S. (*An Introduction to New Testament Christology,* Paulist Press, 1994), draws our attention to the gospel's overriding premise that:

> The Johannine Jesus is clearly conscious of having preexisted with God before the world began (17:5) and of having come into this world from that world of previous existence in order to say and do what he heard and saw when he was with God. . . . The notion of preexistence is apparent in different forms in other New Testament works, but John alone in the New Testament brings this into the heart of a Gospel account of Jesus' public life, inviting readers to see in a visible human figure functioning in this world, the stranger from above who is not of this world.

Some form of the word *father* appears over 120 times in the fourth gospel. These citations are typical: "The Father loves the Son and has placed all things in his hands" (3:35) and "Jesus said to them, 'If God were your Father, you would love me, for I came from God and now I am here. I did not come on my own, but he sent me'" (8:42).

Possibly the most telling comments come from the prolonged Last Supper discourse Jesus delivers in John: "Jesus said to him [Thomas], 'I am the way, and the truth, and the life. No one comes to the Father except through me. If you know me, you will know my Father also. From now on you do know him and have seen him.' Philip said to him, 'Lord, show us the Father, and we will be satisfied.' Jesus said to him, 'Have I been with you all this time, Philip, and you still do not know me? Whoever has seen me has seen the Father. How can you say, 'Show us the Father?'" (14:6–9ff)

Remember the "I am" phrase you filed away awhile back? It just resurfaced in the quotation above. And there are more:

- "I am the true vine, and my Father is the vinegrower" (15:1).
- "I am the resurrection and the life" (11:25b).
- "I am the good shepherd. I know my own and my own know me" (10:14).
- "I am the bread of life" (6:48).

Clear and present are the echoes of Moses' encounter with God at the burning bush, where he was commissioned to return to Egypt as leader of the Israelites. "But Moses said to God, 'If I come to the Israelites and say to them, "The God of your ancestors has sent me to you," and they ask me, "What is his name?" what shall I say to them?' God said to Moses, 'I AM WHO I AM.' He said further, 'Thus you shall say to the Israelites, "I AM has sent me to you" ' " (Exodus 3:13–14).

"Jesus, who is one with the Father, is able to reveal the Father in a unique way," says *The New Jerome Biblical Commentary.* "Only because this is true can he be described as the vine, the life, the resurrection, the way, the gate, the good shepherd, the truth, and the bread of life . . . the unique saving revelation of God among men and women" (83:49).

Something as subtle as the twist of a verb tense can deliver a powerful message. " 'Your ancestor Abraham rejoiced that he would see my day; he saw it and was glad.' Then the Jews said to him, 'You are not yet fifty years old, and have you seen Abraham?' Jesus said to them, 'Very truly, I tell you, before Abraham was, I am' " (8:56–58). Grammar carries precise meaning in chapter 6, "Then Jesus said to them,, 'Very truly, I tell you, it was not Moses who gave you the bread from heaven, but it is my Father who gives you the true bread from heaven' " (6:32). Jesus' comment here is lifted from his Bread of Life discourse (6:22–71), which may well be the most strongly eucharistic portion of any Second Testament book. Interestingly, the consecration so significant to the Last Supper in all of the synoptics is missing entirely from John's version. Did he, perhaps, believe he had already covered that in this impressive dissertation?

Other patterns or figures of speech to watch for in John include Jesus' hour, spoken of most intensely in 12:20–27. Check 8:20b as well for new insight into John's portrait of Jesus. "[N]o one arrested him, because his hour had not yet come." Nothing happens to Jesus in this gospel by chance, nor does anything take him by surprise. Jesus is always in control of his situation. Whatever occurs happens with Jesus' full knowledge, and his nobility is preserved throughout unless he chooses to set it aside as he does shedding tears over his friend Lazarus' death (11:33–35). The reader has no trouble believing this majestic figure to be one with the Father. Even during the trial before Pilate, Jesus seems more in charge of the situation than the Roman procurator. "Pilate therefore said to him, 'Do you refuse to speak to me? Do you not know that I have power to release you, and power to crucify you?' Jesus answered him, 'You would have no power over me unless it had been given you from above; therefore the one who handed me over to you is guilty of a greater sin.' From then on Pilate tried to release him" (19:10–12a).

Following the prologue, John's gospel is commonly partitioned into two major divisions, the Book of Signs (1:19–12:50) and the Book of Glory (13:1–20:31). With those titles, two more leitmotifs surface. Jesus' works are never termed miracles but, instead, signs. The function of a sign is to serve as a directive, pointing to something . . . or, in this case, someone . . . beyond itself. Functioning in somewhat the same manner as Mark's messianic secret, John's signs direct attention much more to who Jesus is than to what Jesus does.

The words *glory* or *glorified* are found more than thirty times in John's text, primarily in the latter section so named. *Glory* is one of those words that gets bandied about without, for the most part, being clearly understood. Doing something for "the glory" seems to us arrogantly overbearing, a blatant effort to gain the spotlight and remain in it for as long as possible. To glory in something is to delight in it, which is infinitely more positive. But most agreeable is the idea of giving glory to in the sense of honoring or praising. It is this connotation which is found most often in John. It can refer to Jesus or to the Father, but then, the two are one here. Chapter 17, Jesus' high priestly prayer, could also be dubbed the glory chapter, beginning as it does with five verses exemplifying glorification.

Another such segment all but concludes Jesus' four-chapter Last Supper discourse as he intercedes on behalf of his disciples, "The glory that you have given me I have given them, so that they may be one, as we are one, I in them and you in me, that they may become completely one, so that the world may know that you have sent me and have loved them even as you have loved me. Father, I desire that those also, whom you have given me, may be with me where I am, to see my glory, which you have given me because you loved me before the foundation of the world"

(17:22–24). As Jesus' life draws to a close, John returns to his timeless existence with the Father, thereby utilizing a literary technique known as inclusion, which acts somewhat like parentheses—an aid John also makes good use of (as do I). When an idea is stated both early and late in a text, the implication is that the entire work is somehow suffused with it.

This eternal existence of Jesus flows into everlasting life for his followers as well, a dominant pattern in his speech in the fourth gospel. Possibly the best remembered verse in all of Scripture, judging by bumper stickers and placards held up at sporting events at least, is 3:16, "For God so loved the world that he gave his only Son, so that everyone who believes in him may not perish but may have eternal life." Yet this comment to Nicodemus is only one of many. Jesus tells the Samaritan woman at the well, "Everyone who drinks of this water will be thirsty again, but those who drink of the water that I will give them will never be thirsty. The water that I will give will become in them a spring of water gushing up to eternal life" (4:13b–14). In his Bread of Life discourse, of paramount importance in this gospel, Jesus again says, "This is indeed the will of my Father, that all who see the Son and believe in him may have eternal life; and I will raise them up on the last day" (6:40).

Still later, consoling Martha upon the death of her brother Lazarus, "Jesus said to her, 'I am the resurrection and the life. Those who believe in me, even though they die, will live, and everyone who lives and believes in me will never die. Do you believe this?" (11:25–26) Never mind what Martha replies. How do you respond? How do I? The Third Big Question is front and center here, and the development of thought in this sphere over the two millennia of biblical history is truly astounding as we shall see in greater detail in chapter 13.

God's Love Is Here to Stay

The final composition George Gershwin left in his too-brief career was the ballad "Our Love Is Here to Stay." It could have been Jesus' final assertion in his too-brief time among us as well. His love . . . God's love . . . is here to stay. We can't earn it. We don't merit it. We can ignore it. We can even refuse it. But we can't do away with it. It's here to stay, and John's gospel has a lot to say about that. And if the love of the Father and the imposing Johannine Jesus flows from many a gospel passage, it's as nothing by comparison with the three compact letters attributed to the same writer(s) (see chapter 9).

Representative of Jesus' statements on love is this from the Last Supper: "As the Father has loved me, so I have loved you; abide in my love. If you keep my commandments, you will abide in my love, just as I have kept my Father's commandments and abide in his love" (15:9–10).

There may be a certain irony in the knowledge that one of the tenderest passages on this subject lies in John 21, a chapter almost certainly a later addition. A quick look at 20:30–31 indelibly impresses the reader with the sense that this is where a modern film director would bark, "Cut! Roll credits." No matter how it got there, chapter 21 contains that incomparable scene in which a repentant Peter is forgiven and reinstated by a kind and sensitive Risen Christ (21:15–19). Peter's three denials are wiped away by his three affirmations.

We shall soon have to move on, leaving untold layers of this enigmatic gospel unexamined, but before we do, let's drop by for a short visit with four of its most engaging characters. Introducing us to each in turn will be that peerless Johannine scholar, Father Raymond Brown, who recorded his impressions of them in *A Retreat with John the Evangelist: That You May Have Life* (St. Anthony Messenger Press, 1998).

Nicodemus: In the Light, but Seeing Little

The coming of Nicodemus to Jesus [3:1–36] offers a unique moment of reflection. Here was an educated man, a teacher in Israel, a Jewish authority who was involved in Sanhedrin meetings. He was not hostile to Jesus but was one of those at Jerusalem who had come to believe in Jesus because of the miracles he saw [2:23]. Nicodemus saw the physical side of Jesus' signs but not the fullness of what they signified. He saw Jesus as a wonderful teacher who had come from God in the sense that he had God-given power to perform miracles/signs; but he had not understood that Jesus had come from God as the creator Word become flesh, as divine Wisdom incarnate.

Nicodemus, like the others in this group, provides ample food for thought as we grapple with that issue of who Jesus really is and what that actually means in our lives individually and collectively. Read Brown's assessment carefully. Does it now or did it once describe your own position? If it did in the past but no longer does, what changed? If it does now, should it change?

The Johannine Jesus, like his Father whom we came to know in the Hebrew Scriptures, exhibits boundless patience, taking people where he finds them in their spiritual development and allowing them the freedom to decide if, when, and how they will continue to grow. It will take Nicodemus a long time, but then he has a lot at stake: position in the Sanhedrin (the Jewish leadership council), status in the community, affluence. He would naturally wish to answer with great care, "Who is this Jesus really, and what does that mean in my life?" He arrives at night, hoping to keep his visit secret, but John says something more by that: Nicodemus, though supposedly a man of enlightened ideas, comes to Jesus out of the darkness.

When, at last, Nicodemus moves fully into the light, he does so without reservation. Assisting Joseph of Arimathea with Jesus' burial, Nicodemus is right out there "in front of God and everybody," assuring that his decision will make, if not the network news, certainly the Jerusalem grapevine. We are told that he "came, bringing a mixture of myrrh and aloes, weighing about a hundred pounds" (19:39b). Transcribing that Roman weight into a modern equivalent, it still comes out to around seventy-five pounds, which would have set Nicodemus back a pretty shekel. A more subtle inference may be drawn from the "coincidence" that this would have been an amount fit for the burial of a king.

You Talking to Me? A Samaritan AND a Woman?

Immediately following the encounter with Nicodemus in chapter 3, John presents his readers with a decided study in contrasts in chapter 4, where the Samaritan woman awaits Jesus at the well (4:4–42). This episode opens on an unpromising note with, "But he [Jesus] had to go through Samaria" (4:4).

PAUSE: While I'm aware that books don't come with Pause buttons, I'm creating one here anyway to give you time to either find the map section at the back of your Bible or hunt up your biblical atlas. And yes, you do need a set of reliable and readable biblical maps. One all-purpose Lands of the Bible doesn't quite cut it for two thousand years of history. Find the map for Palestine in Jesus' day. Got it? Okay, Pause button off.

Notice that the ancient Palestinian land bridge can be sectioned off north to south as Galilee, Samaria, and Judea. Although often dubbed Galilee of the Gentiles, the northern portion nevertheless had a sizable Jewish population. Jesus lived and carried out much of his ministry there. Judea, a Latinized version of the old tribal name of Judah, remained the southernmost portion and was blessed to contain within its borders Jerusalem with its Temple, recently renovated and enhanced by none other than Herod the Great.

Between the two lay Samaria, the former center of the northern kingdom of Israel. After that nation's sad demise at the hands of the Assyrians in 721 B.C.E., relations between it and its neighbor to the south (and, later, to the north) unraveled. Already suspect for having created a new monarchy, new temple, and new high priesthood following the breakup of the nation, the residents of Samaria (the entire area was now called by the name of its capital city) became more undesirable when those left on the land by the Assyrian conquerors after the bulk of the population had been deported began to intermarry with the foreigners whom the empirical forces settled in their place. The twin notions held by Judeans that Samaritans were, candidly speaking, a bastard race practicing a bastard religion had by Jesus' day had more than seven centuries to fester. Jews traveling between Galilee and Judea assuredly did skirt Samaritan territory whenever possible. A *good* Samaritan (Luke 10:29–37)? That would have been the ultimate oxymoron. The only cleansed leper to return in gratitude to Jesus was a Samaritan (Luke 17:11–19). It would be difficult to depict his Jewish companions in a worse light.

That's more introductory information for John's story than you'd expect from a nineteenth-century Russian novel, but nothing in the story makes much sense without it. Now then . . .

We've already seen some of the implications of Jesus' meeting the woman at the community well at noon. Well, there's another. Women customarily drew water early in the day and might augment their supply in the evening. If the woman was there at noon, something was distinctly rotten in the state of Samaria, as Shakespeare might have mused. Was she intentionally avoiding her neighbors? In view of what we learn about her history, that's not beyond feasibility.

The conversation begins haltingly. That it begins at all is a marvel, and well she knows it. As a Jewish man, Jesus should not speak to her because she is a Samaritan, because she is a woman in public, and because she is a Samaritan woman, thus believed to be impure. It doesn't bode well, or does it? Ultimately, Jesus will have a longer theological discussion with this undesirable outcast than with any other single person. Such an exchange was unheard of in Jesus' world. What are the implications in ours? Writes Raymond Brown in *A Retreat with John the Evangelist* (St. Anthony's Messenger Press, 1998):

> This attitude made her a more realistic model for discipleship than if she were eager to encounter Jesus. After all, many people have a chip on their shoulder in regard to God because they see inequalities in life. Notice that Jesus did not answer her objection; he was not going to change instantly a world of injustice.

As the dialogue continues, Jesus suggests she come back with her husband, knowing full well she's a little short in that department. In the Fourth Gospel, Jesus is routinely acquainted with the histories of supposed strangers and often with their thoughts. This is a woman who has lived, shall we say, unconventionally.

> Again that was a realistic touch, appropriate for reaching out toward all those whose obstacle to conversion is a far-from-perfect past. To be brought to faith, people must acknowledge where they stand, but they can take hope from this story inasmuch as Jesus persisted even though he knew the woman's state. He did not say to the woman, "Come back after you straighten out your life," for the grace that he offered was meant to help her change.

One of the ways in which John's characters gradually move toward the light is found in the terms of address they use for Jesus. As their exchange opens, the Samaritan woman first bluntly calls him a Jew (4:9b). After his comment about a spring of water, which must have sounded as inviting as indoor plumbing, she is more polite: "Sir, give me this water . . ." (4:15b). Next, Jesus startles her with his knowledge of her past, moving her to exclaim, "Sir, I see that you are a prophet" (4:19b). She then ventures, "I know that Messiah is coming . . ." (4:25b). Without hesitation, Jesus affirms, "I am he, the one who is speaking to you" (4:26b). This sends her into town in such a hurry she leaves her water jar, forgets she may lack credibility with the townspeople, and blurts, "Come and see a man who told me everything I have ever done! He cannot be the Messiah, can he?" (4:29) She wants this to be true and, like most of us when we may be eager but not especially hopeful, seeks reinforcement. At the story's climax, she gets her support to an unexpected degree. Many of her fellow citizens buy in, "It is no longer because of what you said that we believe, for we have heard for ourselves, and we know that this is truly the Savior of the world" (4:42b).

Watch for progressions of this type as a feature of John's writing style. Look, too, for the phrase "come and see." As he does with the Samaritan woman, John's Jesus invites those he meets to approach, to come nearer, to see and listen and decide for themselves who he is and whether they wish to come into his light. Our next character might have said, "Define light," as he had never seen any at all. He was born blind.

The Man Born Blind Sees More Than Most

A person blind from birth has experienced only profound darkness which, in this gospel, means physically and spiritually as well. As this intricately crafted story unfolds, both progression and regression will occur. The obsolete idea that tragedies such as blindness are the direct result of sin is challenged. The fear many late first-century Christian Jews felt regarding their synagogue status surfaces. The pomposity of those presumed (certainly in their own minds) to be enlightened is deflated, and the hero wins out in the end. There's something for everybody, and John the dramatist is in rare form.

The actual healing is really auxiliary to the story. Jesus effects it with a mud paste made from his saliva (saliva was thought to have healing properties). It is after the fact, when the poor man should have been allowed to delight in his wonderful new eyes, that the fun begins. First, is this the same man or a phony? (9:8–9) Then the Pharisees join the fray, demanding that he explain why this was done on the Sabbath. Still not convinced of his identity, some onlookers fetch his parents to identify him and explain what happened (9:18–23). Beyond, "That's our boy," they can contribute little. His tormentors circle back for another round (9:24–34), by which time the newly sighted man is becoming a tad testy. Finally Jesus rescues him (9:35–38), and the episode concludes with a few words from Jesus to the Pharisees which do not make their day (9:39–41).

Like the Samaritan woman, the man born blind only gradually grasps who Jesus is. When he is first asked who healed him, he replies, "The man called Jesus" (9:11b). To the Pharisees, he proclaims, "He is a prophet" (9:17b). Toward the end, as Jesus himself inquires, " 'Do you believe in the Son of Man?' He answered, 'And who is he, sir? Tell me so that I may believe in him.' Jesus said to him, 'You have seen him, and the one speaking with you is he.' He said, 'Lord, I believe.' And he worshiped him" (9:35b–38).

Lazarus, the Man Who Died Twice

"The Samaritan woman illustrated an initial coming to faith; the man born blind illustrated an incipient faith that acquired depth only after testing; the Lazarus story illustrates *the deepening of faith that comes through an experience of death* (italics his), " says Brown. Lazarus, the brother of Martha and Mary, receives no mention in Luke's account (10:38–42). This seems strange in light of the sisters' urgent message to Jesus in this gospel, "Lord, he whom you love is ill" (11:3b). For John, not only is Lazarus important, his story becomes the ultimate sign, the sign which seals Jesus' doom.

The Johannine Jesus, never taken by surprise, lingers two more days before setting off to help his friend. During this time, he speaks again of glory (11:4), and John sets up another misunderstanding (11:11–15). This one assures that it will be crystal clear in the minds of disciples and readers alike that Lazarus will already be dead upon Jesus' arrival. Dead, dead, dead! No one will be able to later insinuate recovery or even resuscitation. The emphasis placed on this simple truth always reminds me of the opening lines of Charles Dickens' *A Christmas Carol,* "Marley was dead, to begin with. There is no doubt whatever about that." He could have been writing about Lazarus.

The personalities of the two sisters as portrayed here are remarkably consistent with Luke's brief sketch. Martha, the Type A who gets things done with dispatch and efficiency, is pleased to see Jesus, but her irritation at his tardy appearance lurks just beneath the surface, "Lord, if you had been here, my brother would not have died" (11:21b). She recovers quickly with, "But even now I know that God will give you whatever you ask of him" (11:22). Already a believer in the resurrection of the dead (11:24), Martha needs only reassurance from Jesus before reaffirming her faith, "Yes, Lord, I believe that you are the Messiah, the Son of God, the one coming into the world" (11:27b).

Mary, Martha's gentle sister, greets Jesus in almost the same words, but one senses a quieter intonation (11:32b). Now it is Jesus' turn to "come and see" (11:34b) as Mary escorts him to the cave tomb. John's imposing "Jesus began to weep" (11:35) shows this Jesus, who spoke so often and so effectually about eternal life, reduced to tears at the death of a person dear to him as are we all.

When he asks that the stone be rolled from the entrance to the cave, the ever practical Martha suggests this might not be a great idea since Lazarus has been dead four days (11:39). Once again, the fact that Lazarus is dead, dead, dead is underscored. Lazarus' emergence from the tomb is almost anticlimactic after all the buildup, but the story was never so much about him as it was about faith. Lazarus does get to enjoy a celebratory dinner (12:1–2), which seems like the very least they could do.

Coming as it does a matter of days before Jesus' own death and resurrection, the Lazarus account invites comparison. While there are similarities, there is one conspicuous difference. Lazarus returned unchanged to the life he left and at some point in his future got to repeat the process, whereas Jesus moved from his human life to a cosmic existence. As Paul wrote to the Romans, "We know that Christ, being raised from the dead, will never die again; death no longer has dominion over him" (6:9).

"Thus," writes Brown, "although the raising of Lazarus was a tremendous miracle bringing to culmination Jesus' ministry, it was still a sign. The life to which Lazarus was raised is natural life; Jesus meant it to symbolize eternal life, the kind of life that only God possesses and that Jesus as God's Son made and makes possible. . . . In the instance of Lazarus, Jesus was not simply renewing a life that ends in the grave, but offering eternal life."

Life, not death, is always the last word, and this is our last word on John.

Letters to the Churches

My mother's brother died at twenty on a battlefield in France long before my birth. The sadness never entirely left my mother, and her brother's framed photograph sat on her bedroom dresser all the years of my growing up. To me, however, the serious young man in uniform had no more identity than a magazine photo. Upon my mother's death, as I was sorting through the tangible remains of her life, I came across a packet of letters written by and to her younger brother. As I read his sometimes hasty notes to her, my uncle began to take shape as a real person. By the time I finished, I felt as though I had actually met him, which in a way I had.

Letters can have that effect, or at least they used to before e-mail blew such letter-writing skills as we once possessed out the window. We may be the poorer for that, and coming generations almost certainly will be.

Communication by letter has been the accepted form of correspondence since the written word was devised, becoming a genuine art form in the hands of the truly gifted. It is this literary genre that will occupy us during this chapter, which is only fitting since it occupies so much of the Second Testament, twenty-one of its twenty-seven books. In some cases, it may be a stretch to call these books. The Letter to Philemon, the Letter of Jude, and the Second and Third Letters of John are more notes, taking up a page or less in a modern Bible, and possessing no chapter divisions.

There are, notwithstanding, other divisions in this section. The letters attributed to Paul make up the first grouping. They are ranked from longest (Romans) to shortest (Philemon). These are followed by the Letter to the Hebrews which bridges the two major divisions while itself defying definition. It belongs neither to the Pauline set nor to the catholic (small "c") letters that follow. *Catholic* simply means "universal." The letters of James, Peter, John, and Jude are classified as catholic because they are not addressed to specific faith communities the way Paul's tend to be. All of them, even Paul's, may have been intended for a broader audience than appears at first glance. It's entirely possible that they were passed around among the new and struggling Christian communities, each group sifting any letter received for such enlightenment it might provide. We may owe our possession of these letters to this practice. The letters were carefully preserved as timeless treasures. Remnants of this custom endure within Catholicism even now in the form of papal encyclicals. From the Greek *en* ("in") *kyklos* ("a circle"), the word denotes a letter meant for broad, general circulation, i.e., the universal church.

The letters of the Christian Scriptures "correspond" to the writings of the Hebrew Bible in several important ways. Not unexpectedly, their content varies widely, dependent in large part on situations faced by the individuals or groups to whom they are addressed. Their tone fluctuates as well, ranging from highly theological (Romans, Hebrews) to rubber-hits-the-road practical (Timothy, Titus, James). And for all this Paul is associated with about half of the books in the Christian canon and thirteen of the letters—his is far from the only voice speaking through the letters . . . even his own. There are quite a number written under Paul's name (that pseudonymous business again). One could assume, then, that the letters contain a vast store of information helpful in dealing with the three B-I-G questions plus the two-part Jesus question. Indeed they do.

It should be noted that, although *letter* and *epistle* are often used interchangeably, they're not completely synonymous. As a rule, an epistle is a more formal document than a letter. The Letter to the Hebrews no doubt qualifies as an epistle while Paul venting his frustration to the Galatians does not. In the ancient world, as in ours, letters generally followed an established form. Ours is fairly straightforward: an opening (Dear . . .); the body of news, information, gossip, and assorted tidbits; and a close (Sincerely . . .). The Greek form incorporated around the Mediterranean differed to a degree. It, too, opened with a salutation, but that customarily included the sender's name as well as the recipient's, and a formal greeting (Grace and peace to you . . .). A short passage of gratitude usually ensued, followed by the letter's central message. The formal closing contained personal news, regards to and from friends and family, and a final blessing. Just as our own dispatches stray from the format, so did theirs.

Delivery systems in the first century give new meaning to snail mail. Where possible, the best bet was to place your communiqué in the hand of a trusted courier. Travel, either by land or sea, was tough enough for humans. It could be murder, literally, on goods being transported. It's reasonable to surmise that some letters to the churches from Paul's pen or any number of others did not survive. That these did is reason enough to see the hand of God at work. Of course, that's only my own opinion, but it's one I respect.

Saul/Paul: A Big Name Either Way

Because he has been called the single most prominent figure in the Christian Scriptures next to Jesus himself, Paul deserves a little "ink" as pre-computer journalists used to say. Thomas Cahill turns the spotlight on Paul in *Desire of the Everlasting Hills: The World before and after Jesus* (Doubleday, 1999):

> Over the last century much has been made of Paul as the inventor of Christianity, the man who took the unfocused, anti-intellectual messianism of the bubble-headed followers of Jesus and constructed it into an effective theological weapon, which Christians would eventually use to beat not only the Jews but the whole of the ancient world. This is only partly true. Paul did not *invent* the faith of the early Church in the continuing reality and presence of Jesus. If Paul became in his own lifetime the most articulate spokesman for this faith, he was never much more than an articulator who knew how to zero in on the most essential elements of his argument and could thread his discourse with the welcome colors of his own personal experience. If Paul had never left the pharisaical school, the Jesus movement that became Christianity would have survived and probably even prospered (if with a more limited scope), but it would have been a

Christianity that lacked (at least for some time) Paul's intellectual edge as well as his emotional edginess.

Paul could have written the first organized account of Jesus' life and been remembered as the creator of the gospel form instead of Mark. "Paul," continues Cahill, "sets himself the task of being not another storyteller but a theologian . . . that is, someone who can articulate clearly the intellectual affirmations that lie behind the stories."

Glimpses of Paul's own story can be found in his correspondence, but it is Luke who tells us more than anyone about this controversial figure in his second work. The Acts of the Apostles comes up for review in chapter 10, so we'll table the Pauline biography until then and look instead at the remarkable output of written communications he left to the early churches and, by extension, to us.

Pigeonholing Paul

The thirteen letters identified with Paul split almost exactly down the middle in terms of genuine versus pseudonymous. Seven are credited to Paul with little argument; three are doubtful, and three more are almost surely not his work. The seven bearing the Pauline stamp of authenticity are:

- 1 Thessalonians
- 1 and 2 Corinthians
- Galatians
- Romans
- Philippians
- Philemon

Those where a disciple's hand is more likely than Paul's are:

- 2 Thessalonians
- Colossians
- Ephesians

Those generally agreed to be non-Pauline are:

- 1 and 2 Timothy
- Titus

Each is significant in its own way, and all of the letters, Pauline and catholic, taken together make up a body of work so well respected that, in post-Vatican II Catholicism, they are the renderings of choice as the second Scripture reading at nearly all weekend liturgies.

As long as we're on this subject, a short aside. Unlike the first and third readings at eucharistic celebrations, which generally find a common focus, the second reading pretty much has a life of its own, particularly during Ordinary Time. Take Cycle A, for example. Readings from Paul's Letter to the Romans commence with the Ninth Sunday in Ordinary Time and march right along through the Twenty-fourth Sunday. Commonality of themes among all three readings is rare. And, as long as we're here, another little bird walk. The English language falls victim to that old translation bugaboo when it comes to Ordinary Time. *Ordinary* here refers to the numbered or ordinal Sundays and in no way infers that the two "Ordinary" seasons are of less consequence than the others.

We'll glance at each letter in the Pauline corpus in the order they are listed above.

1 Thessalonians

In the First Letter to the Thessalonians, we have the oldest document in the Christian canon. Written in either 50 or 51 C.E. from Corinth to the community in Thessalonica (today's northern Greece), this letter embodies the earliest evidence of Christian belief and practice. Remember, the first gospel is still fifteen to twenty years away. What this letter contains represents the thinking of believers a mere score of years distant from Jesus' lifetime. Where did their concentration of thought lie?

First, as Ronald D. Witherup points out (*The Bible Companion*, Crossroad Publishing, 1998), "The primary focus of the body of the letter (2:1–3:13) is to reinforce the fidelity of the Thessalonians in spite of the challenges that sometimes appear." Fortification of belief will be the underlying motivation behind many of Paul's communiqués, and understandably so. New and inexperienced converts, left by necessity to fend for themselves, would constantly face situations for which they had no precedent and questions for which they had no answers. We can scarcely imagine what this would be like, with our practically instantaneous access to a blizzard of web sites, not to mention some two thousand years of thought on every conceivable nuance of Christian theology by everyone from Ambrose and Augustine to Teilhard de Chardin and Karl Rahner. The only "search engine" available to the

Thessalonians, and to their colleagues in similar communities, was Paul. They turned to him, of course.

1 Thessalonians also provides a fascinating glimpse into the earliest understanding of Jesus' return. Members of their initial group are dying and so will not be on hand when Jesus comes again. Their companions are concerned about their fate (4:13–5:11). Paul reassures them but seemingly shares their conviction that Jesus could arrive at any moment. His later writings reflect a more extended outlook.

Paul's description of Jesus' arrival (4:16–17) falls back on traditional imagery from theophanies of old. He will "descend from heaven" (4:16b), a reminder of the abode of the god(s) in ancient cosmology. "Then we who are alive, who are left, will be caught up in the clouds . . ." (4:17a), meeting the cosmic Christ in that typical cloud-embellished setting. Among evangelical Christian sects, this experience is known as the "rapture." Catholic and mainline Protestant denominations view the portrayal in a figurative rather than a literal sense.

Galatians

It is not the authorship that is murky here, but the locale. Paul wrote it, we can be fairly sure, but what was the zip code on the letter? Galacia was an established Roman province, but its mixed population ranged over a much broader area, then known as Asia Minor, now Turkey. Since the concerns of the letter are probably directed toward Gentile converts toying with Judaism, an more northern locale is likely. In any case, this, too, is an early letter, possibly written from Ephesus c. 54 C.E.

Regardless of the wheres, the whens, and the whos, the what is manifest from the opening line: Paul is furious! He manages to sputter out a civil five-verse greeting before landing on them with both sandals. "I am astonished that you are so quickly deserting the one who called you in the grace of Christ and are turning to a different gospel—not that there is another gospel, but there are some who are confusing you and want to pervert the gospel of Christ" (1:6–7).

Paul's apostolic credentials are being questioned, so he sends along his vitae curriculum in more detail than we receive from him anywhere else (1:13–2:21). "You foolish Galatians! Who has bewitched you?" (3:1a) And he's off again, this time reaching back to Abraham to demonstrate that the Law alone may have sufficed until Jesus, but that it is no longer the case (3:6–5:6). "You were running well; who prevented you from obeying the truth?" (5:7)

Eventually, the tone begins to cool. "See what large letters I make when I am writing in my own hand!" (6:11) Paul seems to have availed himself of a standard practice of his day and used a scribe or secretary. As we might do with a typewritten message placed on the desk for our signature, Paul adds a passage in his own hand for emphasis. No one can accuse him of lack of emphasis in this letter. Upon completion, he couldn't be blamed if he sent the secretary out to get him a couple of aspirin.

Philippians

Paul first brought his message to Europe c. 50 C.E. when his second missionary journey brought him to Philippi. What we know as the Letter to the Philippians was penned by Paul, probably at Ephesus, somewhere between 54 and 58 C.E. The odd phrasing of the preceding sentence is due to considerable speculation on the part of Pauline scholars that the letter as it now appears is, in fact, a compilation of two, even three missives.

If Paul exhibited his, shall we say, forceful side to the Galatians, his appeal to the Philippians is the diametric opposite. As in Galatians, he hustles through the preliminary niceties (1:1–2) so that he can get on with the enjoyable task of telling them how highly he thinks of them: "I thank my God every time I remember you," (1:3), and how much he misses them: "For God is my witness, how I long for all of you with the compassion of Christ Jesus" (1:8). Paul has a definite soft spot for the Philippians (not to be confused with, as one lector solemnly intoned, the Philippinos), made wistful, perhaps, by the fact that he writes to them from prison. Philippians is one of four so-called captivity letters in which imprisonment is mentioned, the others being Ephesians, Colossians, and Philemon.

Paul speaks as you would expect him to when addressing dear friends, supporting and encouraging them in their faith, bringing them news of his own travels, thanking them for their generosity. One of the most exquisite appeals to virtue to be found anywhere in Scripture is situated near the end of this letter: "Finally, beloved, whatever is true, whatever is honorable, whatever is just, whatever is pure, whatever is pleasing, whatever is commendable, if there is any excellence and if there is anything worthy of praise, think about these things" (4:8).

In closing, Paul fondly bids them: "Greet every saint in Christ Jesus. The friends who are with me greet you. All the saints greet you" (4:21–22a). The saints alluded to are obviously very much alive. They were not then canonized (since the process was unknown), nor have any of them been canonized since. So what do we really mean when we designate someone a saint? Rock bottom, what is a saint? If someone walking by tossed this at you, "Hi there, Saint Fred," or "Good to see you, Saint Carrie," would you smile, burst out laughing, faint dead away, or write them off as slightly deranged? I've experimented with greeting students this way (on good days) and the most frequent reaction was alarm. I expected phone calls from irate parents, "What did you call my child?" Why does something so praiseworthy elicit such a peculiar response? It may be that we equate saintliness with perfection and, recognizing our many imperfections, shy away lest we taint the term by association. But saints on earth weren't perfect. Read a few of their lives (Augustine, Teresa of Avila, Ignatius of Loyola, etc.).

In his introduction to *All Saints: Daily Reflections on Saints, Prophets, and Witnesses for Our Time* (Crossroad Publishing, 1997), Robert Ellsberg reminds us:

> While there are recognizable patterns in the lives of the saints, each one was in his or her own way an "original." They achieved their holiness with the material at hand . . . material, in many cases, of apparently dubious quality. Many of them struggled hard to invent a new style of Christian witness in response to the needs of their time . . . not infrequently needs obvious to themselves alone. Even among the canonized saints, it is striking how many of them paid dearly for the originality of their vision. Along with the many certified martyrs, there are countless others who suffered persecution or humiliation . . . not from ostensible "enemies of the faith" but at the hands of their fellow Christians. All this is easily forgotten.

Paul's living, breathing saints weren't perfect. What he attempted to do was to move them along in this direction. And isn't this what a saint is . . . someone who directs the whole of his or her life to God, imperfectly but sincerely, right here, right now?

1 and 2 Corinthians

The letters to the Corinthians contain some of Paul's most penetrating and prudent insights, all of them apparently greatly needed by a community whose problem areas were as diverse as rival Christian factions and troublesome liturgical practices, marital responsibilities and questionable sexual practices.

Corinth was quite a town. Barely a century old when Paul arrived, the Roman Corinth he knew replaced a previous municipality which had stood for millennia. Elbowing two seaports, Corinth was not surprisingly multi-cultural. Because of this, Raymond Brown writes in *An Introduction to the New Testament* (Doubleday, 1997), "Attempts to live according to the gospel in the multiethnic and crosscultural society at Corinth raised issues still encountered in multiethnic, multiracial, and crosscultural societies today."

In the eyes of some observers, Corinth was Sin City, where all the sailors went on shore leave. This description may be overblown, but there is no doubt that a strange mixture of races, religions, and social classes blended there with varying degrees of success. Little wonder, then, that this community, of which Paul was very fond, also caused him to at least figuratively pull out what little hair he had (Paul is traditionally thought to have been bald).

In what we know as two letters may lie the remains of as many as seven. Over the space of nearly a decade, commencing c. 56–57 C.E., Paul was often in contact with the Corinthians. The first letter as it is now formulated takes up such issues as the competing groups who are causing division (1:10–17) and segues from there into a number of related topics to the end of chapter 4. For the next two chapters, he deals with the distasteful question of incest and, on a related note, casual sex. The body of the letter, chapters 7–14, constitute a Q & A session with Paul doing his best to respond to queries put to him.

All of chapter 15 is devoted to a justification of resurrection as a tenet of belief. As in his First Letter to the Thessalonians, Paul reassures novice Christians about the trustworthiness of their conviction regarding resurrection. In fact, he stakes everything on it:

For if the dead are not raised, then Christ has not been raised. If
Christ has not been raised, your faith is futile and you are still in
your sins. Then those also who have died in Christ have perished.
If for this life only we have hoped in Christ, we are of all people
most to be pitied (15:16–19).

It is in the second letter that we see the most evidence of parts of
several letters merging. Chapters 1–9 are thought to be from one letter
while chapters 10–13 are probably from another, since the tone is so
different, and there is little continuity. In the first, Paul explains himself
and his ministry with equanimity, whereas at chapter 10 he suddenly
goes on the defensive. But whatever their original form or subsequent
evolution, the letters to the Corinthians remain among Paul's most
important writings.

Romans

Still, if you can read only one of Paul's letters in its entirety and take the
time to study it carefully, few would disagree that the choice should be
his Letter to the Romans. "Longer than any other NT letter, more reflective in its outlook than any other undisputed Pauline letter, more calmly
reasoned than Galatians in treating the key question of justification and
the Law, Romans has been the most studied of the apostle's writings . . .
indisputably Paul's theological chef d'oeuvre," writes Brown (*The New
Jerome Biblical Commentary,* 1990). ". . . this letter has played a major role
in the development of theology."

By c. 57–58 C.E., when he composed this letter, probably from
Cenchreae near Corinth, Paul was anxious to travel west to the imperial
capital, Rome, and beyond to Spain. "I remember you always in my
prayers, asking that by God's will I may somehow at last succeed in
coming to you. For I am longing to see you" (1:9b–11a). Paul did not
found the Christian community at Rome, and it is uncertain how much
was known about him there, so one of the purposes of this letter may
have been to introduce both himself and his theology prior to his actual
arrival. As he has yet to establish personal contact with the Roman
community, Paul tends to address issues that have arisen elsewhere and,
he must have assumed, would have surfaced there as well. However, the

eschatology expressed in 1 Corinthians in regard to the Resurrection is missing here as is comprehensive treatment of the Eucharist or, for that matter, the church in general. The Holy Spirit comes into unusual prominence in chapter 8, and the responsibilities of disciples are treated at some length in chapters 12–15. Ronald Rolheiser writes (*The Bible Companion,* Crossroad Publishing, 1998):

> The most "meaty" issue that Paul tackles in Romans, is the notion of justification by faith alone. This used to be a dividing line between Catholics and Protestants. Supposedly, Catholics thought you could earn salvation by good works, while Protestants thought it was a gift of God that required nothing else. Both positions were inaccurate, nothing more than caricatures. Fortunately today, Catholics and Protestants alike have a more nuanced appreciation of Paul. Romans does teach that justification by faith is God's free gift, but Paul also insists that people must live out that faith by their good actions. Christian freedom, in fact, is not the license to do whatever you will but to do God's will freely because it is the right thing to do.

Philemon

Scarcely long enough to even be considered a letter, this might be better termed a quick note to a friend. Highly personal in nature and bereft of the methodical development of thought found in Paul's more extended works, this little gem could be overlooked. This would be unfortunate because gem it is.

The crux of the situation is clearly stated. Paul has come to know a runaway slave, Onesimus, who belongs to Philemon. Much as he would like Onesimus to remain at his side, Paul acknowledges Philemon's rights as a property owner, asking only that the slave not be punished for going AWOL. If we expect more of Paul somehow regarding the slavery issue, we again need to allow for the sizable gap that exists between his time and our own, between his culture and our own.

Ron Witherup clarifies the predicament:

> So what is so revolutionary about Paul's letter? It does not attack the institution of slavery as such, as we might expect (or hope).

In Paul's day, slavery was an accepted fact of society. Slaves were property. By rights, Philemon could have punished Onesimus severely or sold him to another owner. But Paul insists that baptism into Christ changes relationships. By baptism Onesimus had become a "brother" to Philemon. He was now to be treated as one of the community. If it is ever true that "big things come in little packages," I think this saying applies to [the Letter to] Philemon. Deep down it provides testimony to how truly revolutionary Christianity can be when we recognize the implications of our faith.

2 Thessalonians

The authorship of the Second Letter to the Thessalonians is problematic. If it is genuinely Pauline, it may date from shortly after the first letter to Thessalonica. If it is not, both date and writer are up for grabs. Scholars suspect pseudonymous authorship when the style, the vocabulary, the subject matter, or the tone of a document is markedly different from those favored by a particular writer—in this case Paul. We all have speech patterns that we use repeatedly whether we are conscious of it or not. You've doubtless become well acquainted with some of mine by now. When these do not appear or when others show up that an author seldom uses, it raises a red flag. The same is true of vocabulary, etc.

In Second Thessalonians, certainly the tone is noticeably changed. The warmth of the first letter is replaced by cool detachment. A late date of composition is also hinted at by the strongly apocalyptic spirit of chapter 2, characteristic of the latter years of the first century, making the ongoing conflict between good and evil central to this short letter.

Colossians

Colossae was an important textile center noted for its purple woolens. Purple dye, excreted from tiny mollusks found along the Phoenician (Lebanese) coast, was scarce and expensive, causing it to be associated almost exclusively with royalty or, at the very most, the extremely wealthy. Located southeast of Ephesus, it would have accommodated assorted ethnic and religious groups.

If Paul wrote this letter, it would have been late in his career, somewhere in the early 60s C.E. If it is pseudonymous, the date could shift as far as the 80s. Written in Paul's name, the letter simulates his style passably. As always, it is necessary to bear in mind that it is not so much who wrote certain biblical books as what they contain. Here, the focus is Christology, specifically the cosmic Christ rather than the human Jesus. Colossians 1:15–20 cites what was, in all probability, an early Christian hymn—nor is this the only instance of this in the Pauline corpus (see Philippians 2:6–11).

Typical of these letters, Colossians serves the dual purpose of strengthening the faith of the young community (1:27–2:18) and rectifying faults stemming from opponents (3:2–4:9). *The New Jerome Bible Handbook* (Liturgical Press, 1992) states that since "a complex of Judaism, paganism, Christianity, magic, astrology, and mystery religion forms the cultural background of the letter, there is no way of identifying the opponents at Colossae with any one group. However, most scholars connect the error with Judaism in some form."

A commentary of this nature promotes the kind of attitude adjustment most of us require from time to time. It's easy to allow ourselves to think that living as Jesus' disciple would have been so uncomplicated in the decades immediately following his death because the factions, positions, sects, and variant beliefs that have plagued us ever since did not yet exist. Oh, but they did! The circumstances our forebears in faith encountered were in all likelihood no easier than ours, nor more difficult—simply different. Signing on with Jesus rarely insures that our lives will be comfortable, just better both here and hereafter.

Ephesians

Ephesus was one of the great cities of the Mediterranean world. From its position on the Eastern shore of the Aegean Sea, Ephesus held sway as capital of the Roman province of Asia (Minor) and as commercial, religious, and cultural hub as well. In the latter part of the first century, it may have boasted a population as high as a quarter of a million. The church at Ephesus is the first of the seven churches addressed at the outset of the Book of Revelation (2:1–7). The fabled Temple of Artemis (Diana), one of the seven wonders of the ancient world, drew devotees from far and wide, and got Paul himself in considerable hot water when his Jesus advocacy cut into the local flourishing trade in silver statuettes of the goddess (see Acts 19).

So Paul knew the city without a doubt. Whether he actually wrote a letter to the Christians there is doubtful for all the reasons mentioned earlier. If he did, it was very late, mid-60s C.E. If he didn't, then like Colossians, the date could be pushed well down the line toward the end of the century.

The body of this letter is devoted in large part to the church, its oneness and its calling, with firm emphasis on the parity of Gentiles with Jewish converts: "[T]he Gentiles have become fellow heirs, members of the same body, and sharers in the promise in Christ Jesus through the gospel" (3:6). Everyone is admissible, and everyone brings his or her individual gifts. "The gifts he gave were that some would be apostles, some prophets, some evangelists, some pastors and teachers, to equip the saints for the work of ministry, for building up the body of Christ, until all of us come to the unity of the faith and of the knowledge of the Son of God, to maturity, to the measure of the full stature of Christ" (4:11–13).

The verse which ensues is, for me, among the most noteworthy in the entire Christian canon, prodding me to persistently strive to delve deeper, see further, assimilate better, with the sure knowledge that I will never entirely get off square one this side of the Great Divide: "We must no longer be children, tossed to and fro and blown about by every wind of doctrine, by people's trickery, by their craftiness in deceitful scheming. But speaking the truth in love, we must grow up in every way into him who is the head, into Christ" (4:14–15).

1 and 2 Timothy

The two letters to Timothy, together with their companion letter to Titus, are grouped under the heading "Pastoral Epistles" or "Pastoral Letters" because of their common thread of instructions concerning ministries and ministers.

In these letters, the accent shifts from greater missionary effort over a wider area to the care and maintenance of existing communities. In much the same manner as parents trying to secure the future of their children when they are no longer on the scene, these pastoral letters look to ways of ensuring that the young churches will grow and prosper. One of their most pressing needs will remain stable, well-taught leadership, an issue that has never ceased to be a concern at some level throughout the long centuries of Christianity and certainly remains paramount in our own.

But think what we have at our disposal which would have been undreamed of then. Christianity today has not only found acceptance; it is far and away the largest religious body on the globe. Interaction within this body is nearly instantaneous, thanks to rapid transportation and high-tech communication. Pastoral staffs on the parochial and diocesan levels serve local churches, exhibiting a care and devotion only beginning to unfold when these letters were written. Over a span of two thousand years, great minds have set about elucidating every aspect of Christian belief and practice. Their conclusions are at our fingertips. Advances in educational opportunities have made our age, on a broad base, the best informed in history.

The Timothy in question was one of Paul's converts, companions, and sometimes emissaries. Of Jewish/Gentile descent (Acts 16:1–3), Timothy is dear to Paul: "For this reason I sent you Timothy, who is my beloved and faithful child in the Lord, to remind you of my ways in Christ Jesus, as I teach them everywhere in every church" (1 Corinthians 4:17). Second Timothy is intended specifically for him in contrast to the more general nature of the first letter. In it, Timothy is cautioned about the damage inflicted by false teaching and factions and is implored to stand firm: "[P]roclaim the message; be persistent whether the time is favorable or unfavorable; convince, rebuke, and encourage, with the utmost patience in teaching . . . always be sober, endure suffering, do the work of an evangelist, carry out your ministry fully" (4:2, 5).

Titus

The final entry in the Pauline sequence is the letter to another of Paul's companions, Titus, who accompanied Paul to Jerusalem on one occasion (see Galatians 2:1–3). It was also Titus who evidently smoothed some troubled waters for Paul and the church at Corinth (see 2 Corinthians 7–8). Consistent with the other pastoral letters, the Letter to Titus concentrates on maintaining faithful adherence to the faith (1:5–16) and the marks of effective pastors and others in leadership positions (2:1–15). In today's parlance, we would say such leaders should be role models. The terminology may be contemporary, but the basic idea is as old as, well, the Letter to Titus.

With this, our far too concise visit to the world of Pauline correspondence ends. It does so in the hope that your interest has now been piqued sufficiently that you will pay a more extended call to one or another of Paul's communities.

The Letter to the Hebrews

Once considered Pauline, the Letter to the Hebrews now wanders the earth orphaned, though not for lack of speculation regarding its parentage. Prominent names in the first-century church have been brought forward, including Barnabas, Luke, Apollos, Priscilla (Prisca), Aquila, and Clement of Rome. The nonconformist nature of Hebrews is also seen in its style. We may err in calling this a letter at all as it is less epistle than sermon. The customary salutation is missing. The text begins with the first word and does not follow the accepted letter form.

Whoever the writer was and whatever configuration he or she intended the text to take, this much is clear: Hebrews is directed toward Jewish converts to Christianity, building a solid case for the sacrifice of Jesus overruling the Mosaic covenant. Jesus is shown as superior to Moses in chapter 3 and as the eternal high priest in chapter 5. The author harkens all the way back to the mysterious figure of Melchizedek (Genesis 14:18–20) in establishing Jesus' preeminence. This persuasive emphasis on priesthood leads some to think the letter was composed prior to the destruction of the second Temple, and with it the Jewish priesthood in 70 C.E. Others see it as a literary device used in a much later work.

The crown jewel of this letter/sermon (if writings can possess such things) awaits the reader in chapter 11, which we already previewed in regard to Abraham in chapter 5 of this volume. Few are unfamiliar with 1 Corinthians 13, the ode to love. At her daughters' weddings, my close friend and professional associate memorized the entire chapter and directed Paul's timeless words couched in her own love directly to each bride and groom. It gave new meaning to the *living* word of God. Hebrews has a similar treat in store, but instead of love, the author here creates an elegy of faith: "Now faith is the assurance of things hoped for, the conviction of things not seen" (11:1).

There follows a sketch of the faith of many figures from the Hebrew Scriptures, drawing the conclusion that "therefore, since we are surrounded by so great a cloud of witnesses, let us also lay aside every weight and the sin that clings so closely, and let us run with perseverance the race that is set before us, looking to Jesus the pioneer and perfecter of our faith, who for the sake of the joy that was set before him endured the cross, disregarding its shame, and has taken his seat at the right hand of the throne of God" (12:1–2).

Our growing appreciation of who Jesus really is and what he should mean in our lives receives ethereal illumination in the Letter to the Hebrews, portraying a Jesus in the Johannine tradition. No matter how great the First Testament heroes were, Jesus surpasses them all, even Moses.

The Letter of James

With the Letter of James, we enter the territory of the catholic, or universal, letters. This is something of an oversimplification inasmuch as recipients are occasionally hinted at, if not directly addressed. Authors' names are provided in this section, but you're probably putting very little credence in these by this time.

Entering the domain of James, I abandon any pretext at objectivity. I have been captivated by this letter for years in much the same way and for much the same reason that I enjoy Amos in the Hebrew canon. These boys are nothing if not candid. You could even say frank—oh, let's face it; they're downright blunt. Diplomatic service careers wouldn't have suited either one.

Who is the James of the straight talk? Now don't sigh; we can come pretty close here. He's clearly not the son of Zebedee who was part of Jesus' inner circle. That James' death is recorded in Acts 12:1–2 and occurred early on. The other apostolic James, son(?) of Alpheus, is so inconspicuous we know practically nothing about him. The best candidate is the James who was related to Jesus and who rose to prominence as the leader of the Jerusalem church, where his judgment turns the tide at the Council of Jerusalem (Acts 15). His actions there coupled with the concerns expressed in this letter point to a level-headed, "real world" kind of guy. The Jewish historian Josephus mentions in his *Antiquities* (20.9.1) that this James was stoned to death in the year 62 C.E.

If so, this letter is one of the Christian canon's earlier works, and works are what got it in trouble on more than one occasion.

You see, James has no use for the axiom, "Don't just do something, stand there." For him, profession of faith is so much hot air if not backed up by fitting deeds. "What good is it, my brothers and sisters, if you say you have faith but do not have works? Can faith save you? If a brother or sister is naked and lacks daily food, and one of you says to them, 'Go in peace; keep warm and eat your fill,' and yet you do not supply their bodily needs, what is the good of that? So faith by itself, if it has no works, is dead" (2:14–17). This might make us squirm, but there's not much wiggle room here!

Martin Luther was not fond of James's theology, writing it off as "a right strawy epistle" and writing it right out of his Christian canon (it found its way back in due time). Luther subscribed firmly to the doctrine of faith as gift. This issue kept Lutherans and Catholics at arm's length for some four centuries although, as noted earlier, neither's position was ever as hard and fast as sometimes portrayed.

James also heavily promoted the virtue of knowing when to keep one's lip zipped:

> Anyone who makes no mistakes in speaking is perfect, able to keep the whole body in check with a bridle. . . . How great a forest is set ablaze by a small fire. And the tongue is a fire. . . . it stains the whole body, sets on fire the cycle of nature, and is itself set on fire by hell. . . . From the same mouth come blessing and cursing. My brothers and sisters, this ought not to be so (3:2–10).

The comfort level when James was preaching must have been rather low. In respect to style, James, like Hebrews, more resembles a sermon than an epistle.

For so short a writing, James manages to speak to a variety of issues. He talks astutely about the causes of division within a community:

> Those conflicts and disputes among you, where do they come from? Do they not come from your cravings that are at war within you? You want something and do not have it; so you commit murder. And you covet something and cannot obtain it;

so you engage in disputes and conflicts. You do not have, because you do not ask. You ask and do not receive, because you ask wrongly, in order to spend what you get on your pleasures (4:1–3).

I defy anyone to read James and not fidget a little from time to time. Procrastination is not an option either:

Come now, you who say, "Today or tomorrow we will go to such and such a town and spend a year there, doing business and making money." Yet you do not even know what tomorrow will bring. What is your life? For you are a mist that appears for a little while and then vanishes (4:13–14).

In light of our own hectic existences, replete with day planners and Palm Pilots, this has a surprisingly contemporary ring. More on the folly of basing life on the accumulation of wealth is found in 5:1–6.

We may be tempted to conclude that riches are inherently evil and poverty infinitely desirable, but this is not the sense of Scripture. The oft misquoted verse from 1 Timothy reads: "For the *love of money* [emphasis mine] is a root of all kinds of evil" (6:10a). Luke's parables about the rich man and Lazarus (16:19–31) or the rich fool (12:16–21) do not condemn affluence in and of itself; it is the attitude toward it and use or misuse of it that come in for condemnation. Perhaps this is why Matthew's first beatitude reads "poor in spirit" instead of merely "poor" as Luke has it. "In spirit" has to do with outlook, implying that one might be steward of the world's greatest fortune and remain poor in spirit. Conversely, it's possible to be clutching and grasping even if there are few, if any, assets to clutch and grasp. In any case, warns James, watch it; nobody's here for long anyway.

"Are any among you sick? They should call for the elders of the church and have them pray over them, anointing them with oil in the name of the Lord" (5:14). In this succinct verse is found the basis for the Catholic sacrament of anointing of the sick. Over time, this sacrament became so closely associated with the dying, i.e., last rites, that priests were at times reluctant to visit seriously ill parishioners lest their mere appearance send an unwarranted signal of impending demise. Vatican II reshifted the focus to more closely reflect James's injunction, advocating that the sacrament be administered not only to the dying, but to any whose age or state of health warrants special prayer (see the *Constitution on the Sacred Liturgy,* #73–75). The grace attendant upon this sacrament is thus invoked primarily on its healing properties, be they physical or spiritual or both. So James winds up being a comfort after all.

The Letters of Peter

If the notion of pseudonymous writing has remained ambiguous up to now, clarification is about to burst upon the horizon. It is scarcely possible to imagine two writings, ascribed to the same author, which have less in common than those attributed to Peter. If you didn't see the same name topping them, it would never occur to you to link them. While it cannot be said with certainty that Peter, the apostle, wrote the first letter bearing his name, he unquestionably could have. If so, it would have to date from c. 60 C.E.

Arguing in favor of Petrine authorship is the letter's subject matter. The *New American Bible* places a major subtitle at 2:11: "The Christian in a Hostile World." This covers everything in the letter from this point until the concluding three verses and sums it up nicely. The intended recipients of this letter are patently undergoing tough times which could conform to Nero's persecution to which Peter himself fell victim. The sub-subheadings in the *NAB* show that helpful advice is included for nearly everyone: Christian Examples (2:11–12), Christian Citizens (2:13–17), Christian Slaves (2:18–25), Christian Spouses (3:1–7), Christian Conduct (3:8–12), Christian Suffering (3:13–22), Christian Restraint (4:1–6), Christian Charity (4:7–11). Every indication is present of a shepherd doing everything in his power to protect, defend, guide, direct, and instruct his flock.

The Second Letter of Peter is something else entirely and took a good deal of flack in the early church, even undergoing outright rejection. Few would impute it to Peter. Because? "It includes parts of Jude which makes it seem unlikely that it is an original letter. It speaks of a 'collection' of Paul's letters which did not exist until the end of the century; . . . it speaks of 'your apostles' as if the writer did not belong to that group" *(The New Jerome Bible Handbook).*

Still another consideration is the letter's attention to the supposed delay of Christ's return which occupies almost the whole of chapter 3, a concern that did not make itself felt to any degree until after Peter's death. False teachers who became more of a problem with the passing of time likewise receive consideration. One senses an undercurrent of impatience flowing through the target audience which the writer attempts to quiet: "But do not ignore this one fact, beloved, that with the Lord one day is like a thousand years, and a thousand years are like one day. The Lord is not slow about his promise, as some think of slowness, but is patient with you, not wanting any to perish, but all to come to repentance" (3:8–9). A charming image of God for our collection from a work dating from the closing days of the biblical period.

The Letters of John

The three short letters of John have long been joined to the gospel of the same name, and Johannine motifs such as light and love do surface, but for many of the reasons already recorded regarding dubious authorship, they may or may not share a common creator after all. Even so, they have value in their own right.

If you feel you're experiencing the incredible shrinking letters, you are. As with the Pauline letters, the catholic missives are arranged from longest to shortest in the Christian canon, so we're now getting down to notes you can hang on the refrigerator door.

The gist of these letters demonstrates the distress brought about by splits or schisms. That these are apparently pronounced and painful hints at a very late date. All three Johannine letters stem from the closing days of the first century.

The first two letters make use of an expression found nowhere else in the Bible: *Antichrist*. Surprised? You're not alone. For many people, the term instantly brings the Book of Revelation to mind; yet it never arises there. In 1 John 2:18–23 and 4:3, the Antichrist(s) designate the person(s) who, upon leaving the community, plunge back into the darkness. 2 John 7 (there are no chapters in 2 and 3 John) sets a similar tone. If anything, 2 John is a little sharper, perhaps indicating a continuous worsening of the problem. A great sadness pervades these discussions of separation.

Opening as it does with a poetic preface on the order of John's gospel, 1 John is less a letter than an instruction. 2 and 3 John are definitely letters, each addressed to a mysterious unknown recipient: "the elect lady and her children" (2 John 1a) and "the beloved Gaius" (3 John 1a). Whether these were real people or were contrived as literary devices may never be known.

If nothing else, the three concise Johannine letters paint a picture of a community trying valiantly to cope with problems from within and without, with resentment and with dejection. The message throughout is: hang in there. We can read these letters with profit as our modern church meets and copes with comparable challenges. What I hear murmured across time and distance is: "leaving is not the answer." Or, as a wise Jesuit spiritual director wryly remarked, "Who told you you're allowed to quit?"

The Letter of Jude

Rounding out our visit to the biblical correspondence file is the terse little letter from someone named Jude, not the apostle since he speaks of that generation as historical (17), but more likely the brother of another letter writer, James. This would make him a relative of Jesus.

Jude assumes knowledge of the Torah (3–16), but it is his use of two apocryphal books that is most interesting. Verse 9 refers to an incident recorded in the Assumption of Moses, and verse 14 cites the Book of Enoch. These works and other such literature were evidently still in circulation in the late first century when this letter was composed, although most have since been lost. For various reasons, they were never accepted into the canon of the Hebrew Bible just as similar writings failed to make the cut in the Christian Scriptures. A number of these do survive. The best known are the "Gospel of Thomas," the "Protevangelium of James," and the "Gospel of Peter." Far from containing the secret messages sometimes ascribed to them, they are readily available but theologically do not possess the credibility of their four canonical relatives.

The letters that did survive and ultimately became part of Christian Scripture paint a broad and varied picture of the Mediterranean first-century secular and religious world, a world surprisingly like our own, probably because it was peopled by folks surprisingly like ourselves.

CHAPTER TEN

Revelation from Opposite Directions

P airing the Acts of the Apostles with the Book of Revelation in a single chapter may be a first, and perhaps I should have titled it "The Odd Couple." These two works are undeniably polar opposites in many respects, but it is because of this that they are interesting viewed in juxtaposition.

Should we venture to group the books of the Christian canon in a fashion corresponding to the Hebrew set of four, it would look like this:

- Gospels
- Narrative (Acts of the Apostles)
- Letters
- Apocalypse (Book of Revelation)

The analogy is a little shaky as there are only two actual groups. Those we've covered. The other two categories consist of a single book each. They couldn't be more disparate in style and content. But we get a fascinating behind-the-scenes look at the widely divergent ways in which God chooses to be revealed. Revelation, as we have seen, comes in all kinds of packaging, and within each particular wrapper is to be found the gift of God—and the gift is God.

Luke: Volume Two

Luke's is the only gospel with a sequel, although some believe his two works were originally one. No matter, really. What counts is that we have the Acts of the Apostles, for without it, biblical history would be truncated. For the most part, the lessons learned in Acts are available to us only there. So this book could be a total disaster in terms of style and form and remain of inestimable value. This is a moot point obviously since the author is Luke, master of the written word.

As you've undoubtedly committed every word read thus far to memory, it may be unnecessary to remind you that Luke has a penchant for parallelism. Look for it to appear in Acts as well. In fact, the two books are themselves parallels of one another. Again there is a nod to the enigmatic Theophilus and a quick recap of the closing verses of his gospel (1:1–5).

Take note of the geography. Geography? Indeed. We didn't mention this particular quirk of Luke's in examining his gospel, but we would be remiss to omit it now. Luke uses geography theologically. He's not the only biblical writer to utilize this technique, but he may be the most skillful. Like the other evangelists, Luke places Jesus' death and resurrection in Jerusalem. Unlike others, he stays right there, entertaining no postresurrection appearances away from the city. Luke has had Jesus on one continuous journey to Jerusalem for most of his gospel (Luke 9:51ff).

That Luke's Jesus requires a certain grit to embark on a trek which may not end well is implied by, "he [Jesus] set his face to go to Jerusalem" (Luke 9:51b). Jerusalem! Ancient Jebus first captured by the legendary David! Capital of the united kingdom and, later, Judah! Seat of the Davidic kings! And above all else, site of the first glorious temple constructed by Solomon and the second rebuilt temple newly refashioned and refurbished by Herod the Great! Jerusalem, the holy city, religious hub of Judaism. For Luke, it was essential that the defining events of Jesus' life should not only take place there but remain there.

When Acts picks up the story, the scene is unchanged. Of Jesus' post-resurrection appearances, Luke says, "While staying with them, he ordered them not to leave Jerusalem" (1:4a). But within a few verses, Luke puts the apostolic team on the road. Immediately prior to his ascension, Jesus promises the impending arrival of the Holy Spirit (a Lucan theme, remember?), after which "you will be my witnesses in Jerusalem, in all Judea and Samaria, and to the ends of the earth" (1:8b). Like a pebble dropped into a Jerusalem pond, the ripples move out to ever-distant destinations. Recalling who was calling the shots in Jerusalem at that time, it takes less than rocket science to determine what is meant by "the ends of the earth." By the end of this book, the venue will have moved to the political, economic, "everything" center of the Mediterranean world, Rome. The inference in Luke's wrapping up his literary endeavors there might be that once established in the imperial capital, Jesus' message could reasonably be expected to travel those remarkable Roman roads to the furthest reaches of the empire.

Expect from the apostolic figures of Acts the same kinds of words and deeds associated with Jesus in Luke's gospel, another example of parallelism. Themes, too, can be counted on to replicate themselves. If the gospel as literary form is not to be confused with biography, Acts should not be looked to for biographical information on the apostles, any or all. This book is a narrative; it might be titled *The Birth and Early Years of the Church*. The incidents recorded are selective, reminiscent of the historical books of the Hebrew Bible.

Acts may be unique in the Christian canon, but its form is quite common in literary circles. The acts of great personages were regularly set down and preserved for later generations. Retaining this idea, this book might more logically be titled *Acts of Peter, Paul, and James,* as these are the central figures. Other members of the apostolic community put in an appearance from time to time, but only peripherally. The spotlight shines first on Peter; then, when he peters out, on Paul with an extra-large cameo by James. If this is good enough for Luke, it's good enough for me, so we'll focus our condensed visit to Acts on the final incident involving the earthly Jesus, plus that promised visitation by the Holy Spirit, then one each on Peter, Paul, and James.

Rising to the Occasion

The village of Bethany, home to Jesus' friends Martha, Mary, and Lazarus, lies just over the Mount of Olives from Jerusalem, thereby retaining Luke's laser focus on the city. It is there, according to his gospel (Luke 24:50–53), that Jesus in his physical state departs. The Lucan narrative continues in Acts, recounting the same incident in slightly different form (1:6–11). During these final moments with Jesus when one imagines the apostles entertaining the hope that he was about to distribute catechisms and apostolic instruction manuals, the Eleven chose instead to send Jesus off with his teeth clenched, "Lord, is this the time when you will restore the kingdom to Israel?" (1:6b) Yet again those deeply entrenched messianic expectations come to the fore. When we become frustrated at the time it takes to alter mindsets, it could be helpful to recall that Jesus didn't have a lot of luck with it either.

"As they were watching, he was lifted up, and a cloud took him out of their sight" (1:9b). The cloud theophany is once more in evidence, making this episode a favorite with artists. Should we take their depictions literally? Current understandings make this doubtful. That antediluvian up-down cosmology runs up against a wall of scientific knowledge. If science and religion are not incompatible, if a benevolent God is total truth, resolution of quandaries of this sort must be possible. That it doesn't seem to be possible at this moment can be disappointing but does not threaten faith. Something happened. Precisely what . . . exactly how are questions for another day.

Essential to living as both people of intellect and people of faith is the avoidance of extremes: refusing to consider any notion beyond Luke's few words on the one hand; jettisoning the story as unworthy of rational belief on the other. When questions of a "Why does God do . . . ?" nature arose in courses I once took from a Jesuit whose intellect was as brilliant as his smile, his standard rejoinder was, "I don't know. When you see him, ask him." Like you, I have plenty of questions, but according to reports, there will be an eternity in which to learn the answers. Impatience sets in, but with it comes the realization that an ever-increasing store of questions should result from any attempt to comprehend, let alone grow in a relationship with the creator of the universe. For now, answers are good, questions are better.

Happy Birthday, Christianity

Chapter 2 tells the tale of the first Pentecost, except it wasn't the first Pentecost at all. A time-honored observance dating to Leviticus 23:15–22, Pentecost, or the Feast of Weeks *(Shavuot),* marked the completion of the grain harvest. It was one of the three pilgrimage festivals when all observant Jews who were able traveled to the temple in Jerusalem. That's why all those folks who heard Peter in so many languages (2:5–13) were on hand. A particularly pivotal occurrence caused Jesus' followers to associate their origins with this event and, ultimately, to appropriate its name. *Shavuot* in more recent centuries, by the way, has come to commemorate Moses' receiving the Torah at Sinai.

So what happened? The Holy Spirit happened! As promised by Jesus, the Spirit of God took hold of a distinctly dispirited group and lit a fire under them—or above them—or within them as the case may be:

> And suddenly from heaven there came a sound like the rush of a violent wind, and it filled the entire house where they were sitting. Divided tongues, as of fire, appeared among them, and a tongue rested on each of them. All of them were filled with the Holy Spirit (2:2–4a).

Wind! Fire! There are theophanies everywhere you look in these opening chapters. In addition to wind and fire, the Spirit also brought sufficient spinal starch to turn that timid band into intrepid proclaimers of the word. In effect, they became apostles at last. Although we often use them interchangeably, *apostle* and *disciple* have quite different definitions. *Apostle* means one who is sent; *disciple* indicates a follower. It "follows," therefore, that all apostles must first be disciples, but the reverse is not always the case.

Pentecost came to be seen as the birthday of the church since, emboldened by the Spirit's timely call, Jesus' tiny core of followers now stood a real chance of making him known to the world. Catholicism sees these and other events documented in Acts to be of such consequence that they are substituted for the Hebrew Scriptures as the first readings at weekend liturgies during the seven Sundays of the Easter season in all three cycles.

Peter, the Jewish Apostle, Meets Cornelius, the Roman God-fearer

Peter is traditionally viewed as first among the apostles as he is invariably named first on biblical apostolic lists. He and Zebedee's boys, James and John, also made up that inner circle of three privileged to share experiences with Jesus no one else did. Being first among equals, as his successor in the Vatican is considered today, didn't mean that Peter was always right or even that he always had a solid grip on the situation. But he learned. Chapter 10 reviews one of his most crucial lessons.

The Roman centurion Cornelius was a God-fearer, a Gentile attracted to Judaism's monotheism and high moral standards. As such, he was devout and could have paid homage to God on the Temple Mount in the Court of the Gentiles. Praying one day in the city of Caesarea, he was jolted by a vision of one of those imposing Lucan angels we encountered in the gospel annunciation stories, and told to summon one Peter who is staying with a tanner in Joppa. That would have made him reasonably easy to find as places of business occupied by leather workers tended to be graced by an aroma which could be detected, if not appreciated, for some distance.

Soon after, Peter, daydreaming about what he'd like for lunch, gets an entire menu of fresh food set before him—three times! You'd think he'd be overwhelmed; instead, he's decidedly underwhelmed. When told, "Get up, Peter; kill and eat," Peter is aghast, protesting, "By no means, Lord; for I have never eaten anything that is profane or unclean" (10:13–14). Peter's dilemma lies in the smorgasbord before him, containing "all kinds of four-footed creatures and reptiles and birds of the air" (10:12). Included presumably were a number of nonkosher items off limits to Jews on the basis of the age-old dietary laws (still in force among Orthodox Jews and some others to this day).

Don't you get the feeling that there is something more than just lunch at stake here? Foods long held to be ritually unclean (unacceptable) are no longer to be viewed that way. With timing that would do a spaghetti western proud, Cornelius's emissaries arrive while Peter is still puzzling over clean versus unclean foods. Off he goes to Caesarea.

Upon arrival, Peter enters Cornelius's home, which certainly indicates he's been doing some thinking while on the road. As a Jew, he was forbidden to associate with a Gentile, much less accept his hospitality. Cornelius explains his experience with the startling angel. Wedded to Peter's own encounter with the lunch buffet, awareness begins to dawn.

> "I truly understand that God shows no partiality, but in every nation anyone who fears [is in awe of] him and does what is right

is acceptable to him. You know the message he sent to the people of Israel, preaching peace by Jesus Christ—he is Lord of all" (10:34b–36).

Gentiles, like unclean foods, have long been dismissed as outside the pale. Now, Peter learns, not only are they to be included, they are to be regarded as equals. Had this and other similar episodes not occurred, post-Jesus history would have to be rewritten almost entirely. Think of the influence Christianity has exerted on all of Western civilization, and a good deal of Eastern as well. Had Gentiles never been admitted and welcomed to the developing communities of Jesus' disciples, the Way would have remained a small Jewish sect, this book and thousands more would never have been created, and you and I would be vastly different people. The story of Cornelius and his household is one of the most significant in Acts and, for that matter, in all of early Christianity.

Saul, the Persecutor, Becomes Paul, the Apostle

Shortly thereafter, Peter's place at center stage is gradually usurped by Saul/Paul. This is not the same type of name change found in the Torah. Because it was not uncommon for residents of vassal states to have two names, one Roman and one stemming from their own culture, this man shares the name of Israel's first king, Saul, yoked to the patrician Paulus (Paul). Commencing at chapter 13 of Acts, copious quantities of ink are devoted to Paul's exploits and accomplishments. Here, the reader is able to find some of the answers to questions raised by reading the Pauline letters. Without Acts, little would be known of the man himself. We would have to content ourselves with the scattered personal comments made in the various letters. In Acts, we travel with him, share his hardships, and come to know him rather well.

It is not these adventures, however, which we will reflect upon in depth. It is the amazing, if repetitive, story of how Saul the persecutor became Paul the apostle. For this, we seek first a grisly scene, the execution of Stephen, one of those commonly regarded as the first deacons. Convicted of blasphemy, a crime automatically punishable by stoning, Stephen is hauled outside the city (executions, like burials, never took place within city walls): "[A]nd the witnesses laid their coats at the feet of a young man named Saul" (7:58b). As the first disciple to die for his faith in Jesus, Stephen is honored on December 26, the day after Jesus' birth is celebrated.

> And Saul approved of their killing him. That day a severe perse-cution began against the church in Jerusalem, and all except the apostles were scattered throughout the countryside of Judea and Samaria. Devout men buried Stephen and made loud lamenta-tion over him. But Saul was ravaging the church by entering house after house; dragging off both men and women, he committed them to prison (8:1–3).

The scattering or dispersion of Jesus' flock had begun. As is often true of calamitous happenings of this nature, good ultimately comes of it, not because God wills the adverse results of poor human choices, but because God can and very often does find ways even there to promote the ultimate good. The insular little band has begun to fulfill Jesus' prediction that they will move beyond Jerusalem to Judea, Samaria, and the ends of the earth. Luke's geographical/theological sojourn is under way.

Saul/Paul, having left a path of death and destruction in his wake in Jerusalem, hungers for new worlds to conquer:

> Meanwhile Saul, still breathing threats and murder against the disciples of the Lord, went to the high priest and asked him for letters to the synagogues at Damascus, so that if he found any who belonged to the Way, men or women, he might bring them bound to Jerusalem (9:1–2).

Chapter 9 constitutes a turning point, not only for Saul, but for Christianity, a prospect that would have been singularly unappealing to him at the time.

Parents and teachers routinely employ the same stratagem to assure that certain information is forever engraved upon the memory: repeti-tion. Tell them. Then repeat what you said. Then say it again for emphasis. Luke applies this approach to the story of Saul/Paul's conver-sion, reprising the chapter 9 events in 22:3–16 and 26:2–18. Yet another version of it comes from Paul's own lips in Galatians 1:11–24. Why all the fuss? It is not unusual to hear Paul characterized as the Christian Scriptures' most influential figure next to Jesus himself. As remarked earlier, Christianity would unquestionably have survived without Paul, but it would have been a much slower process with a far different result.

Meanwhile, back on the road to Damascus, the hotheaded Pharisee from Tarsus is about to get knocked for a loop, not knocked from his horse. This is another of those "biblical certainties" that people will sometimes firmly defend: Paul was knocked off a horse just as Adam and Eve ate apples and three magi showed up at the Holy Family's door. Nowhere are any of these allegations ever made, but artistic depictions often portray them that way.

"He fell to the ground and heard a voice saying to him, 'Saul, Saul, why do you persecute me?' He asked, 'Who are you, Lord?' The reply came, 'I am Jesus, whom you are persecuting' " (9:4–5). Interesting, isn't it, that Paul is not accused of harassing Jesus' followers, but rather Jesus himself. A good bit of time might be spent pondering the question of our purpose on this earth in light of this disquieting phraseology.

Saul is blinded as "light from heaven flashed around him" (9:3b). The light that has led him all his life has suddenly been extinguished. As he would later say: "I am a Jew, born in Tarsus in Cilicia, but brought up in this city at the feet of Gamaliel, educated strictly according to our ancestral law, being zealous for God" (22:3). Tarsus was an important seaport on the southern coast of modern Turkey. Saul had evidently shown considerable promise, intellectually, religiously—or both—for him to have been sent to Jerusalem to further his education at the feet of so respected a rabbi as Gamaliel.

If his family was not wealthy, it must have at least been well off because poor boys didn't often receive such an opportunity. "I am a Jew, from Tarsus in Cilicia, a citizen of an important city" (21:39a). To be a citizen of a Roman city was no mean thing. Roman citizenship carried with it valuable prerogatives, not the least of which was immunity from crucifixion, which may be the reason Paul is said to have been beheaded at about the same time Peter was crucified. Whether this precious citizenship was inherited or earned is unknown, but it stood him in good stead late in life when "the chief priests and the leaders of the Jews" (25:2a) appealed to the Roman governor Festus to have Paul sent to Jerusalem, a journey almost sure to prove fatal: "I appeal to the emperor," said Paul (25:11b). Only a Roman citizen possessed that right. Festus, probably relieved to have a legitimate way out, ruled: "You have appealed to the emperor; to the emperor you will go" (25:12b).

So the person sprawled in the dust of the Damascus road was no ordinary man. If his life up to this point had been noteworthy, it was merely a prelude to what lay ahead. For the rest of Paul's conversion experience—see any one of the accounts listed above—especially the remainder of chapter 9. As a carnival pitch man might say: "See a blind man regain his sight. See a blind soul enlightened. See a life transformed. See God work in mysterious ways with the most inauspicious raw material." It's quite a story.

The Church's First Ever Council

And now James moves into the spotlight. There's a speck of conniving afoot on my part, I should admit, as Peter and Paul both play a role here as well, providing an excuse to return them to the stage. The star of this show, in actuality, is not of the human persuasion, but is instead an event: the Council of Jerusalem. There, for the first time in a single location, the leaders of the Jesus movement come together to hash out thorny difficulties of importance to them all. In this council can be detected the vague outlines of councils to come for hundreds of years, the most recent of which was the Second Vatican Council.

The year was 47–48 C.E. The chapter is 15. The immediate concern is pretty straightforward:

> Then certain individuals came down from Judea and were teaching the brothers, "Unless you are circumcised according to the custom of Moses, you cannot be saved." And after Paul and Barnabas had no small dissension and debate with them, Paul and Barnabas and some of the others were appointed to go up to Jerusalem to discuss this question with the apostles and the elders" (15:1–2).

Heading the Jerusalem church at this time was James of the family of Jesus.

Peter, fresh from his theology lesson of the deli lunch and the Roman God-fearer, comes down on the side of Gentile inclusion without the messy initiation ceremony (15:7–11). If this seems obvious to us, we should remember that these first followers considered their faith in Jesus the fulfillment of their ancient Jewish faith. That they firmly believed it impossible to have one without the other is entirely understandable.

Barnabas and Paul then take the floor, underscoring Peter's position. But it is James who issues the final judgment:

> Therefore I have reached the decision that we should not trouble those Gentiles who are turning to God, but we should write to them to abstain only from things polluted by idols and from fornication and from whatever has been strangled and from blood (15:19–20).

The choice of prohibitions may seem strange to us, but as *The New Jerome Biblical Commentary* clarifies, "The four clauses seem to be four of the things proscribed by Leviticus 17–18 for aliens residing in Israel: meat offered to idols, the eating of blood and of strangled animals (not ritually slaughtered), and intercourse with close kin" (44:83).

"Then the apostles and the elders, with the consent of the whole church, decided to choose men from among their members and to send them to Antioch with Paul and Barnabas" (15:22a). This delegation carried a letter "to the believers of Gentile origin in Antioch and Syria and Cilicia" (15:23b). "When they gathered the congregation together [at Antioch], they delivered the letter. When its members read it, they rejoiced at the exhortation" (15:30b–31).

The Council of Jerusalem assembled the leaders of the universal church (whose "universe" was extremely narrow at that point) to discuss questions of belief and practice applicable to all believers, not merely a local church. This body, having reached consensus, proclaimed its edict to the wider church. The methodology may have changed in light of the Internet and telecommunications, but the process is much the same when councils convene in our own age. Yet, this landmark council rarely leads the list of Catholic ecumenical councils, perhaps because techni-cally these councils of bishops are convoked by the pope, which was not the case here (Peter would have had no understanding of this title) as the council revolves around James.

If you're wondering, there have been twenty-one ecumenical councils in Catholic history, starting with the First Council of Nicea in 325 C.E., which gave us the Nicene Creed and ending (up to this point) with the Second Vatican Council in 1962–1965, which gave us a new lease on life. Councils have not always made lasting contributions to the church for their own and later times, but they can exert tremendous influence. The Council of Trent in 1545–1563 was Catholicism's response to the Reformation for good or for ill, and it was the dictates of this council that shaped Catholicism up to Vatican II. "It's always been this way" usually means "it's been this way since Trent."

Something else we shouldn't overlook in evaluating our earliest council is pointed out by Raymond E. Brown, S.S., in *An Introduction to the New Testament* (Doubleday, 1997):

> More significant is a deafening silence about Jesus. No one who favors admitting the Gentiles without circumcision mentions the example of Jesus, saying, "Jesus told us to do so." And, of course, the reason is that he never did tell them to do so. Indeed, one may suspect that the only ones likely to have mentioned Jesus would have been those of the circumcision party, arguing precisely that there was no authorization from him for such a radical departure from the Law. Even Paul remembers Jesus as "born under the Law" (Galatians 4:4).

> This may have been the first of many times when those who have resisted change in the church did so by arguing that Jesus never did this, whereas those who promoted change did so on the import of Christ for a situation that the historical Jesus did not encounter. . . . The road was now open for free and effective evangelizing to the ends of the earth. In fact that road would also lead away from Judaism. Even though the Savior for Gentiles was a Jew born under the Law, Christianity would soon be

looked on as a Gentile religion quite alien to Judaism, especially to a Judaism for which the Law would become ever more important once the Temple was destroyed.

The quick stops made at a handful of episodes in Acts can do no more than provide the flavor of the book. Like movie trailers (approved for all audiences) in theaters, the idea is to lure you into spending more time mining the riches of these sometimes neglected pages. Trust me, it won't be a chore. As gleaning our own genealogy has taught many of us, investigating familial roots teaches us as much about ourselves as it does about our ancestors.

Revelation: The Book of Hope . . . or Despair?

We have now arrived at our final scriptural book, literally and figuratively. Literally, this is the counterpart to Genesis as, together, they form the bookends of the biblical library. Figuratively, we have no more Christian works to visit in these pages.

It is appropriate, I think, that Genesis and Revelation are positioned as they are. Certainly for our purposes it is. Genesis: "In the beginning, God . . ." Revelation: "Then I saw a new heaven and a new earth" (Revelation 21:1a). If in Genesis more attention was paid to origins, in Revelation the accent is increasingly on endings (eschatology). The First and Third Big Questions have to some degree found homes within these writings. I suppose it wouldn't be entirely unreasonable in applying the literary ploy of inclusion to say that just about everything between Genesis and Revelation pertains to the Second Big Question somehow. This may be a shade simplistic, but it's not far off the mark.

A Road Map to Revelation

Opening the Book of Revelation brings most of us smack up against a fanciful world of swirling images and imaginative creatures whose like we haven't met since our last visit to *Alice in Wonderland*. Actually, this is not a bad reference point. With any luck at all, no one takes the Cheshire Cat, White Rabbit, Mad Hatter, and Queen of Hearts to be historical characters. We're perfectly aware that they're representative. Return with me to Wonderland-tea-party mode and prepare to embark on a similar adventure to a land where almost nothing is what it first appears and practically everything has a broader symbolic connotation. Try to erase as many as possible of the downright peculiar things you've heard about this book and get ready to take the plunge with objectivity and enthusiasm. As I used to say to a small boy whose oft-heard wails were due to a proclivity to hypochondria, "You know what? You're going to live right through it."

Another 98-Cent Word Marked Down from $1.00

As the Irish Dominican scholar Wilfrid Harrington suggests in *Revelation: Proclaiming a Vision of Hope* (Resource Publications, 1994):

> Let us come to grips with the terms. *Apocalypse* is a literary genre or form . . . the kind of literature in which apocalyptic views are expressed. *Apocalyptic eschatology* may best be understood in comparison with *prophetic eschatology. Apocalypticism* is the world-view of an apocalyptic movement or group. [Please don't cast this aside in favor of a little light reading, i.e., Einstein's theory of relativity. The literary skies begin to clear as we move along.]

> Apocalyptists had largely opted out of history. For them, there was no future in any human institution. The only hope was in a divine intervention which would radically challenge the status quo and, in fact, bring about a new situation involving the definitive vindication of the suffering elect. Apocalypticism is, in practice, a gospel of the marginalized. It proclaims, "God is on our side. Here we are . . . the minority, whether in relation to an alien power or in face of a power-group within our own society. We have no clout. But right is on our side, and a God who looks not to might but to right has to be on our side." When one takes God seriously, it is a powerful argument. The question, of course, is whether one might be tempted to make God into whatever one wants God to be.

If eschatology has to do with humanity's ultimate goal, individually and collectively, and those events leading up to it, apocalypticism is occupied with arriving at that goal (the wrap-up of human history, eternal life with God) as rapidly as possible.

The apocalyptic style developed late in the biblical period, spanning three or four centuries from 200 B.C.E. to 100–200 C.E. As noted earlier, Revelation is not the only example of this form in Scripture, merely the most obvious. Other prominent examples include sections of the books of Ezekiel and Daniel. Snatches of apocalyptic imagery spice up a good many other books as well.

Apocalyptic writings generally pit manifest good against equally evident evil. If it were being written today, there might be lots of heroes in white hats countered by just as many villains in black hats. There may be no more effective literary technique than symbolism, providing everybody "gets" it. When a symbol is replaced or forgotten, a modern-day Tower of Babel is just around the bend. This is the predicament most of us are in when we first tackle an apocalyptic book.

So, before we tackle, let's turn to Tickle. In *The Book of Revelation: A Catholic Interpretation of the Apocalypse* (Liguori Publications, 1983), Father John Tickle points out apocalyptic writing's "very specific characteristics":

> Apocalyptic writers take the past, the present, and the future and mingle them all together. Hence it is almost impossible to discern when they are talking about the past or when they are talking about the present. Once this has been done, they use cryptic symbols to concoct images that reflect this combined perspective. Next, they look to the future and predict it, based on past and present experiences. (In the Book of Revelation those experiences are the sufferings of the early Christian community.) They say, "Here we are, and this is how we're suffering, and this is what's going on, and these are the promises of the Lord to us during his life; therefore, this shall take place in the future."

You may have heard someone speak of the prophesies in the Book of Revelation. Does this imply that apocalypticism and traditional Hebrew prophecy are two sides of the same coin? Not really, because the style is entirely different. But there are definitely similarities. As Tickle continues:

> The Book of Revelation is prophetic in this sense: "Here's what Jesus promised, this is what you are doing, and this is what will

result." Prophecy ends on a note of hope: "Just get with the program and change your heart, convert and go back to what the covenant demands. Go back to God and do what he says, and this bleak future will not happen." But apocalypse—especially *the* Apocalypse—by stressing death and destruction appears to eliminate hope . . . seems to be saying, "You don't have a chance." Is there any way to change this gloomy apocalyptic attitude about salvation? Fortunately, there is, because Revelation concludes by saying, "Don't worry. Jesus has already done it. You didn't do it, and you weren't ever going to do it. So I'll do it myself." Jesus Christ will bring us to fulfillment.

To vividly illustrate Christ's victory and what awaits us beyond this life, this earth, the confines of this time and place, the writer of Revelation becomes the forerunner of George Lucas, proposing an amazing universe of his own making on the order of *Star Wars*. It's not unlike what we saw in the creation stories of Genesis where divine truths that defy our finite minds or for which we lack specific data are conveyed through other means, i.e., myths, allegories, new apocalyptic scenarios. Whereas Lucas presumably dreamed up his own story lines and characters, much of the imaginative symbolism of Revelation is drawn from similar literature in the Hebrew canon. "Just as prophecy is not fortune-telling, so the Book of Revelation is not fortune-telling," says Margaret Nutting Ralph in *The Bible and the End of the World: Should We Be Afraid?* (Paulist Press, 1997). "The book of Revelation is not prognosticating inevitable future events which will precede the 'end of the world.' "

The John Question Again

Who exactly is this ancient George Lucas? Surely you can't be surprised at this point to learn it's uncertain. He identifies himself as "John, your brother who share[s] with you in Jesus the persecution and the kingdom and the patient endurance, [and who] was on the island called Patmos, [an island used by Roman governors for exile] because of the word of God and the testimony of Jesus" (1:9). For a great many years, this John was assumed to be the John of the gospel and/or the letters. This notion has been abandoned for the most part today although there are certain Johannine likenesses, and all of the books with a John connection are late compositions, springing from the decade of the 90s C.E., some say even later. The literary form of Revelation resembles that of the gospel not at all. Granted, clever writers, such as the Johannine authors, are perfectly capable of working in a variety of styles, but this doesn't seem to be happening here as vocabulary, language usage, and other elements of style are so sharply contrasted. All that is actually known of this John is that he wrote from the island of Patmos in the Aegean Sea. It's safe to say he wasn't a politician, a military strategist, a crystal ball gazer, or an oracle with the ability to read history still centuries away. Yet people have been confining John to one or another of these archetypes in every Christian era, especially our own. Writes Ralph:

> We are all familiar with some people's attempts to apply the symbolic language of the book of Revelation to institutions and people of our own time. No matter what institution or person is the object of such an interpretation, the person offering the interpretation is simply revealing his or her own hate and prejudice. The interpretation has absolutely nothing to do with the purpose or meaning of the book of Revelation.

The forthright narrative of Acts told us a lot about the first years after Jesus' departure: the birth of the church, what and who Jesus' followers considered themselves to be, how the fledgling faith made its way around the Mediterranean, who the major players were, how incipient beliefs and practices began to develop. Now we step into a dreamlike world (indeed, John is said to see it in a vision [1:9–10]), by turns fantasmagorical and frightening. A direct story with a logical plotline? Hardly! Here, there is almost no plotline, and direction is chancy as it's hard to know which end is up. But, just as you do entering a carnival fun house, bear in mind that things are not always what they seem—simply enjoy the experience.

Seven (the Perfect Number) Letters

The book opens with a series of letters "to the seven churches that are in Asia [Minor]" (1:4a). Already we've come upon the first symbolic element: numbers. Numerical values customarily were assigned characteristic significance in the ancient world. It wasn't the connotation of lucky or unlucky numbers bandied about today. It was simply that numbers had purpose. Seven was the perfect number; six was the number of imperfection. Closely allied was twelve, the number of fulfillment, and so there are twelve tribes, twelve judges, twelve apostles, and so on. In reading apocalyptic literature, keep an eye out for not only the whole numbers, but combinations which involve them, i.e., three plus four. Chapter 7 speaks of 144,000, "sealed out of every tribe of the people of Israel: From the tribe of Judah twelve thousand sealed, from the tribe of Reuben twelve thousand, from the tribe of Gad twelve thousand . . ." (7:4b–5). The square of twelve multiplied by one thousand equals the population of the new Israel. It is simply God's kingdom fulfilled. Certain present-day sects read this passage as proof that a mere 144,000 will squeak through the pearly gates (21:21).

Other numerical meanings that will be handy to file away are forty, which is a round number rarely intended to be exact; four, which encompasses the entire world (four winds, four corners of the earth, etc.); and one thousand, which denotes a very long time. We still use this one today, as in, "I haven't seen you in a thousand years." But seven is the big one, especially in this book. It appears ten times in the first chapter alone.

Jesus Christ is named in 1:5b and "his God and Father" in 1:6b, but such clear-cut names will be infrequent in apocalyptic writing. An indication of what's to come follows in 1:8: " 'I am the Alpha and the Omega,' says the Lord God, who is and who was and who is to come, the Almighty." Euphemisms for God and Jesus abound, the most prevalent of which may be "the one." Alpha and Omega, the first and last letters of the Greek alphabet, identify Jesus, the Christ, as the eternal "one." In this book, the human Jesus is barely discernible. Here, the cosmic Christ reigns . . . literally. His description, couched in imagery taken in large part from Daniel 7:9–15, begins at 1:13 as John sees "one like the Son of Man" standing among seven golden lampstands, one for each of the churches. Tickle unravels the symbols:

> His "robe" symbolizes priesthood; his "sash of gold" kingship;
> his "snow-white hair," eternalness; his "eyes [blazing] like fire,"
> infinite knowledge; his "feet—like polished brass," unchange-
> ableness; his "voice—like the roar of rushing waters," divine

authority. The "two-edged sword" refers to the word of God which will reward and punish on Judgment Day. And "his face [shining] like the sun at its brightest" indicates divine majesty. . . . The seven stars in his "right hand" are an allusion to contemporary imperial power; the emperors' crowns were decorated with the seven planets of the world, indicating that the emperors were the power of the universe. But Jesus has seven stars in his hand. . . . Truly he has the whole world in his hands.

The seven churches to whom the letters are addressed are located in real geographical cities. The first, Ephesus, we've visited before with Paul. All of them are clustered in a relatively small area of what is today southwestern Turkey. The letters are formulaic, recognizing first the obstacles and distress each community has experienced and commending efforts made for good. "But I have this against you . . ." (2:4a, 14a, 20a). The gaze that has been fixed on these churches is penetrating and uncompromising. Their shortcomings are exposed to the light with no attempt made to soften the glare. I live in a small city comprised of seven parishes. I can't help wondering what would be said to each of them, my own included. If we heard the formatted opening, "I know your works . . ." (2:2a, 19a, 3:1b, 8a, 15a), how would we greet those words?

Welcome to the Throne Room

When the curtain rises on the body of the book in chapter 4, John is told: "Come up here" (4:1b) (remember the up-down cosmology). Upon his arrival, "there in heaven stood a throne, with one seated on the throne! . . . Around the throne are twenty-four thrones, and seated on the thrones are twenty-four elders, dressed in white robes, with golden crowns on their heads" (4:2–4). Some of this imagery is reminiscent of Jesus, suggesting that the elect will share his attributes. Twenty-four is indicative of the entire church (the twelve apostles added to the twelve tribes).

"[I]n front of the throne there is something like a sea of glass, like crystal" (4:6a). The proverbial glass ceiling of today forms a fair analogy. The glass separates one party from the other, but not to the extent that it is opaque. God can look "down" upon humanity just as an ambitious corporate executive can look up toward the objective.

"Around the throne, and on each side of the throne, are four living creatures, full of eyes in front and behind" (4:6b). The mental picture drawn by this is self-explanatory. The more eyes, the better to see you with, my dear. The creatures, which embody traits of God, show forth God's ability to see all and know all. In our world, parents and teachers are sometimes thought to have eyes in the back of their heads. Would that this were true! With God, it is. The creatures are borrowed from the apocalyptic opening of the Book of Ezekiel (1:5–14), accenting that symbols found in one example of this genre can be easily shifted to another. In Revelation, they represent Christological traits: the lion, majesty; the ox, power; the human, wisdom; and the eagle, soaring and graceful, speed. In the early centuries of Christianity, the same four creatures came to stand for the writers of the four gospels: the lion for Mark, the ox for Luke, the human for Matthew, and the eagle for John— imagery that endures to this day.

Revelation could be the most musical biblical book next to Psalms. There's a lot of singing, enough to make those of us with limited vocal abilities wonder whether we can expect to make the cut. The bulk of these choral recitals are hymns of praise, similar in nature to the praise songs of the Hebrew Psalter. Two of them conclude this chapter— 4:8, 11. Each alludes to the curious blend of past, present, and future typical of apocalyptic writings.

Other Notes to the Symbol-minded

It is impossible here to continue working systematically through each chapter of Revelation. We shall have to make do with a few more notes on common symbols to look for in the ensuing chapters, plus another comment or two on apocalyptic writing in general.

- **Colors:** Colors as well as numbers have specific meanings. White = purity. Black (sometimes green) = death. Red = either indulgence or wantonness.
- **Angels:** We've met these beings many times throughout the Hebrew and Christian Scriptures, but they are everywhere in Revelation. The word means "messenger." Are they winged? Probably not, but we're accustomed to seeing them that way as

artists attempt to depict their fleetness. It should be noted that angels are not deceased humans. They are noble, majestic beings of an order all their own. There are, thankfully, innumerable good people who share our planet, but they are precisely that, good people, not angels; nor do they become angels at their deaths.

- **Lamb:** This reference to the sacrificial Passover lamb is, of course, Jesus, who sacrificed himself for us during the season of Passover. Applied to the enigmatic suffering servant of Isaiah 53:7, the term is applied to Jesus by John the Baptist in the gospel of John 1:29b, 36b.
- **Sea:** This imagery may not be strictly apocalyptic since large expanses of uncharted water had long been viewed with apprehension by ancient people. Who knew what those waters held? Leviathans (sea monsters), most likely. Watery chaos was feared. The pillars of the earth plunged into just such a realm and harbored the dread abode of the dead, Sheol.
- **Horns:** These are authority symbols and, as such, would also be recognized outside the apocalyptic arena. Numerous references are made to Israelite altars having horns (see Leviticus 4:7, 18, 25, 30, 34 and Joshua 6:4–20 for examples) on which the blood of sacrifices was poured. While no one is sure what these altars looked like, it is generally assumed that the horns must have been protuberances at the four corners.
- **Bride:** the people of God; the church.
- **New Jerusalem:** the dwelling place of the people of God.
- **Woman giving birth (12:2–13):** Two allegorical interpretations surface here: the covenanted Israel bringing forth the Messiah, or Mary, the mother of Jesus, doing likewise. While either reading is valid, the former may more closely reflect the author's intent.
- **Virgins:** those who have remained faithful to the end.
- **White robes washed in blood:** the garb of the redeemed, often martyred.
- **Dragon:** the forces of evil or Satan himself.

- **Beast:** Just as we use the term *beastly* today to signify someone or something intrinsically evil, so the beast of Revelation denotes those who join forces with Satan and his minions.
- **666:** "[L]et anyone with understanding calculate the number of the beast, for it is the number of a person. Its number is six hundred sixty-six" (13:18). Throughout the course of history, as one by one persons who appeared to be the epitome of evil wreaked havoc on the world, each was thought to be the "666" personage of Revelation. Within the past century, both Stalin and Hitler have earned the title in many minds. In all probability, however, the person in question here was the Roman emperor Nero. In both the Hebrew and Greek languages, letters of the alphabet had numerical counterparts. Determining a person's number was simply a matter of doing the math. Total the numerical equivalents for each letter of the person's name, and there you are. In Hebrew, Caesar Nero adds up to 666. Why the secrecy? Because casting aspersions on the absolute, if slightly mad, monarch of the empire was not conducive to long life. Apocalypses can take the form of underground writing, complete with code words easily understood by the reader but hopefully not by outsiders. To continue the Hitler analogy, this would be on the order of World War II clandestine communiques between units of the resistance. The use of actual names and places was unwise.
- **Babylon:** And this was one of those places. By the time Revelation was composed, Babylon had long since ceased to be a world power. It was no threat to anyone, so why excoriate it? Because the reigning superpower was imperial Rome, and it would be foolish to annoy this Goliath needlessly. Babylon was a logical euphemism, for the mere mention of the name aroused latent anger, hurt, and resentment among a people who never forgot its exile there some six centuries earlier. In the same way, place names like Auschwitz and Hiroshima and events such as the Holocaust and D-Day will unquestionably continue to stir up raw emotion generations, even centuries, from now.

Unsettling Concepts Which Should Be Settled

Rapture! Antichrist! Armageddon! Three more terms which seem trouble-some even if we're not entirely sure what they mean. The first two have already been discussed to some degree, but it may be helpful to allow Bishop Kenneth Untener to expand on them here (*Catholic Update*, C0993, St. Anthony Messenger Press, 1993):

- **Rapture:** We normally use *rapture* to signify spiritual or emotional ecstasy. However, the more basic meaning of the word is "to seize, to transport." End-of-the-world prophets use it in this latter sense. Matthew's gospel speaks of two women grinding meal; one is "taken" and the other is left (see 24:41). Literalists do not accept this as symbolic language, and they expect that at the end of time the just will be plucked from the earth by God (see 1 Thessalonians 4:17).

- **Antichrist:** The term *Antichrist* appears only in the first and second epistles of John. It is clearly a term symbolic of the forces working against Christ in all periods of history, not a clue about a specific individual.

- **Armageddon:** The prospect of Armageddon had been scaring the wadding out of people for a good many centuries before Hollywood turned it over to the special effects experts. Mentioned only once in the Bible (Revelation 16:16), Armageddon is portrayed as the climactic pitched battle between good and evil. In actuality, it is the region immediately surrounding the Israelite city of Megiddo, long a crossroads for caravans due to its advantageous locale and the scene of many an armed conflict because its plains lent themselves admirably to military maneuvering. Megiddo was associated with combat the way Las Vegas is associated with gambling, making it a predictable site for Ground Zero in the ultimate cosmic clash.

Re-creation

As the Book of Revelation winds down in a flurry of angels and voices and "the Word of God" mounted on a white steed leading the armies of heaven (19:11–16), the victory of the "King of kings and Lord of lords" is assured. To the beleaguered first readers of this book persecuted by Emperor Domitian, the message rang loud and clear: Jesus has already won the victory; don't give up and don't lose hope; you'll win in the end because Jesus' victory is yours as well.

The seer then paints a rosy future. "I saw a new heaven and a new earth; for the first heaven and the first earth had passed away, and the sea was no more. And I saw the holy city, the new Jerusalem, coming down out of heaven from God" (21:1–2a). The first book of the Bible began with *creation;* the final book closes with *re-creation.* This may be the most profound example of inclusion found in Scripture, suggesting that first, last, and always God is creator, and the work of his creating hands never ends, shaping and reshaping, molding and mending. I once heard a composer congratulated on having written over four thousand songs. Singularly unimpressed by his achievement, he shrugged and quietly observed: "It's what I do." Creation is what God does. Revelation urges its readers not to dwell on death and destruction, but on life and ongoing creation.

The distinguished French theologian and anthropologist Pierre Teilhard de Chardin wrote extensively of the culmination of human history. Although he died seven years before Vatican II was convened, his vision explored the broader horizons Pope John XXIII deemed necessary to an ever-deeper understanding of God. De Chardin saw the wrap-up of humanity's great drama as an Omega point, a great culmination of humanity's development. Reading chapters 20–21 of the Book of Revelation, de Chardin exclaimed, "Shout to the theologians that this is exactly the idea that I have. Your Christ is too small! Let me make him larger . . . as big as the whole world."

The swooping, soaring final chapters of Revelation furnish glimpses of the new creation. With chapter 22, the book "comes" to a close in more ways than one. Some form of the word *come* is used seven times (no surprise there!), about equally divided between references to Jesus' coming back to humanity and allusions to humans coming to Jesus.

What this *parousia* ("coming") of Jesus will ultimately be no one can say. We can surmise that he will be more readily recognized than he was when he arrived the first time. During the liturgical season of Advent, which also means "coming," the church invites us to ponder the various comings of Jesus, not merely his Bethlehem birth, but this second coming, as well as other means through which he comes into our lives. The Eucharist is foremost for Catholics, but we also meet Jesus in those people and occurrences that "come" into our lives every day. Bishop Kenneth Untener writes (ibid.):

> We don't really know what it will be like when Jesus, already present among us, fully manifests himself in glory at the end of the age. It will probably be as different from our expectations as was every other "parousia," including the incarnation. Is the end of the world near? No one has any idea. It could be forty million years away (the sun has at least that much fuel) or it could happen a week from Tuesday.

There may be no more appropriate conclusion than the one John chose to end his book and with it, unknown to him, the biblical canon, "The grace of the Lord Jesus be with all the saints. Amen" (22:21).

Intermission

Except for such citations as must be included in our consideration of the Third Big Question in chapter 13, this completes our visit to the Hebrew and Christian Scriptures. It has been all too short, but at least the introductions have been made in the hope that revisiting will continue for years to come and that with each visit our grasp of God will broaden and deepen. Such knowledge is indispensable to a mature faith. But, imperative as it is, it is never the sole consideration. So as we close this section, I leave you with the words of two prayerful contemporaries.

In *Living God's Word: Reflections on the Weekly Gospels* (St. Anthony Messenger Press, 1999), Father David Knight has this to say:

> God sent the Holy Spirit to guide the Church and each of her members along the practical path to life in its fullness. God's intent is not just that we should know but that we should

grow . . . grow in understanding by the gift of understanding; grow in appreciation of the things of God by the gift of wisdom; grow in response to God by free acts of the will supported by the gifts of awe, piety, and courage. To guide us in our choices the Holy Spirit enlightens us with the gifts of counsel and knowledge.

And John Shea, storyteller par excellence, adds in *Gospel Light* (Crossroad Publishing, 1998):

I am not a scripture scholar but, as with most people who have preached and/or taught Christian faith, I am a voracious consumer of scripture scholarship. Over the years I have settled into a double sentiment about what I have consumed. First, I am appreciative and grateful. There is so much to know and so many women and men have scrutinized these ancient texts and uncovered their intricate workings and complex connections. Learning from them is always a pleasure. Second, these scholarly efforts are not a substitute for personal engagement. They are a beginning, positioning the spiritual seeker on the Jesus path. However, in order for some illumination to occur, there must be creative interaction with the text. Spiritual development is not a second-hand enterprise. We cannot borrow it from the bright. We can only apprentice ourselves to the emerging wisdom of the story, sitting at the feet of the story—Christ.

CHAPTER ELEVEN

Viewing the World from the Near East

All day I think about it, then at night I say it.
Where did I come from,
and what am I supposed to be doing?
I have no idea.
My soul is from elsewhere, I'm sure of that,
and I intend to wind up there. . . .
I didn't come here of my own accord, and I can't leave that way.
Whoever brought me here will have to take me home.

—*Jelaluddin Rumi*
thirteenth-century Islamic mystic/poet

Judaism and Christianity are by no means the only religious traditions that ponder the Three Big Questions. The yearning voice of the lyrical Rumi is but one raised from the third great monotheistic belief system born in the Near East, Islam. We will turn our attention to the growing Muslim presence in both East and West but, because it is the youngest of the three, we will look first at Judaism, which grew out of biblical history and continues to exert an influence well beyond its numerical adherents. Thomas Cahill discusses this and, indirectly, those three pivotal questions in *The Gifts of the Jews: How a Tribe of Desert Nomads Changed the Way Everyone Thinks and Feels* (Doubleday, 1998):

> In a cyclical world, there are neither beginnings nor ends. But for
> us, time had a beginning, whether it was the first words of God

in the Book of Genesis, when "in the beginning God created heaven and earth," or the Big Bang of modern science, a concept that would not have been possible without the Jews. Time, which had a beginning, must also have an end. What will it be? In the Torah we learn that God is working his purposes in history and will *effect* its end, but in the Prophets we learn that our choices will also *affect* this end, that our inner disposition toward our fellow human beings will make an enormous difference in the way this end appears to us.

The way things appear to us germinates in our worldview. Cahill continues:

The worldview of a people, though normally left unspoken in the daily business of buying and selling and counting shekels, is to be found in a culture's stories, myths, and rituals which, if studied aright, inevitably yield insight into the deepest concerns of a people by unveiling the invisible fears and desires inscribed on human hearts.

As children of Judaism, Christianity and Islam share much of its worldview. From this common heritage, nonetheless, the offspring, like human progeny, have taken some very divergent paths, resulting in an unhappy family history. On the plus side, serious attempts at reconciliation are now being made as our commonalities come to be featured at least as much as our differences. On the minus side, it has taken centuries for the rifts to become so profound, so we cannot expect to repair our relationships overnight. We all have a long way to go, but perhaps direction is more important than speed, and the fact that we are beginning to move toward one another rather than further apart (sometimes at any rate) is encouraging. How did we arrive at this point? Who are our neighbors who turn in at the synagogue or mosque each weekend as we turn in at our church?

Being Jewish Today

Living as an observant Jew in the twenty-first century is strikingly different from doing so throughout the biblical centuries, yet in some ways remarkably similar. Here's how Rabbi Harold Kushner opens his study of Jewish being and thinking in *To Life!* (Little, Brown, 1993):

> This is a book about Judaism, a 4,000-year-old tradition with ideas about what it means to be human and how to make the world a holy place. Yet despite its age, perhaps because essential human nature hasn't changed that much over the centuries, because issues of life and death, parents and children, human hopes and human failures remain constant over the generations even as the surrounding landscape changes, the ideas of Judaism are important to us today. Anyone who takes his or her destiny as a human being seriously has to be acquainted with these ideas."

As we have seen, Christians *are* acquainted with a profusion of these ideas if they are on speaking terms with their Bible. As we have further recognized, Jesus, thoroughly Jewish himself, was steeped in them as well and came "not to abolish but to fulfill" (Matthew 5:17b). Antisemitism, then, amounts to hatred of Christianity's spiritual grandparents. How on earth did this happen?

The late humorist Sam Levinson, also Jewish, once taught high school history classes and commented wryly on answers he'd seen on tests, which, while not exactly wrong, were not exactly right either. One student, asked for the rationale behind the decline of Rome, allegedly replied: "The fall of the Roman Empire was caused by carelessness." If there's a modicum of truth in this, there may be about the same amount in saying that the rupture in Jewish-Christian relations was initially predicated by misunderstanding.

Early followers of the Way were stunned to find themselves expelled from their synagogues (John 9:22). John's gospel became itself a source of dissension when his frequent allusions to "the Jews" were interpreted as meaning any and all Jews rather than specific individuals or groups. Such stereotyping gave rise to the conviction that the Jews (any and all) killed Jesus (John 18:28–19:15), a tragic error that was only officially renounced during Vatican II in *The Declaration on the Relationship of the Church to Non-Christian Religions:*

And, while certain ones among first-century Jews did not accept the Gospel and some outrightly opposed its spread, nevertheless the Jews remain dear to God, who never takes back a gift and who has given the Jews many! God likewise never takes back a decision and God has decided to choose the Jews as history clearly reveals. . . . For even though certain Jews did favor and press for the death of Jesus, that death cannot rightly be blamed on all Jews either living then or, certainly, living now. . . . We reject completely any persecution against the Jews, and we deplore the hatred, persecution and anti-Semitism of the past *(Nostra Aetate, 4)*.

According to the web site www.adherents.com, which is an excellent source of statistical information regarding religions, contemporary Judaism consists of approximately fourteen million people worldwide. So small a number comes as a surprise to many, raising the question why a tradition that represents a rather miniscule percentage of the world's population makes the short list of world religions at all. The answer, of course, lies in the influence Judaism has exerted over roughly four millennia, an effect far outstripping its size.

As early as Genesis 45:7, the term *remnant* began to be used to describe God's people. It pops up in biblical texts nearly six dozen times thereafter as a reminder that the Hebrews/Israelites/Jews would never be able to rely on sheer numbers to pull them through. Their strength lay elsewhere. If they couldn't rely totally on themselves, they were compelled to depend on their God. This unwavering faith has been the key element in delivering at least a remnant from one perilous situation after another. In the end, the wonder may be not that so few Jews remain today but that any do. If anything testifies to the Jews' designation as the "Chosen People of God," it is that they're still here.

The Wandering Jews

Jewish life was no cake walk during nearly two thousand years of Hebrew history. We've taken a look at some of this. By Jesus' time, the Jews were neither geographically nor religiously homogeneous. About as many Jews lived outside Palestine as within, and the Jewish belief system maintained a variety of views. Among the predominant sects were two we meet in the gospels and Acts of the Apostles, the Pharisees and the Sadducees, and one we only recently encountered in their library of Dead Sea Scrolls, the Essenes.

The Jewish dispersion actually began nearly eight centuries prior to Jesus' era with the strewing of the ten northern Israelite tribes across the vast landscape of the Assyrian Empire. The term "Ten Lost Tribes" that is used to describe this calamity is not strictly accurate, even if it is safe to say they were lost as tribal entities. Certain individuals and families survived, although quite a few intermarried with the foreigners the Assyrians implanted in the land. In the case of the Levites, a sizable number lived in the southern kingdom of Judah. As dedicated as the Tribe of Levi was to the service of God, some were priests and numerous others performed an assortment of functions at the Temple in Jerusalem. Still, following the Assyrian invasion of 721 B.C.E., the Israelite focal point shifted primarily to Judah, and in the course of the ensuing years Israelites would increasingly be known as Judahites (Jews).

Of course, Judah, too, would suffer a similar fate when the Babylonians came knocking at their city gates in 587 B.C.E. and carted most of them off to Mesopotamia. Upon their release by the Persians in 538, many returned to rebuild ruined Judah, but some remained in Babylon, creating additional dispersion.

One cataclysmic event in 70 C.E. may have done more to accelerate the *diaspora* ("dispersion") than anything else, and this was the destruction of the second Temple by the Roman general Titus, part of a heavy-handed crushing of the first Jewish revolt. This changed Judaism forever.

From Temple to Synagogue . . . Priest to Rabbi

The Roman sweep through Judea (the Latinized form of Judah) ended the role of the Temple as the heart of Jewish worship permanently. It was never rebuilt. All that remains today is the Temple Mount, the huge walled landfill created in order to provide an adequate level surface on which to construct the Temple. The Temple Mount itself has become a sacred site. Jews pray before the Western Wall, slipping written prayers into the cracks between its mammoth stones. The Western Wall is also known as the "Wailing Wall" because in its shadow Jews still lament the loss of the Temple.

241

Atop the Temple Mount now stands the Dome of the Rock/Al Aqsa Mosque, among Islam's holiest shrines. From there, according to Islamic tradition, Muhammad ascended to heaven. Some sects of Orthodox Judaism advocate the rebuilding of the Temple, believing that the Messiah will not come until this is accomplished. So deeply devoted are both Jews and Muslims to the spot that neither is apt to move far toward compromise or concession. Horrendous clashes have occurred there in recent years. Deep emotions are attached to a fair number of issues that divide the two religions. To brush them aside or trivialize them is a disservice to everyone concerned. Believers will fiercely defend their tradition, which is why, in an increasingly interdependent global society, it becomes more and more urgent that we respect others' convictions and understand them accurately even—perhaps especially—when we do not share them.

With the demise of the Temple and its sacrificial forms of worship, the Jewish priesthood passed into history as well. The rabbinic Judaism that began to emerge from the Exile with its emphasis on prayer and readings from the Torah became the accepted practice and remains so today.

From Jerusalem to the Ends of the Earth

Ironically, Jesus' admonition to his disciples to move beyond Jerusalem, Judea, and Samaria "to the ends of the earth" (Acts 1:8b) proved applicable to the Jews as well. On the other hand, it may be entirely reasonable inasmuch as:

- Jesus' early followers considered themselves Jews who saw in Jesus the fulfillment of Hebrew history and the ultimate "Way" to be Jewish;
- the schism between Jews and Christians was not a single event but occurred gradually over time;
- the Roman repression of the First Jewish Revolt (66–70 C.E.), and later the Second (132–135), scattered across the empire all manner of Jewish sects, including Christians.

The inclination to term the Promised Land Palestine (derived, in a wry twist, from the name of the Israelites' mortal enemies, the Philistines) escalated. The area would not again be a Jewish homeland until the creation of the new state of Israel in 1948. For close to eighteen hundred years, the Jews were dispersed among the nations of the earth and they were seldom welcoming.

In light of their limited numbers and lack of authority within the sundry host nations, it seems almost inevitable that the Jews would ultimately be assimilated into the larger mass and exit the world stage, much as the ten northern tribes did long before. This didn't happen. No single rationale explains why, but several meaningful elements combine to account for it. Chief among these are:

- that being Jewish was a twofold thing, involving race and religion;
- the Jews' sense of themselves as the chosen of God;
- their grounding in their own history and in the history of the wider world;
- their instinct for survival, honed by long experience with hostile societies;
- their commitment to learning.

We shall expand on each of these factors, fully realizing that it is not possible to do more than scratch the surface.

Being Jewish

Judaism's rituals and disciplinary doctrines are strictly for Jews, but its ethics are meant to be universal for all believers in God. The injunctions codified in the Ten Commandments not only are taken over whole by the other two great Western traditions but also are found seeded throughout every positive philosophical and theological system in history.

This succinct and accurate condensation of Judaism is offered by William J. O'Malley, S.J., in *God, The Oldest Question: A Fresh Look at Belief and Unbelief—and Why the Choice Matters* (Loyola Press, 2000). Judaism is a curious mixture of the exclusive and the universal.

Although geographical strictures limit the ethnicity of several world religions, Judaism is the only one in which race and religion are so closely intertwined. If Judaism in its most rudimentary form originated with the patriarch Abraham (c. 1850 B.C.E.) and if Judaism as a proper religion did not emerge until the time of the Exodus (c. 1250 B.C.E.), it is crucial to know who these people were. More to the point, who was Abram (Abraham)? His hometown, Ur, was an influential Sumerian city in Mesopotamia, the cradle of civilization nestled in the confluence of the nurturing Tigris and Euphrates Rivers. Water lines were virtual blood lines in the arid Near to Middle East. Without the Nile, there would have been no magnificent Egyptian civilization at the western end of the Fertile Crescent; without the Tigris and Euphrates, there would have been none at Mesopotamia in the east. Throughout the Hebrew Scriptures, wherever "the River" is mentioned with a capital "R," it means the Euphrates. More often than not, great rivers equal great civilization.

People had been pouring into the region we know as Mesopotamia since time immemorial. "Since the earliest times there had undoubtedly been nomads on the western fringes of the Euphrates valley," states *The New Jerome Biblical Commentary*: "and since the fourth millennium they had pressed in, in increasing numbers, and by the third millennium constituted an appreciable portion of the population. These people were Semites and are known as *Akkadians*. They intermingled with the Sumerian population, adopted and modified their culture, and even became rulers in some city-states."

All of this was long before Abraham's time, of course, but it is from these roots that he, and with him his familial and religious descendants, sprang. Since the Sumerians were entirely unknown to us little more than a century ago, much research into the remarkable culture they created lies ahead.

Genesis 14:13 refers to Abram as "the Hebrew," a designation found almost exclusively in the first two books of the Torah and one that is somewhat unclear. Were these the Apiru or Habiru spoken of in writings from ancient sites as far flung as Tel Amarna in Egypt and Ugarit in modern Lebanon to Mari at the northern edge of the Arabian desert and Assyrian Nuzi in today's Iraq? Possibly, but it's one of these questions that remain open and await better evidence.

The name fades, except in respect to the language, early in the biblical saga. In its stead, we find an appellation whose origins are easier to trace, "Israelite." Its citation in Genesis 32:32 is the first of 762. If you recall, one of Abraham's twin grandsons was named Jacob. In one of those meaningful name changes, Jacob became Israel after his legendary struggle with a mysterious adversary: "Then the man said, 'You shall no longer be called Jacob, but Israel, for you have striven with God and with humans, and have prevailed' " (Genesis 32:28). Linguists question whether this statement accurately reflects the etymology of the word *Israel*, thinking it might be something closer to "may God rule" (*El*, the name of the chief Canaanite deity, is retained to apply to the Hebrew/Israelite God and is found in such names as the archangels—Michael, Gabriel, Raphael, Uriel, etc.).

So by patriarchal times, Abraham's genealogy is ethnically Semitic-Sumerian and that's about the extent of it. Israel begins as a lone individual, and the name becomes attached to his immediate family of twelve sons and at least one daughter and, as the generations pass, is extended to the tribal units founded by each son and ultimately to the nation.

The Chosen

As time passed, Jacob's extended family was extended to be sure, but never was it a secular power. The growing realization of themselves as chosen among nations brought with it a corresponding sense of responsibility. As we have seen, there was an obligation for this relatively modest clan in this relatively remote part of the world to live in compliance with the covenant they had entered into with their God, a duty not always taken as seriously nor lived out as meticulously as might have been desired. Still, at some level, the Israelites were always aware of the charge they had been given.

In order to discharge this trust and occupy their special place wherever in the world they happened to be, it was urgent that the Israelites, later Jews, survive . . . and survive more or less intact. This fairly basic assignment would present great difficulty at almost every step of their historical journey, and managing to carry it off at all remains one of their most noteworthy achievements.

Intermarriage with those who lived among them was taboo from the dawn of Israelite history (Deuteronomy 7:1–4). A large part of the animosity that existed between the northern and southern kingdoms subsequent to Israel's subjugation at the hands of the Assyrians was due to the propensity of the surviving Israelites to marry their newly arrived, imported neighbors. As it turned out, the Judahites had no room to talk as they, too, fell into this trap around the time of the Exile.

Upon their return and as a major concession to the requirements for the restoration of their culture, the Judahites bowed to the demands of Ezra, who admonished them:

> The people of Israel, the priests, and the Levites have not separated themselves from the peoples of the lands with their abominations. . . . For they have taken some of their daughters as wives for themselves and for their sons. Thus the holy seed has mixed itself with the peoples of the lands, and in this faithlessness the officials and leaders have led the way (Ezra 9:1b–2).
>
> We have broken faith with our God and have married foreign women from the peoples of the land, but even now there is hope for Israel in spite of this. So let us not make a covenant with our God to send away all these wives and their children . . ." (Ezra 10:2b–3a).

Strong medicine!

The experience of biblical Israel has resonated down the long centuries among Jews. Scattered for most of their history over an assortment of host nations where it was generally made quite clear that they didn't belong, the Jews acquired the habit of staying together and maintaining a low profile. Occupying specific districts of cities made it easier to sustain cultural practices and religious beliefs. Urban sectors populated by minorities are by no means rare, nor are they necessarily negative in nature. Remnants of them remain in American metropolises, especially in the northeast, reminders of a time when immigrants were streaming through Ellis Island from every European port. Enclaves from Little Italy in New York City to Over the Rhine in Cincinnati waited to welcome them, offering much of what was familiar and loved at home.

When this type of segregated living is no longer voluntary or beneficial, however, the situation darkens. *Ghetto,* the word associated most often with these settings, has come to denote something undesirable at best. From the Middle Ages on, Jews became all too familiar with ghettos. Life there could be restricted to the point that it bordered on persecution. Even under the most favorable conditions, the mere existence of ghettos fostered an "us and them" mentality that bred suspicion and distrust.

Physical persecution was always a threat and, frequently, a reality. Jews suffered at the hands of those who called themselves Christians and yes, sadly, Catholics during the Crusades, the Inquisition, the Russian pogroms, and, of course, the Shoah, or Holocaust. This bitter history was reenacted on the Broadway stage in the musical *Fiddler on the Roof.* A Russian pogrom seems an unusual setting for such a production, yet it presents such an endearing portrayal of Jewish life in a small backwater that it has become a classic of the American stage. Listen to the lyrics of its songs. In them, you will learn more than you might previously have imagined about Jewish beliefs and practices of the era.

But there's no big finish to this show, no flags flying, no pull-out-all-the-stops production number. Instead, the characters pick up to move yet again as their little town of Anatevka is threatened by the approach of the tsar's troops, and the tough little band of villagers tries to make the best of the situation, assuring one another that they didn't have much to leave behind anyway and would no doubt be better off elsewhere. Each family departs, burdened with the thought that they may never see their longtime friends and neighbors again.

During World War II, Poland's Warsaw ghetto generated disease, fear, famine, and death as more and more Jews were rounded up and herded within its walls. When Nazi forces at last arrived to ship the remaining occupants to camps and obliterate the ghetto itself, they were met with unexpected resistance from within its walls. Hungry, sick, and nearly unarmed, the Jews staved off superior enemy forces for days. *The Warsaw Concerto* was composed to honor their heroism.

Stick together? It's one of the things Jews have always done best. Living in today's pluralistic society, especially in the United States, problems still present themselves, which, if less lethal, are nonetheless troubling. More and more Jewish young people intermarry with Gentiles professing all sorts of beliefs and/or disbeliefs. Some elements of Jewish society continue to bar mixed marriages; all discourage it. In this respect, nothing much has changed. The chosen remain a remnant, only fourteen million or so, striving to survive unassimilated into alien cultures. The chances that they will succeed have been redoubled by the establishment at last of a Jewish homeland. Finally, there's somewhere they belong. But just as it was when Joshua led the Israelites across the Jordan River into Canaan, the land wasn't open and unoccupied when the newcomers arrived laying claim to it. The former inhabitants, in our age the Palestinians, have rights as well, rights that invariably seem at odds with their Jewish neighbors. Resolution is not easily achieved.

Telling and Retelling the Story

Each year, when Jewish families gather for the Seder during the Passover celebration, the story of the Exodus is retold. Those present at the meal are given copies of the Haggadah, Hebrew for *telling*. The Haggadah explains the ritual and how it will unfold (*Seder* itself means "order"). Repetition in the form of ritual has a place in all religious traditions. In some, it finds greater favor than others. All three monotheistic religions of the Near East make extensive use of ritual, none more than Judaism. Recitations form part of ancient rites, and through them the story of a people is engraved in memory. This shared history becomes a bond, linking members of the group across generations and across the world. It is another of the strengths which have contributed to the survival of "the remnant," and there is no better illustration of that than the Seder.

Consistent with the other principal components of the Passover observance, the Haggadah has its origin in the Book of Exodus when Hebrew firstborns were passed over during the tenth plague. "You shall tell your child on that day, 'It is because of what the LORD did for me when I came out of Egypt.' It shall serve for you as a sign on your hand and as a reminder on your forehead, so that the teaching of the LORD may be on your lips; for with a strong hand the LORD brought you out of Egypt. You shall keep this ordinance at its proper time from year to year" (Exodus 13:8–10). In keeping with this injunction, the youngest child present begins by asking: "Why is this night different from all other nights?" The father or the adult assuming the role of father figure then recounts the great Exodus saga in much the same fashion as his forebears have done for hundreds of years.

No one will ask for your dietary preferences at a Seder. The food, too, is rich in symbolism and may be served on a beautifully decorated plate reserved solely to this occasion. On the plate will be:

• a roasted shank bone of lamb, a reminder of the lamb eaten prior to the departure for Egypt and its many successors sacrificed at the altar of the Temple;

- wafers of unleavened bread *(matzoth),* recalling the order to eat with "your loins girded, your sandals on your feet, and your staff in your hand; and you shall eat it hurriedly" (Exodus 12:11) (people about to take flight cannot wait for bread to rise);
- bitter herbs (see Exodus 12:8b), tokens of the bitterness of slavery to the Egyptians;
- a roasted or hard-boiled egg, long a symbol of new life as Christians now use it at Easter, demonstrating the free will offering of the people;
- parsley, its greenery another reminder of new growth;
- salt water, into which the parsley is dipped, an appropriate sign of the tears shed under Egyptian oppression;
- *haroseth,* a sticky mixture of finely chopped apples and nuts mixed with cinnamon and wine which stands for the mortar used by Hebrew slaves to erect Pharaoh's cities.

The Seder table is centered by a ceremonial cup of wine, known as Elijah's cup. Due to his mysterious departure from planet earth (2 Kings 2:11), a legend grew up around Elijah, predicting that he would return to announce the coming of the Messiah (see Matthew 11:14, Mark 9:4–5, Luke 1:17, John 1:21, 25, among others). The cup sits at the center of the Seder table in the hope that the Messiah will soon appear and, with him, the dawn of a new age.

The story remains fresh and deeply personal because the storyteller relates it as if he had experienced it. Lines of past, present, and future blur, connecting all generations and merging them into the common experience of a single people. This sense of self has contributed greatly to the durability of a relatively small group. It also lends insight into what it must have meant to followers of the Way to find themselves no longer part of what had always been their whole identity.

The synoptic gospels understand the Last Supper to have been a Seder meal. If so, Jesus remained an observant Jew to the end.

To Life!

The familiar Jewish toast "To Life!" comes close to expressing the essence of Hebraic philosophy. Determined to live, to survive despite forced baptisms, organized pogroms, attempted genocide, and insidious covert discrimination, the Jews have become adept at enduring no matter what the circumstances. A standing joke claims that if a person can simply create a filing system no one else in the office can decipher, this is called job security.

The Jews have frequently been just as creative, making themselves useful even where they were not wanted. For instance, in medieval times, money lending was not deemed to be a proper profession for a Catholic. The charging of interest was thought to be usury, and thus un-Christian. Nonetheless, bankers were necessary to trade, with the result that Jews were actually invited to act as financiers, an occupation they continued to engage in thereafter. At a time when a middle class was all but nonexistent, the aristocracy benefited most from the loaning of money, and negative stereotypes such as Shakespeare's Shylock sprang up. Typecasting is always harmful and can be deadly. The notion of the Jews controlling capital was still prevalent when Hitler came to power in Germany in 1932 and was one of the inflammatory accusations he made against them.

The People of the Book

Gentiles called biblical Jews the people of the Book. The book in question was, of course, the Hebrew Scriptures to which they were attentive in a manner puzzling to outsiders. Furthermore, they possessed little literature aside from the Torah, the Prophets, and the Writings. Those three sections taken together comprise the *Tanak,* or Jewish Bible. The love of Scripture has remained their hallmark. The Torah is read continuously in Jewish synagogues. Just as Catholics progress through three cycles of Sunday gospel readings and then start all over again, so Jewish congregations, upon completing Deuteronomy, begin again with Genesis.

> Keep these words that I am commanding you today in your heart. Recite them to your children and talk about them when you are at home and when you are away, when you lie down and when you rise. Bind them as a sign on your hand, fix them as an emblem on your forehead, and write them on the doorposts of your house and on your gates (Deuteronomy 6:6–9).

Jews continue to take these words of Moses to heart. At their Bar Mitzvahs, as they take their rightful places in the adult assembly, Jewish boys are often gifted by their families with *phylacteries* or *tefillin,* especially if they follow the Orthodox tradition. These consist of two black leather cubes attached to long leather straps. Inside the small black cubes are tiny parchment scrolls, hand inscribed in Hebrew with passages from the Torah.

Adult males wear *tefillin* at morning prayer, winding the straps of one seven times around their left arms, positioning the box on the upper arm in such a way that it faces the heart. The other cube is centered on the forehead between and above the eyes with the straps wrapped around the head. Thus, the word of God as enjoined by Moses remains always next to head and heart.

On those doorposts Moses mentioned, visitors to a Jewish home find a *mezuzah*, a small case, usually metal. Ranging from unadorned to lavishly embellished, mezuzahs, too, carry small (in this case, 2" x 2") parchment scrolls of handwritten Hebrew, bearing Deuteronomy 6:4–9 (cited above) and Deuteronomy 11:13–21. The mezuzah is touched each time a person enters the house as a reminder of the centrality of God and his Law in a Jewish home. Few rival Jewish reverence for God's word and its place in everyday life.

No other writings rival the Tanak, but second place would have to go to a collection called the *Talmud,* translated "study" or "instruction." The Talmud is made up of interpretations of the Torah by learned rabbis largely from the first to fifth centuries C.E. Two versions of the Talmud exist, one originating in Palestine, the other in Babylonia. This voluminous work records discussions, disputes, and decisions intended to assist Jews to live out in their own lives what the Torah teaches. To this end, it deals with marriage and dietary laws, religious rites and festivals, history and folklore, the effects engendered by changing circumstances encountered living as aliens in a cultures of great diversity, and much more.

Jewish learning is not confined to matters religious. Jewish thinkers, writers, and scientists have flourished in surroundings good and bad. One of the most esteemed was the twelfth-century philosopher Moses ben Maimon, better known as Maimonides, whose work from the Jewish perspective is often compared to that of Thomas Aquinas from the Catholic. Although Judaism is not essentially a credal religion, Maimonides drafted a sort of unofficial credal statement for Judaism by codifying thirteen articles of belief. The twentieth century saw the emergence of another notable philosophical mind in the person of

Martin Buber who hoped to see movement toward cooperation on matters of concern to Jews and Christians alike.

Judaism Today

Judaism in the modern world is no more homogenous than it was in Jesus' world. Rarely does any major religion come down to a single strand of tradition adhered to by all believers. Under the overarching umbrella of any sect are found, as a rule, from two to four great arms. These, in turn, branch out into a host of smaller factions. Judaism today consists of:

♦ **Orthodox:** Among the primary camps of any belief system, there is likely to be a group who see themselves as the authentic representation, the keepers of the flame as it were—the orthodox. The validity of this claim varies from group to group but within Judaism there is little doubt that among Jews these are the Orthodox. As the guardians of their tradition, the Orthodox stress strict observance and are wary of change. This conservatism may be more understandable in Judaism given its history and its sense of its special role among the nations and religions of the world. They number about two million.

♦ **Conservative:** Actually, these are the middle-of-the-roaders. More lenient than the Orthodox, the Conservative arm of Judaism, some four million five hundred thousand strong, attempts to retain all that is essential to Jewish belief and practice while adapting, where possible, to the secular societies in which they find themselves.

♦ **Reform:** Little more than a century old, Reform Judaism is far and away the most liberal, going so far as to ordain women. Reform congregations, often called temples though they are really synagogues, have experienced exceptional growth in the United States which is home to a Jewish population second only to Israel's. There are about three million seven hundred fifty thousand Reform Jews worldwide.

The numerical estimates above total only ten million two hundred fifty thousand and do not take into consideration the sizable body of Jews who either consider themselves secular or are unaffiliated with any particular branch. A rough guess would place their numbers at around four million five hundred thousand.

Israel Lives Again

In the wake of the near annihilation of European Jewry under Hitler, the need for a Jewish homeland was inescapable. The idea wasn't new. Zionism, named for Mount Zion, began its push for a Jewish state in the late nineteenth century. In 1948, three years after World War II ended, a new Israel was founded on the site of its biblical predecessor, a move not without controversy as thousands of Palestinians were displaced in the process. Wars ensued with neighboring Arab states. Peace remains fragile as the Jewish offspring of Isaac struggle to coexist with the Arab, and largely Muslim, posterity of Ishmael.

Islamic Peace and Submission

Last, in terms of longevity, of the three great Near Eastern faiths among the world religions is the Muslim world of Islam, dating from the seventh century C.E. Its late arrival, however, has not hindered its rapid rise numerically and geographically. Muslim ranks have swelled to approximately one billion three hundred million, second only to Christianity's estimated two billion. From its origins in modern Saudi Arabia, Islam has extended its presence throughout the Near East, across Africa, over much of southern Asia, and, more, recently into Europe and the Western Hemisphere. Some thirty million Muslims dwell today in Europe with another six to eight million in the United States (for the most recent demographics, go to www.adherents.com). Figures like these lead some to characterize Islam as the fastest growing religion in the world today.

Islam is variously translated to read "peace and submission to the one almighty God, peace through faith and surrender," etc., and stems from the Arabic *salaam*, meaning "peace." Yet the most recent Islamic influence is often seen as less than peaceful. As I introduce Islam to groups of adolescents and adults, I ordinarily ask them to provide a noun to follow the adjective *Islamic*. Sad to say, the reply is almost always *terrorist*. If Islam, like Christianity, is the child of Judaism; if Muslims worship the same God as Jews and Christians; if there are marked theological similarities; and if Islam is growing rapidly around the world, there must be more to it than that and, of course, there is. If you have never come face to face with Islamic belief and culture, it's safe to say you soon will.

The Prophet

Not all religions have founders, but there is no question but what Islam did. His name was Muhammad, and he was born in the Arabian city of Mecca *(Makkah)* in 570 C.E. Orphaned by the age of six, the boy moved around in his large family until finally coming under the care of an uncle whose spice caravans traversed the territory from the Arabian peninsula to Syria and Palestine on the Mediterranean shore. Muhammad was unschooled, serving as a camel driver in a caravan crew made up of Jews and Christians. The stories and beliefs they either shared or argued over many evenings in camp had a profound effect on a youngster who was by nature engrossed by such matters. From his multireligious unofficial tutors, Muhammad learned of a single benevolent God who holds humankind accountable for its actions.

This held immense appeal for the young Muhammad who was repelled by some of the practices he experienced at home. The poor were made poorer by the need to buy idols and sacrificial animals. Female infanticide was common. Societal structures were rigidly stratified. To the idealistic boy, religion as he knew it was base and purposeless.

Muhammad's fortunes improved, materially at any rate, upon his marriage to the wealthy and much older widow Khadijah. Tragically, only one of the six children born of the union survived to maturity, a daughter named Fatimah. Grief occasioned by these compound misfortunes led Muhammad to spend more and more time wandering alone, pondering the meaning of life and death.

In a cave close to Mecca, c. 610 C.E., Muhammad is said to have been visited by the angel Gabriel who announced to him that he was to be the one prophet of the one God. This turning point is honored by Muslims as the "Night of Power and Excellence." Over the course of a decade, Muhammad received many more revelations which were set down in what would become Islam's most sacred writing, the Qur'an (Koran).

Just as Paul had trouble with the silversmiths of Ephesus when his preaching threatened their lucrative trade in idols, so Muhammad incurred the wrath of merchants who lived off the same livelihood in Mecca. In time, he was forced to move to Medina, a city some two hundred fifty miles distant. This event, called the "Hegira," stands at the head of the Islamic lunar calendar. Years are clocked from the Hegira in the same way they are registered from the supposed birth date of Jesus in the Christian world.

Eventually, Muhammad returned to Mecca, where a shrine called the "Kaaba" had stood from antiquity. Muhammad retained it, believing that a meteorite set in its corner had in actuality been bestowed on Abraham by Gabriel. This became the "Sacred Black Stone." Pilgrimages to Mecca and the Kaaba with its venerated stone later became central to Islamic practice.

Muhammad's teachings were popular. Conversions were many and swift. Christians and Jews were tolerated because of their devotion to the same God, although it was believed that both groups had misinterpreted his teaching. Huston Smith writes of doctrinal conflict between Jews and Muslims in *Why Religion Matters: The Fate of the Human Spirit in an Age of Disbelief* (HarperCollins, 2001):

> Truth to tell, the religious differences between these two faiths are so small that Muhammad could hardly have been more surprised when he discovered that the Jews and Christians of his day did not accept him as an addition to their own prophetic lines.

Openmindedness toward Jews began to wane following an assassination attempt by a Jewish woman who tried to poison Muhammad and very nearly succeeded.

By the time of his death in 632, Muhammad had pulled Arab states into a loose confederation, which amounted to a theocracy, a government based on the laws of God as interpreted by leaders who are regarded as inspired. At no time did Muhammad ever make any claim to divinity himself, remaining so humble a figure that it is said he mended his own clothing and milked his own goat. Like his followers, Muhammad worshipped Allah (God). Even now, Muslims resent being called Muhammadans for, as they will quickly remind offenders, they venerate Allah, not Muhammad. This, indeed, is the Muslim creed, short and to the point: "There is no God but Allah, and Muhammad is his prophet."

The Holy Book

In congruity with Judaism and Christianity, Islam centers much of its belief on the contents of its holy book, the Qur'an (Koran). Believed to be a precise transcript of Gabriel's words to Muhammad, not a single word of its one hundred fourteen chapters *(Surah)* has ever been altered. Because Muhammad was not formally educated, he is thought to have memorized the Qur'an's passages, dictating them to scribes who later checked their accuracy with him.

In his introduction to *The Essential Koran* (Castle Books, 1997) Thomas Cleary asserts:

> The Qur'an is undeniably a book of great importance even to the non-Muslim, perhaps more today than ever, if that is possible. One aspect of Islam that is unexpected and yet appealing to the post-Christian secular mind is the harmonious interplay of faith and reason. Islam does not demand unreasoned belief. Rather, it invites intelligent faith, growing from observation, reflection, and contemplation, beginning with nature and what is all around us. Accordingly, antagonism between religion and science such as that familiar to Westerners is foreign to Islam.

In light of earlier chapters of this book, *should* such antagonism ever have existed? And if it still persists, why?

Qur'an means the "Recital or the Reading." Cleary cites Sirdar Ikbal Ali Shah:

> The Qur'an is nothing but the old books refined of human alloy and contains transcendent truths embodied in all sacred scriptures with complete additions necessary for the development of all human faculties. It repeats truths given in the Holy Vedas [Hindu], in the Bible, in the words of the Gita [Hindu], in the sayings of the Buddha and all other prophets and adds what was not in them and gives new laws to meet the contingencies of the present time when the different members of God's family who lived apart from each other in the days of old revelations had come close one to the other.

Just as Jesus' initial disciples saw themselves as observant Jews following a more fulfilling Way, so Muslims never saw their religion as new. The same truth revealed through Judaism and Christianity is held to be expanded through the prophet Muhammad.

Notwithstanding, Muhammad is only one of twenty-five prophets revered in Islam. Jews and Christians will find a lot of familiar names here: Adam, David, Jonah, and Ezekiel. Five are most esteemed: Noah, Abraham, Moses, Jesus, and, naturally, Muhammad. Surprised to see that Jesus made the list? His teachings are honored by Muslims though he himself is regarded as a great man, no more. Christian acceptance of his divinity causes Muslims to question their monotheism.

Huston Smith comments in *The Illustrated World's Religions* (Harper SanFrancisco, 1994):

> Following Ishmael's line in Arabia we come eventually in the later half of the sixth century, A.D. to Muhammad, the prophet through whom Islam reached its definitive form, Muslims believe. There had been authentic prophets of God before him, but he was their culmination, so he is called *The Seal of the Prophets*. No legitimate prophets will succeed him.

Islam on the Move

"Proselytization," a fancy word for conversion, is a cardinal tenet of some religious traditions; for others, it matters little, if at all. As you might imagine, it has never been allowed in large segments of the Jewish world, although today it is possible for Gentiles to join Reform or Conservative congregations. Christians have considered proselytizing an important part of their mission from the beginning, based on passages such as Matthew 28:19–20: "Go therefore and make disciples of all nations, baptizing them in the name of the Father and of the Son and of the Holy Spirit, and teaching them to obey everything that I have commanded you."

Muslims, too, sensed a responsibility to spread the teachings of Muhammad to all parts of the world. This they did with remarkable speed, making tremendous inroads into other parts of the Near East and North Africa; then pushing east into Asia. The Qur'an's injunction, "Let there be no compulsion in religion" (2:257), was not always obeyed. The lofty ideals promulgated by any religion are usually practiced imperfectly at best by its adherents, making it crucial for members of each tradition to understand the others' beliefs *accurately*. Then, when a faction behaves in a manner inconsistent with its religion's doctrine, it is seen as an aberration, not as representative of the group.

One reason for Islam's rapid acceptance lies in its universality. Everyone is accepted as a child of Allah. Another impetus is its simplicity. Although Muslims have an inordinate dedication to learning, like Jews, deep theological study is not required in order to practice Islam, nor are strict ascetic practices and complicated rituals. One need only grasp certain basic beliefs and strive to live according to the "Five Pillars."

Principles of Islamic Thought

For Muslims, all things center on and revolve around Allah, the one, the only God. They have ninety-nine names for Allah: the Gracious, the Lord of the Universe, the Creator, the Beneficent, the All-Wise, and so on. Like Christians and Jews, they believe in a single omniscient, omnipotent deity. Unlike Christians, they do not accept a trinitarian concept, finding in that the seeds of polytheism. Nonetheless, the Jewish Yahweh, the Christian Father or First Person, and the Muslim Allah are one and the same.

Muslims also hold that this God has made his message known via many messengers over time, but that this message has been skewed and distorted. Only Islam retains it flawlessly.

Again paralleling the other two Near Eastern world faiths, Islam assumes humanity, individually and collectively, to be accountable for its actions, a culpability which will earn a corresponding reward or chastisement on a final day of judgment.

This notion, naturally, presumes a doctrine of sin. The majority of Christians, certainly Catholics, accept the idea that sin is impossible for those too young to grasp the concept. At puberty, Muslim youth become responsible for the morality of their choices. Original sin is unknown among Islamic tenets.

In a manner reminiscent of the theocratic state of ancient Israel, Muslims draw no line between the secular and the religious in matters of state. All aspects of life fall under the purview of Islam. Some nations that are predominantly Muslim are more committed to this principle than others, but there is often a concerted effort to bring these countries with a middle-of-the-road stance into the conservative fold.

Observances and Festivals

The three monotheistic Near Eastern traditions celebrate a special day of prayer weekly, but each does so on a separate day. Using the time-honored lunar calendar, Jews and Muslims begin and end their days at sunset. The Jewish Sabbath, therefore, commences at sunset Friday and ends at sunset Saturday. Muslim observance starts at sundown Thursday and continues until sundown Friday, usually with special congregational prayer in a mosque at noon. Christians, once separated from their Jewish roots, made Sunday their Sabbath in deference to the foremost event in their history, the resurrection of Jesus.

Islamic places of worship are called "mosques." Whether these structures are simple or lavish, the decor is characterized by beautiful geometric patterns consistent with the ban they share with Jews against the depiction of living beings.

Three cities are holy to Islam: Mecca and Medina in Saudi Arabia and Jerusalem, all because of their association with the prophet Muhammad.

Only two annual celebrations, called *eids,* mark the Islamic calendar, in contrast to the many Jewish and Christian holidays. The Eid of Sacrifice commemorates Abraham's willingness to sacrifice his son. The Eid of Fast Breaking marks the close of the month of fasting, Ramadan.

The Five Pillars of Islam

Muslim lives are firmly anchored by the Five Pillars of Islam. Attention to these is not optional. If even one is neglected, one's religious duty is deemed incomplete.

◆ ***The Creed:*** This is simply total allegiance to Allah and to Muhammad as the messenger of Allah. Everything in the Muslim world stems from this uncomplicated statement of belief.

◆ ***Prayer:*** Five prayer periods grace the Muslim day. The long tradition of Catholic monastic prayer, whose use was recommended by Vatican II to laity and religious alike, is comparable. Both find their basis in the parent, Judaism. Graceful, slim spires known as "minarets" dot the Muslim landscape. From their pinnacles, *muezzins* have for centuries called the faithful to prayer at the appointed times. High tech has made its way up these slim towers in many Islamic cities of today, introducing microphones and speakers.

Proper prayer requires the devout to:
1. cleanse the exposed parts of their bodies as purification;
2. dress modestly (shoes are never worn during prayer);
3. pray in a place that is unsullied (prayer rugs are often used);
4. pray facing Mecca, Islam's holiest site;
5. recite the requisite prayers while standing, sitting, bowing, or prostrating themselves with foreheads touching the floor.

Men and women pray separately. In a mosque, an *imam* who is a lay scholar may act as leader, and prayer rugs cover the floor. When these often beautifully woven rugs are used in other localities, they become in effect portable mosques, and their pattern often reflects that idea. Mosques are devoid of altars, statues, fixed seating, and other fixtures commonly found in sacred spaces. Unique to mosques is the niche in one wall indicating the direction of Mecca.

◆ **Fasting:** The ninth month of the Islamic calendar, Ramadan, is a time of fasting. There are certain corollaries with the Christian Lent both in purpose and practice, especially the stringent Lenten practices of centuries past. It is a period of self-purification through self-denial. The requirements for Ramadan are demanding and obligatory. Abstinence from all food, drink, and sexual intercourse from sunup to sundown is the rule for all, except the sick, children, pregnant women, the elderly, and travelers. Only imperative business is transacted because of the demands of the fast and to allow additional time to meditate on passages from the Qur'an. Those failing to observe the fast are required to feed an impoverished person for each day missed. The Eid of Fast Breaking celebrates the conclusion of Ramadan.

◆ **Zakat:** In concert with Judaism and Christianity, Islam teaches that all creation ultimately belongs to God. Everything humanity possesses comes from God, and it is the responsibility of humans to act as stewards of these gifts. To remind themselves of this, Muslims are required to contribute a fixed $2^1/_2$ percent of their annual capital to meet the needs of the poor. The word *Zakat* can mean either "purification" or "growth." It is hoped that making a substantial offering of material wealth will promote both. Necessary as financial donations are, they do not constitute the whole of Zakat. Said Muhammad: "Even meeting your brother with a cheerful face is charity." Giving of this nature, whether monetary or what we would call sweat equity, is seen as a legitimate and indispensable form of worship.

◆ *The Hajj:* At least once in their lifetime, Muslims should make the pilgrimage to Mecca. Only if physical or financial burdens make the trip prohibitive are they exempt. Travel to holy sites has a long history among the three Near Eastern world faiths. As we have seen, pilgrimage feasts loomed large on Israelite calendars from the time Solomon built the first Temple. Their importance was accented even more during the second Temple period, which included Jesus' lifetime. If at all possible, the people of Israel were to trek to Jerusalem to celebrate Passover, Pentecost (the Feast of Weeks), and Sukkot (the Feast of Tabernacles/Tents/Booths).

The Passover journey of Jesus' family is recorded by Luke in 2:41–52. A gathering for Pentecost is detailed in Acts 2:1–12. Early in the Christian era, pilgrims began to visit their holy places. One of the most famous such early travelers was Helena, the mother of Constantine, who was dedicated to finding and preserving the sites most closely connected to Jesus. During the Middle Ages, Christian pilgrims prominently displayed a scallop shell on their hats, purses, or belts, identifying them as sojourners to the sacred. (The emblem is still associated with travel in its use by a major oil company.)

• About two million pilgrims descend on the city of Mecca yearly from all parts of the world during the twelfth month of the Islamic calendar. Upon their arrival, they exchange their customary attire for simple white garments which instantly erase distinctions based on wealth and privilege and emphasize equality in the eyes of Allah. Over a three-day period, pilgrims go through prescribed rites, gathering first in the courtyard surrounding the Kaaba. News footage always shows a sea of white flowing around the great black shrine. Tradition calls for pilgrims to circle the Kaaba seven times, kissing or touching the Sacred Black Stone each time around, recalling how the Kaaba was built by the patriarch Abraham and his first son, Ishmael, son of Hagar.

- Next, pilgrims walk to the hills of Safa and Marwa, where it is thought that Hagar sought water for herself and her son in the desert following their dismissal from Abraham's camp. There is a critical difference in the interpretation of the Isaac/Ishmael story by Muslims as opposed to that of Jews and Christians. Where the latter focus on Isaac as the legitimate heir and their ancestral patriarch, Muslims concentrate on the misused Ishmael. To this day, attitudes between the two groups can be deeply affected by this rift of long ago.

- Finally, pilgrims stand together on the Plain of Arafa, praying for Allah's forgiveness in a kind of precursor of the Last Judgment when all peoples of all times and places will stand together before God. The Hajj closes with the Eid of Sacrifice, one of Islam's two primary festivals during which gifts are exchanged.

Sunni and Shia

Islam is composed of two major divisions, Sunni and Shia, or Shiite. The Sunnis predominate and are the older of the two. The smaller Shiite sect severed ties with the Sunnis over leadership issues, leaving them distrustful of others' intents. They scan the Qur'an for hidden meanings and evidence of tampering.

They await a messianic figure similar to that expected by some branches of Judaism. They strive to unite the religious and secular under Islamic rule in the lands in which they dominate, i.e., Iran, Iraq, Pakistan, and Lebanon. Sunnis often feel that all Muslims are painted with the same brush by the wider world, and the picture is more often than not Shiite. They see this as inaccurate and unfair.

Religious mystics, long part of Jewish and Christian tradition, have a respected place in Islam as well. Sufis are the counterparts of Christian monastics or Jewish Essenes. The name means "wool wearers" because of the simple robes they wear, indicative of their poverty. They may remind Catholics of Francis of Assisi and his brown-robed friars.

Sufism arose a mere century or two after Muhammad's death. Writes Huston Smith (*The Illustrated World's Religions,* 1994):

> These Sufis were drawn to the Koranic disclosure that there is an inward as well as an outward side to the divine nature. God's relatively obvious aspects might suffice for the majority of Muslims, but the Sufis wanted to plumb Allah's depths. And they wanted to experience him now, in this very lifetime, and not wait until the afterlife.

Instead of secreting themselves behind monastery walls, Sufis live relatively normal family and professional lives. They come together to pray, to sing, to dance (the fabled whirling dervishes are Sufis), and to hear the instruction of the Masters *(Shaikhs)*. Their love of poetry is reflected in the writings of Rumi, cited at the beginning of this chapter. Realizing God to be above all language and portrayals, Sufis rely heavily on symbolism as they strive to break through existing mindsets in their quest for deeper, more profound comprehension of Allah. This can lead to friction with other arms of Islam. Huston Smith continues:

> Mysticism breaks through the boundaries that protect the faith of the typical believer. In doing so, it moves into unconfined regions that, though fulfilling for some, carry dangers for those who are unprepared for their teachings.

In the Western Hemisphere, no discussion of Islam would be complete without some mention of the Nation of Islam, frequently termed Black Muslims. Founded in Detroit in 1930, the Nation of Islam came to national prominence under the leadership of Elijah Muhammad, said to be the messenger of Allah for African Americans.

Apart from strict devotion to the teachings of the Qur'an, the Nation of Islam differed radically in several important ways from mainstream Islam. Elijah Muhammad insisted upon the total separation of races, black from white, which was in stark contrast to the usual Muslim promotion of openness to all people. The Nation of Islam also taught that blacks would ultimately inherit the earth, again in opposition to conventional Islamic belief.

On the other hand, Elijah Muhammad did promote such Islamic fundamentals as diet, hygiene, and the highest standards of ethical and moral behavior. These lofty ideals gave a sense of purpose and self-esteem to many within the movement.

Better known, perhaps, than Elijah Muhammad, was Malcolm Little (Malcolm X) who, until his assassination in 1965, turned the Nation of Islam onto a more moderate path. While making the Hajj, Malcolm was struck by the wide diversity of pilgrims, concluding:

> The brotherhood! The people of all races, colors, coming together as *one*! It has proved to me the power of the One God. . . . The true Islam has shown me that a blanket indictment of all white people is as wrong as when whites make blanket indictments against blacks.

This openness may have cost Malcolm X his life, or at least contributed to the animosity which resulted in his assassination. His legacy of acceptance, which is more consistent with mainline Islamic belief, lives on in the organization now called the World Community of Islam in the West.

Islam in the West

Islam is a growing force globally. In recent years, this has become increasingly obvious in the Western Hemisphere. The presence of a mosque in an American city, startling only a few years ago, scarcely evokes a second glance today. The traditionally Judeo-Christian culture of the West may soon need to include the third great monotheistic religion from the Near East as well.

The need for true understanding and respect among the three related faiths has never been greater. The broad foundation of shared belief should provide a strong basis for cooperation now and the footings to bridge differences in years to come. These differences are real, and nothing is accomplished by trivializing them or pushing them aside. Some carry such significance that they may never be surmounted. Still, this great Near Eastern triad has the same God at its center. Agreeing to disagree with courtesy is not always a bad thing.

CHAPTER TWELVE

Viewing the World from the Far East

T hus far, we have confined our explorations to our own backyard, so to speak, pursuing the B-I-G questions of where we came from and what we're doing here from the perspective of our ancestral heritage (Judaism), our fellow heirs to this patrimony (Islam), and our own foundation (Christianity). Now, we are ready to peer over our backyard fence to begin an acquaintance with our neighbors in the Far East. There we will encounter a world unlike our own in most respects. While it's only natural for us to grasp at whatever commonalities we detect, it's essential to remember that this world must be met on its own terms, not on ours. Abandon preconceptions. Peel away stereotypes. Prepare to view religion in a whole new light from an entirely different perspective and in a brilliant array of hues. Minds open wide? Let's see what's on the other side of the fence.

Near and Far

Religion alive confronts the individual with the most momentous option life can present. It calls the soul to the highest adventure it can undertake, a projected journey across the jungles, peaks, and deserts of the human spirit. The call is to confront reality, to master the self (Huston Smith, *The Illustrated World's Religions*).

Every religious tradition, from most primitive to most theological, comes to grips with that call in its own way. "It is clear that once we return to the depth or core of religion we find much more than dogmas, concepts, institutions, commands," says Matthew Fox in *One River, Many Wells* (Orbis Books, 1997). "We find a striving for experience of the Divine, however that can be spoken of; we find both form and formlessness, male and female, experience and practice."

These systems arising in or near the same geographical hub, as the world religions arise in either the Near or Far East, will by nature share underpinnings of belief and practice. We have already seen this to be true in the Near East. What essentially differentiates the world religions of the Far East from those in the Near East? We should examine a few crucial elements prior to visiting these faiths individually. These components do not, of course, apply equally to all of the religious traditions under consideration here, but they compose a pattern to be found in many.

◆ **Monotheism versus Monism:** The cardinal principle of the three Near Eastern faiths considered earlier is monotheism, trust in a single all-powerful, all-knowing, all-caring divinity. Perceptions of this all-encompassing deity may differ; i.e., the trinity of persons comprising the one godhead espoused by Christians smacks of polytheism to Muslims. Regardless, the core doctrine stands. In the Far East, it is possible to find polytheism or practically no weight given to the importance of gods. More often, one comes face to face with monism, a concept foreign to Near Eastern thought and perplexing to Westerners. Monism advocates a single reality which envelops all of creation rather than a single god. The monist umbrella allows for the adoption of many gods or none, as will become more apparent in a later discussion of Hinduism. For the moment, we need only to bear in mind that the monist mentality is every bit as central to Far Eastern thinking as the monotheistic mindset is to our own.

◆ **Creation, Inside and Out:** Chapter 2 sketched the Judeo-Christian notion of God as creator. Islam concurs, listing *God the Creator* among its ninety-nine names for Allah. All agree that, though everything in the universe sprang from the creating mind of God, God himself is above, beyond, and completely separate from that which he has made. God needs no created thing in order to be. God was before creation, keeps creation in existence, and will live on should creation at some point cease. In the Far East, the ultimate reality or world soul of which everything is a part does not subsist disassociated from the created universe. Everything emerges from this one reality; everything is absorbed back into it.

◆ **Survival of the Soul:** As you might imagine, embracing monism leads to seeing the worth and destiny of the individual person in quite a different light than belief in a personal God. Incorporation into the ultimate reality is not at all the same as eternal life in the company of a loving God. Since so much in religious development is predicated on the worldview of those involved, we would be correct in presuming that this major determinant is at work here, especially in regard to time.

◆ **Linear versus Cyclical Time:** Time is to some extent a human contrivance, although the length of days, years, etc., is predetermined. It's designed to keep us out of trouble even if it often seems to have the opposite effect (think of the brouhaha preceding the turn of the year 2000). The way we survey time determines the way we see much of the rest of our world. The Western mind looks at time as linear: past, present, future. Our faith revolves around the conviction that the person whose genetic code was set in place at conception is the person who will live on in some form as an identifiable entity. The theology of afterlife we hold today developed over many centuries as we see in the Hebrew and Christian Scriptures, but it can be fairly accurately summed up this way: "And just as it is appointed for mortals to die once, and after that the judgment . . ." (Hebrews 9:27).

Eastern thought takes a diametrically opposite approach, viewing time as cyclical. To use modern parlance, Westerners might express their idea concisely: "Once over and it's all over." Easterners could succinctly reply: "What goes around comes around." In the cyclical time mode, creation disintegrates and vanishes periodically, leaving a period in which only the sole universal reality exists until a new creation is formed. It may take eons for one cycle to be lived out, but in the end there can be nothing comparable to Pierre Teilhard de

Chardin's Omega point, marking the culmination of human history. It would merely mark the close of one cycle.

◆ **Resurrection versus Reincarnation:** Opposing outlooks on time leave the door wide open to opposing outlooks on human destiny. The Western attitude that each person is an inviolable entity, a creation never to be duplicated throughout the course of history, leads inevitably to the assumption that every human being must either endure perpetually or cease to exist altogether. This philosophy is consistent with the concept of linear time. Eastern philosophies with their accent on assimilation into an impersonal reality at the end of human life are more likely to see the possibility of this life reemerging in another form at some future date, an idea inherently aligned with credence in cyclical time.

For both camps, the choices made in the present life have repercussions for the next, whether this is taken to mean an extenuation of a particular individual life or the dawn of an entirely new one. Christianity teaches that the possibility of eternal life with God, i.e., salvation, though pure gift, is dependent on the use made of free will in accepting or rejecting this gift. Hinduism, on the other hand, argues that the manner in which life is lived at present will determine the quality of the next mortal life. These two positions, undergirding their respective traditions, shed light on the B-I-G question of where we go from here, but the light is diffused as they are polar opposites.

◆ **Monism versus Dualism:** The constant struggle between good and evil, a conflicting dualism, is at the heart of the Western worldview. The war against human weakness and sin is ongoing with the operative word being *war*. While clinging to the conviction that good will triumph in the end, many retain the notion that human history will crash to a halt in a climactic Armageddon pitting the forces of good against the forces of evil (which will put Hollywood special effects studios to shame). From the Far East spring two quite different ideas, monism and balanced dualism. Monism, as practiced in Hinduism and Buddhism, sees all as one and separation as illusion. As one is enlightened, it is possible to see more clearly one's place and one's possible contribution to the whole. Balanced dualism, as found in the Chinese Taoist tradition, acknowledges two interacting forces at work in the world but views them as balancing, rather than opposing, one another. If it is not a question of one being better than the other, then the desirable outcome must be harmony, bringing the two into accord. The enemy is not sin but discord. The dynamics of the natural supersede the dynamics of the supernatural. Sin for Westerners *is* discord as it disrupts humanity's harmonious relationship with God, so there is a common thread even if it proves to be materially different.

◆ **How We Know What We Know:** Throughout these pages, we have examined a number of routes for revelation from the Western perspective:

• sacred writings, notably, the books of the Bible for Jews and Christians and the Qur'an for Muslims;

• the divinity of Jesus for Christians, the prophecy of Muhammad for Muslims;

• tradition for all three.

We have considered as well the necessity of development in theology, which in turn leads to a deeper grasp of the revelation given us. The Eastern faiths, especially those of a monist bent, lean more heavily on those flashes of insight termed "enlightenment" (*Buddha* is a title meaning "the Enlightened One," much as *Christ* *is* a title meaning "the Anointed One"). Enlightenment cannot be commanded any more than we believe the grace of God comes as bidden. All that it is possible is to make oneself available, a waiting and open vessel. Eastern meditation is thus more an emptying of the conscious mind than the Western idea of concentrating the conscious mind. Westerners frequently comment on the extraordinary calm and patience evidenced by their Eastern counterparts. Conversely, Easterners more often than not think Westerners worry too much.

Hinduism

Judaism, the oldest of the Near Eastern faiths, is dated from the time of Abraham, usually thought to be c. 1850 B.C.E. This makes it a newcomer on the world stage when the spotlight swings to Hinduism. No one really knows how far back into the mists of prehistory the beginnings of Hinduism are to be found, but somewhere in the neighborhood of 3000 B.C.E. is not unreasonable. This does not make it the world's oldest religion (religious practice in some form seems to have existed as long as humanity has), but it certainly takes home the longevity award in the category of world religions.

Hinduism arose in the Indus Valley in the northwest corner of the Indian subcontinent. Little is obtainable from its primordial period which extends to c. 1500 B.C.E. This oldest form of the religion apparently featured a mother goddess. As previously noted, mother and/or fertility figures were objects of worship over a wide area. Local deities may have been venerated as well.

The years 1500–600 B.C.E. comprise the Vedic period, for during this time, the first holy writings, the Vedas, appeared. The Vedas show the influence of Aryans who overran the area at the beginning of this era, bringing with them a culture and religion conspicuously different from that of the native population. One of history's most engrossing stories records the migrations, peaceful or otherwise, and resultant intermingling of peoples; when two cultures come together, each is influenced to some extent by the other with the more dominant exerting the greater force for change. The Aryans brought to India an intricate sacrificial system of religious practice and a concept of afterlife closely resembling everyday existence in the here and now.

This changed completely with the arrival of the Upanishadic period, 600 B.C.E. to the present day, named for the second collection of sacred texts. *Upanishad* is a term that can be translated as "to sit before," as disciple to teacher. In Upanishadic writings, liberation from the present world surfaces and influences much of the rest. A third and much loved holy book, *The Bhagavad Gita,* relating the many adventures of the god Krishna, originated much later, probably in the third century C.E.

Until relatively recently, Hinduism remained implanted where the seed originally fell, on the Indian subcontinent. Modern transportation and communication technologies have encouraged wider dispersion of the Indian people and, with them, their religion. Since Pakistan was created as a separate and independent state for Indian Muslims, India's population is reported to be approximately 85 percent Hindu, and the predominant language is Hindi.

One reason Hinduism failed to move far beyond its geographical heartland is its disinterest in proselytizing. Hindus do not seek converts, believing it possible to incorporate religious ideas of nearly every ilk into its own extremely individualized system. Sometimes termed either the "Eternal Religion" because of its great age or the "Umbrella Religion" because of its willingness to embody so many widely divergent beliefs, Hinduism really has no ecclesiastical core, nor does it insist on a set of common doctrines or any particular form of worship. This makes Hinduism difficult for outsiders to comprehend. A visit to one Hindu temple may leave visitors convinced that they have just witnessed authentic Hinduism in action, not realizing that their next Hindu devotional experience may well include none of the elements just experienced.

Temples? Yes. But didn't we say that the emphasis is on one ultimate reality instead of one god? Also, yes. One does not preclude the other. This universal force is called *Brahman* (translation: "ever growing"). Brahman is indeed the absolute, but a pantheon of divinities also exists. One estimate runs to some 330,000,000, some obviously of enormously greater significance than others. So Hinduism is monist at its center but heavily polytheistic in its history and practice.

Inasmuch as Brahman is the only true reality, all else is illusion, or *maya*. The soul or life force of the individual person, *atman*, is in actuality a bit of Brahman and will in time, possibly after a number of lifetimes, be reabsorbed. Atman lives on after the death of the person in which it currently resides, but that person's identity is erased as atman moves on to another life. This is *samsara*, the transmigration of the soul, familiarly termed "reincarnation." What kind of life this will be has already been determined by the choices made in the life just ended. These decisions are grouped under the heading *karma,* or "actions." Whether atman moves up or down the karmic scale at death depends on a well-lived life or one less noble.

There are intimations of the Western free will theology here, but only within strict limits. Hindus do not have total control of the situation. They are restricted by the caste into which they are born. The majority of societies are characterized by some type of class structure, formal or informal. But India's caste system requires a person born into a given level to remain there for life. An American born into less than favorable circumstances might be expected to rise above the situation and make something of an unpromising life, the inbred Horatio Alger complex. A Hindu is more likely to be resigned to living a full lifetime wherever the karmic hand dropped atman.

Since the nation achieved its independence in 1947, the Indian government has formally discouraged the caste system, especially as it applies to the Harijans, who comprise the lowest caste; but a way of life so deeply ingrained for so many centuries will not yield quickly or easily. Even so, globalization continues to make the modernization of time-honored practices unavoidable. As Vatican II nudged Catholicism to express itself in ways more consonant with the post-World War II world, increasing commerce and interaction with the wider world prods Hinduism and other ancient faiths toward ever evolving manifestations of themselves. It may be easier on the one hand and harder on the other for Hinduism to accomplish this balancing act. As the Umbrella Religion, the acceptance of the new is a matter of course, but as the Eternal Religion, its roots run deep.

Can anything be done to improve atman's chances next time? The person can and should live the *dharma,* or "duties," of that caste meticulously. Dharma is defined for each caste, making free will only a partial factor. In time, possibly a great deal of time, atman will arrive at the top of the karmic scale. The highest caste is Brahmin. From there, *moksha,* "liberation," is at hand. Freed from its many samsara incarnations, atman is reassimilated into Brahman.

The vagaries of karma result in a respect for life in all its forms and a doctrine of nonviolence called *ahimsa,* which is especially associated with Mohandas Gandhi. Apart from the karmic possibilities, a conviction that all life is in effect Brahman implies that to take any life would be tantamount to killing Brahman. Jainism, an offshoot of Hinduism, takes this injunction especially seriously, sweeping the path ahead to avoid stepping on insects and wearing masks over noses and mouths to keep from accidentally ingesting them. While Jainism, together with Sikhism, are direct outgrowths of Hinduism, there is little agreement as to whether they should be considered sects of the parent religion or traditions unto themselves. For this reason, it is not uncommon to see them listed separately among the religions of the world.

The seemingly endless turning of the wheel of samsara is not altogether appealing. Over time, several paths have been carved out to accelerate the process: Knowledge, Devotion, and Action. The first might instead be termed the "Path of Discipline" as it requires exacting practices designed to bring body, mind, and spirit together, to yoke them, i.e., *yoga*. Assistance in centering the mind may come through *mantras*, the chanting of a transcendental word or phrase such as *Om*, or *mandalas*, whose elaborate artistic designs quiet mental activity. Such exercises, requiring long years of rigorous preparation, are not for everyone. Neither is the Path of Action, whose four stages (student, householder, hermit, and pilgrim) encompass a lifetime and are open only to men of the three highest castes.

For most, the Path of Devotion holds the most appeal. *Bhakti*, devotion to one particular deity, directs this path. Those who commit their destiny to such a god may pray at home altars, roadside shrines, or temples dedicated to the god they have chosen. Their hope lies in these devotional acts, known as *puja*. *The Bhagavad Gita* ("The Celestial Song") has a special place in the hearts of these worshippers. Sri Prakasa, former governor of the Indian State of Maharashtra, prays tribute in his introduction to an English translation of this classic work:

> The *Gita*, in its own beautiful manner, has portrayed for us the fundamentals of our ancient faith and is of the highest practical value for man. It prevents him from being too elated by success or too depressed by failure. It enables him to try to shed the various passions and emotions that keep us attached to life that

is fleeting and encourages him to seek the eternal by performing his tasks in the world in a spirit of detachment.

Three primary Hindu deities deserve a mention: Brahma, Vishnu, and Siva. Brahma, the creator, is considered far above human worship. Few temples in his honor are to be found. Vishnu holds the world in existence and periodically comes into the world in various forms called *avatars,* one of whom, interestingly, is the founder of Buddhism, and another is the beloved Krishna. And it is Siva, the destroyer, who brings each cycle of creation to a fiery close.

The Hinduism of the twenty-first century will doubtless remain tied to its ageless moorings while at the same time venturing further into uncharted waters. The virtues of self-discipline, duty, meditation, and nonviolence which define it are not always lived out. Regrettably, the same can be said for every great faith. No people ever lives up to its noblest ideals in all times and places. Neither should an entire tradition be judged solely on the basis of its flaws and failures. The effort to grow and grasp continues, sometimes spawning a completely new approach in the process. This is what happened with Buddhism.

Buddhism

In the foothills of the towering Himalayan Mountains of modern Nepal c. 563 B.C.E., a most extraordinary child was born. Exactly how extraordinary would not become obvious for more than thirty years, but even at the moment of birth this child was destined for rare privilege since his father was a local chief and a member of the affluent Hindu warrior caste. The boy was named Siddhartha (his given name) Gautama (his family name) but has become legendary through the title he would acquire later in life, Buddha, the enlightened one.

Local seers predicted great things for the infant as well. In a story with faint overtones of the presentation of Jesus in the Temple (Luke 2:22–38), predictions were made concerning the child's future. Siddhartha's future could take one of two paths, either of which could lead to a life of distinction and honor. He could be the conqueror of the world or its savior. If there was ambiguity in the minds of the fortune-tellers, there was none in the mind of Gautama Senior. World savior was out of the question; world conqueror was the only reasonable course, and if unfolding events and ensuing years had to be tweaked a little to achieve the desired end result, it was a small price to pay.

As a consequence, Gautama Junior (and it is to him we shall refer henceforth) had a most peculiar upbringing. Fearful that once confronted by poverty, illness, aging, and death, his son would naturally want to do what he could to alleviate them and thus be drawn into the role of savior, the father simply made sure the boy never saw such things, growing up in a kind of Nepalese Disneyland surrounded by beauty, luxury, and ease, totally oblivious to what most of us know as real life. When he traveled, runners were dispatched to clear the surrounding area of any sights which might raise questions or prove disturbing.

As was probably inevitable, the system broke down as the boy grew to manhood, and on succeeding days the young Gautama encountered first a frail old man, then a disease-ridden person lying by the wayside, and last a corpse. This would be enough to shake almost anyone, but for the unworldly Gautama the experience was traumatic. What could begin to explain what he had seen? The shelter of his fabricated world lost forever and desperately seeking answers, Gautama renounced all he owned or would ever own, left his wife and child, shaved his head, and set off in search of clarification. He was nearly twenty-nine years old.

How much of this story is fact and how much the stuff of legend is impossible to say, but in whichever category it belongs, the tale nicely sets the stage for Gautama's public life and the unfolding of his teaching. Picking up the thread, Gautama first sought clues to the baffling questions that plagued him through the traditional avenues of his own Hindu tradition. For six years, he practiced the harsh asceticism prescribed by the Hindu thinkers of the time. In fact, he applied himself to these regimens so assiduously that his health was all but broken. Weakened by extreme fasts, he nearly died. As his strength returned, Gautama was struck by the unmistakable truth that all his efforts had had no result. He had now lived at the two extremes of human existence, great luxury and great austerity. Neither had produced the desired outcome.

Seating himself beneath a fig tree (often called the Bo Tree for *Bodhi*, or "enlightenment"), he proposed to remain there until enlightenment came. As the light of the morning sun pierced the darkness, with it came the Great Awakening, and Gautama had become a Buddha. Thereafter, when asked what he was, a question also put to Jesus, if you recall, he answered, "I am awake." As Huston Smith describes it: "While the rest of humanity was dreaming the dream we call the waking human state, one of their number roused himself. Buddhism begins with a man who woke up." Upon this awakening, Gautama spoke to the five companions who accompanied him. This first sermon inaugurated his new role. In it, he shared important insights.

The far ends of life's spectrum, opulence and mortification, having failed, Gautama concluded that wisdom dictated a Middle Path or Way which many regard as revolutionary in religious thought, given the high esteem in which self-denial is held by many faiths. Soon Gautama went out on another theological limb, dismissing references to gods, and therewith the rationale for worship. He believed that keeping to this Middle Path would bring peace and tranquillity, insight and knowledge, perhaps full enlightenment, and, in due time, arrival at Nirvana. This final goal is based on the Hindu Brahman, but unlike it in ways we shall explore later.

Following the Middle Path, Gautama taught, is made infinitely easier through the acceptance of the Four Noble Truths to which his search had led him:

- all life involves suffering;
- much of this suffering is caused by the desire for personal fulfillment (greed);
- such suffering will end only when these greedy, selfish cravings are overcome;
- the way to accomplish this is to follow the Eightfold Path.

So critical to Buddhism is the Eightfold Path that an eight-spoked wheel has become a common symbol for this faith, as the cross has for Christianity. Each of the eight virtues advocated is preceded by the adjective *right*, not right in the eyes of a deity, but right in their contribution to the equanimity of the individual and the peace and order of society.

◆ **Right Understanding (Knowledge, Views):** The substance of what is needed here is already at hand in the Four Noble Truths. Additionally, it is necessary to see clearly what any particular situation is, or any decisions made regarding it will inevitably be skewed. Individuals must do all they can to see themselves and their world objectively.

◆ **Right Intentions (Thoughts, Aspirations):** If the first step is designed to demonstrate where the problem lies, the second spurs the person to decide whether or not he or she is ready to move with single-minded purpose toward a lifetime goal of surmounting the problem. The process begins with a personal commitment to the renunciation of those worldly pleasures that in the end prove harmful.

These initial steps are frequently united under the heading "Wisdom," while the next three together are "Morality," and the final triad "Concentration."

◆ **Right Speech:** Just as the Letter of James decries the damage done by that small but powerful body part, the tongue (James 3:1–12), the Buddhist emphasis on Right Speech advises a person to first and foremost be *aware* of what emerges from the mouth. Before failings can be remedied, they must be recognized. The accent in this step is on truth and charity.

◆ **Right Behavior (Action):** Within this step lies a subset of the Five Precepts, which will bring to mind parts of Western religions' Decalogue. Again, the significance of these commandments covering interpersonal relationships is not to be found in their originality but in their becoming integral to a person's relationship with God. From the Buddhist perspective, God does not enter into it, but what was said in an earlier chapter still holds: these injunctions are basic anywhere community living is found. Buddhism's Five Precepts are:

- Do not kill.
- Do not steal.
- Do not lie.
- Do not be unchaste.
- Do not take drugs nor drink intoxicants.

- **Right Livelihood:** When asked which aspects of Buddhism they found most appealing and instructive, my students almost invariably cited Right Livelihood. While this mandate is clearly part of Near Eastern belief as well, it may not be given quite the force it receives from Buddhism. Simply put, Right Livelihood enjoins one to shun occupations that may be destructive or have a harmful effect on others. These include slave traffic and prostitution for obvious reasons, tax collection because those engaged in this profession enjoyed the same unsavory reputation they did in Jesus' time and place, alcoholic beverage production, and weapons manufacture. Buddhists believe their choice of vocation should be consistent with their religious beliefs, promoting their own spiritual growth and the common good. An extract from the Greek Hippocratic oath works well here: "First, do no harm."

- **Right Effort:** Gautama's teaching is insistent in the matter of exertion. Progress, let alone enlightenment, requires one's constant and diligent application. As Huston Smith explains:

  The only way fetters can be shaken off is by what William James called "the slow dull heave of the will." "Those who follow the Way," the Buddha said, 'might well follow the example of an ox that marches through the deep mire carrying a heavy load. He is tired, but his steady, forward-looking gaze will not relax until he comes out of the mire. Only then does he relax."

- **Right Mindfulness:** "All we are is the result of what we have thought." This sentence opens the revered Buddhist writing, *The Dhammapada,* and provides valuable insight into Gautama's philosophy. For him, the mind constituted the single greatest influence on both the individual and the world. Vice takes a back seat to ignorance as the most pervasive threat. To this can be traced many of humanity's woes. Charles Dickens expressed something of the same sentiment in *A Christmas Carol,* when the ghost of Christmas Present opens his robe to reveal two children, a boy and a girl, "yellow, meagre, ragged, scowling, wolfish." Appalled, the miserly Scrooge asks their identities to which the spirit replies: "This boy is Ignorance. This girl is Want.

Beware them both, and all of their degree, but most of all beware this boy, for on his brow I see that written which is Doom, unless the writing be erased."

Gautama counseled resolute self-examination which would result in self-awareness which would, in turn, result in seeing oneself and the world as it actually is. Buddhists zero in on the sights and sounds, tastes and touches of the moment in which they find themselves in an effort to be mindful of that which is, not that which was or will be. Deception, whether its source is interior or exterior, must in the end fail. Right Mindfulness brings the great wheel nearly full circle in its resemblance to Right Knowledge or Understanding.

◆ **Right Absorption (Concentration):** This eighth and final step involves meditative techniques in many ways similar to Hindu yoga, a tradition Gautama knew well from his years of ascetic practice. Drawing on his ancestral faith, the Buddha advocated quieting the mind and broadening the vision, thereby opening the way to possible enlightenment. "Something happened to the Buddha under that Bo tree," writes Huston Smith, "and something has happened to every Buddhist since who has persevered to the final step of the Eightfold Path. Like a camera, the mind had been poorly focused, but the adjustment has now been made."

In the *Declaration on the Relationship of the Church to Non-Christian Religions (Nostra Aetate),* the bishops of the Second Vatican Council wrote of this ancient faith: "In various forms of Buddhism, too, people understand that the current situation is not sufficient and that there is a path for life on which people can reach greater freedom or enlightenment."

Nirvana

By choosing the Middle Way, acknowledging the Four Noble Truths, and striving to follow the Eightfold Path, a Buddhist can hope eventually to arrive at life's ultimate goal, nirvana. Like the Hindu Brahman from which it derives, nirvana is difficult to explain in words which resonate in Western ears. Like Brahman, nirvana is impersonal and so cannot be defined as God. There is, however, a second definition which sheds a somewhat different light. Huston Smith explains:

Buddologists have compiled a list of characteristics of *nirvana* that seem to place it in the Godhead camp. *Nirvana* is permanent, stable, imperishable, immovable, ageless, deathless, unborn and unbecome; it is power, bliss, and happiness, the secure refuge, the shelter, and the place of unassailable safety; it is the real Truth and the supreme Reality; it is the Good, the supreme goal and the one and only consummation of our lives, the eternal, hidden, and incomprehensible peace.

Got that? Now comes the hard part: Buddha did not believe in the Hindu *atman,* or "soul," but rather in *an-atman,* "no soul." According to Gautama, human beings are not inhabited by any kind of ethereal spirit that continues in existence after their deaths. Without abandoning the notion of reincarnation learned as a Hindu boy, Gautama recast it to allow for the continuation of some elements of personhood. After death, a person is reborn into a life that will be totally new. Still, certain personal traits will survive in some form in the new life. There is a karmic connection, but no substantial element survives. Everything then, and everyone, is transitory.

Given this sense of the radical impermanence of things, we might expect the Buddha's answer to the question of whether human beings survive bodily death to be a flat no, but actually his answer was equivocal. Ordinary persons when they die leave strands of finite desire that can only be realized in other incarnations; in this sense at least these persons live on (Huston Smith, *The Illustrated World's Religions*).

Theravadas, Mahayanas, and Zen Some

As noted earlier, the majority of world religions break down into two or three primary divisions. In the case of Buddhism, there are two, and they are rather colorfully described as vehicles or rafts, denoting their role ferrying believers across the river of life. The Mahayana constitutes the Larger Vehicle or Big Raft, making the smaller group the Hinayana. Understandably discontented with this designation, this faction took instead the title *Theravada,* the "Way of the Elders." To these might be added a third form of Buddhism, that found in Tibet and known as *Vajrayana,* the "Diamond Vehicle." Zen, the expression of Buddhism often most familiar to Westerners, is actually a school of Mahayana, one heavily influenced by Taoism. A sketch of each of the four follows.

◆ **Theravada:** Members of this sect see themselves as the guardians of Buddhism as it was originally conceived. Their counterparts in Judaism would be the Orthodox. Sri Lanka (at one time Ceylon) has until recently been a cultural and religious test case due to its isolation as an island nation. Converted to Buddhism early on, Sri Lanka was, and to a great extent remains, a laboratory wherein Theravada Buddhism continues unchanged, although it is also widely practiced in other southern Asian countries such as Myanmar (formerly Burma), Thailand, Laos, and Kampuchea (once Cambodia). Conservative in its outlook, some would say stern, Theravada Buddhism foregoes devotion to deities in the tradition of Gautama who, incidentally, never made any claim to divinity for himself. To Theravada Buddhists, the Buddha is the "thus gone," not to be prayed to but to be modeled through his writings and through meditation on his teachings.

Those whose practice of Theravada has given them what we might call a saintly aura are known as *arhats,* or "worthy persons," but nearly all young men and some young women of this sect spend at least a few months experiencing the religious life in a monastic setting. Such communities are called *sanghas.* Theravadins number about one hundred twenty-four million and accept as scriptural only the earliest writings in the ancestral Pali language. These writings consist largely of sayings of the Buddha, *The Dhammapada,* where it is written:

The way is eightfold.

There are four truths.

All virtue lies in detachment.

◆ **Mahayana:** The Larger Vehicle is made up of some one hundred eighty-five million Buddhists who can be found in all parts of the world, but whose roots lie deep in Tibet, China, Korea, Vietnam, and Japan. As Loretta Pastva points out it is more liberal in outlook

281

(*Great Religions of the World,* Saint Mary's Press, 1986): "In each of these countries Buddhism has been a powerful civilizing force. In turn, each of these countries has changed Buddhism, each developing a special, national form of the religion."

Mahayana grew out of a council in 390 B.C.E, nearly a century after Gautama's death, after a dispute with the Theravadins over such issues as an increased role for laity, more flexibility in blending with local cultures, and the role of Gautama himself whom Mahayanas view as somewhat more than human. "The more open stance that lay behind these issues," Pastva asserts, "led the Mahayanists to develop a form of Buddhism that was more inclusive, accommodating, and universal in its appeal." It also led to the emergence of gods and goddesses, many of whom were simply absorbed from the prior traditions of Buddhist converts. These deities could be seen as Buddhas themselves and revered as before.

Holy writings, called *sutras,* accumulated over several centuries, eventually reaching such volume that the Judeo-Christian Bible looks like paperback Cliff's Notes by comparison. Formal worship was instituted under a monastic priesthood. In other words, in the hands of Mahayanas, Buddhism became a true religion. Theravadin arhats gave way to the *bodhisattva,* "one whose essence is perfected wisdom." Mahayanist willingness to adapt to particular cultures encouraged a variety of manifestations, one of the most prominent being the Pure Land Buddhism of China. Westerners who may never have heard of Pure Land are usually acquainted with another sect that originated in China but found its natural home in Japan—Zen.

◆ **Zen:** "Entering Zen is like stepping through Alice's looking glass. One finds oneself in a topsy-turvy wonderland where everything seems quite mad . . . charmingly mad for the most part, but mad all the same. It is a world of bewildering dialogues, obscure conundrums, stunning paradoxes, flagrant contradictions, and abrupt non sequiturs, all carried off in the most urbane, cheerful, and innocent style imaginable" (Huston Smith, ibid.).

Like other Buddhist sects, Zen traces its origins to Gautama himself, claiming that there was an element to Buddha's teaching that escaped many of his followers. Pointing to the Flower Sermon in which no words were uttered but a golden lotus was held out to his disciples by the Buddha, Zen practitioners do not depend on words exclusively to bring them to the instantaneous burst of insight they call *satori* ("awakening").

The golden age of Zen began with a patriarchal figure named Hui-neng (638–713 C.E.), who became the abbot of a monastery of five hundred monks in northern China. By the time of his death, his followers numbered in the thousands. His grave marker is inscribed: "According to his doctrine, non-doing is reality, emptiness is the truth, and the ultimate meaning of things is vast and immovable. He taught that human nature, in its beginnings as well as in the end, is thoroughly good and does not require any artificial weeding out, for it has its roots in that which is serene."

Probing Zen spirituality would require a great deal more space than can be allotted here. A succinct overview comes from *Zen for Beginners* (Writers and Readers Publishing, 1985): "Zen Buddhists believe that the universe is a single, dynamic interdependent whole, and that the more distinctly we become ourselves, the more we realize that we each exist only in relation to this whole. Buddhism calls this interdependent condition 'emptiness.' Everything is caused by something and, in turn, is cause for something else."

There is a story of a young man who was being interviewed by a Zen master with a view to becoming his disciple. His host asked his guest to tell him everything he already knew while tea was being poured. The young man began to speak, and the older man began to pour. Soon the tea overran the cup, spilled across the tea table, and cascaded onto the floor. Dismayed, the young man paused in his recitation to inquire whether the Zen master could not see what was happening. "You are too full," said his host regretfully. "Had you stopped talking before the tea cup filled, we could have begun. As it is, you must empty yourself and return another time."

Heavily influenced by China's Taoist philosophy, Zen places great store in even the most humble aspects of everyday life, believing that enlightenment may come under any and all kinds of conditions. Zen is nothing if not practical. If Buddha wisdom cannot be found in the ordinary activities of daily existence, it is unlikely to be found. Should you run across the title *Zen and the Art of Motorcycle Maintenance* (Harper Trade, 2000) or *The Inner Game of Tennis* (Random House, 1997) on a bookstore shelf, it is very real and to be taken seriously, however wry it may at first seem. Humor is not at all out of place in the Zen landscape. In fact, Zen may well be the only widely practiced faith in which humor is prominently featured. Yet, paradoxically, Zen found wide acceptance among Japan's samurai because they taught the concentration required in the martial arts coupled with a philosophy which overcame the fear of death.

These same Zen principles help others to create delicate art and peaceful gardens. Many who know little else about Zen have heard of *koans* and *haiku*. A koan is a sentence, a question, or merely a phrase designed to jar the mind out of its usual manner of thinking. The best known koan is probably: "What is the sound of one hand clapping?" Haiku is a unique form of poetry consisting of seventeen syllables, no more, no less. Perfect examples of the Zen aversion to wordiness, haikus try to capture the essence of one ephemeral moment in the natural world or in human life. Just as Zen borrowed liberally from Taoism, so other religions, including Christianity, today incorporate elements of Zen thought into their own traditions with great benefit.

◆ **Vajrayana:** Like its siblings, this child of Gautama was born in India but quickly migrated to Tibet, where in essence it forms Tibetan Buddhism today. The heart of Vajrayana is something called *Tantra*. This Sanskrit word can be interpreted to mean "extension," as in augmenting the teachings of the Buddha or "weaving," as in the interconnectedness of all things. The Tibetan path can, it is believed, lead to nirvana in only one lifetime by pulling together (weaving) all elements of human potential. The idea is not so much to rise above or overcome the usual sensual distractions as Zen teaches, but to weave these into one's spirituality.

Hinduism's mantras and mandalas help to control and focus speech and sight while *mudras* center on movement through ritualized gesture and dance. Joining every part of human energy into a synchronized whole helps to lift the spirit to a divine elevation, thus hastening nirvana. The spiritual development of the individual is paramount, as can be discerned in the writings of the Dalai Lama. He states in *Ancient Wisdom, Modern World* (Little, Brown & Co., 2001):

> Spirituality I take to be concerned with those qualities of the human spirit—such as love and compassion, a sense of responsibility, a sense of harmony—which bring happiness to both self and others. Whilst ritual and prayer, along with the questions of nirvana and salvation, are directly connected with religious faith, these inner qualities need not be, however. Thus there is no reason why the individual should not develop them, even to a high degree, without recourse to any religious or metaphysical belief system. This is why I sometimes say that religion is something we can perhaps do without. What we cannot do without are these basic spiritual qualities.

Who exactly is the Dalai Lama? *Lama* is the Tibetan form of *guru*. In *Responses to 101 Questions on Buddhism* (Paulist Press, 1999), John Renard defines the role of the Dalai Lama this way: "His tradition holds that the Buddha-nature is reincarnated endlessly in certain chosen individuals whose coming is foretold and who manifest certain signs on their bodies soon after birth." The present Dalai Lama, winner of the 1989 Nobel Peace Prize, fled to India following the Chinese takeover of Tibet in the 1950s. He has become an internationally recognized spiritual leader who quite possibly has done more to advance understanding of Tibetan Buddhism in exile than might ever have been possible under normal circumstances.

Buddhism is an intricate belief system that is not served well by the cursory overview allotted here. If this brief sketch has contributed even a little to a more accurate grasp of this ancient faith and a greater respect for it, it will do for starters. Further exploration of Buddhism, indeed of all the religious traditions introduced here, is highly recommended. Christians can learn much from the teachings of Gautama to enrich their own faith. The late Trappist monk Thomas Merton was convinced of this. In *Thoughts on the East* (New Directions, 1995) he wrote:

> Both Buddhism and Christianity are alike in making use of ordinary everyday human existence as material for a radical transformation of consciousness. Suffering, as both Christianity and Buddhism see, each in its own way, is part of our very ego-identity and empirical existence, and the only thing to do about it is to plunge right into the middle of contradiction and confusion in order to be transformed by what Zen calls the "Great Death" and Christianity calls "dying and rising with Christ."

Two Great Pillars of Chinese Religious Thought: Confucianism and Taoism

One would expect innovative philosophical perspectives from one of the world's foundational cultures, and China does not disappoint. Distant geographically in earlier times and politically in our own, China has remained an enigma in many ways to Westerners. And when we think of China, religion is rarely first on our word association list. Although the free practice of religion is said to be assured today, the past half-century records a history of religious repression, if not outright oppression.

There can be little doubt that the two primary strands of religious belief are no longer practiced to the extent they once were. Truth to tell, a great many modern Chinese have only a minimal acquaintance with them. Nonetheless, the Chinese character has been formed by them in the sense that Confucianism and Taoism have so greatly influenced the formation of Chinese culture. This, together with the staggering statistic placing roughly one-fifth of the earth's population in China, is reason enough to retain these two classical systems on the list of truly "world" religions.

The Way of Taoism

> The Tao moves in every direction at once,
> its essence is fluid and yielding.
> It is the maker of everything under the sun:
> and everything comes out of nothing.
>
> —*Tao Te Ching,* chapter 40

Taoism (the *T* is pronounced *D*) is nicely encapsulated in that pithy excerpt from its most famous writing, but it takes a bit of explaining before it really penetrates the Western mind. Actually, I'm not sure it ever does entirely. It bears repeating that, as is usual with Far Eastern faiths, we are not dealing with a god here. *Tao* is generally translated "Way" or, sometimes, "Path." Its aim is to bring balance to the universe or, more often, to recognize and work within that harmony which already exists. Judith Berling writes ("Taoism, or the Way," *Focus on Asian Studies,* vol. II, #1, "Asian Religious"):

> Taoism can also be called "the other way," for during its entire history, it has coexisted alongside the Confucian tradition, which served as the ethical and religious basis of the institutions and arrangements of the Chinese empire. Taoism, while not radically subversive, offered a range of alternatives to the Confucian way of life and point of view. These alternatives, however, were not mutually exclusive. For the vast majority of Chinese, there was no question of choosing between Confucianism and Taoism. Except for a few straightlaced Confucians and a few pious Taoists, the Chinese man or woman practiced both—either at different phases of life or as different sides of personality and taste.

The founders of the two religions were virtual contemporaries, living most of their years in the sixth century B.C.E. Taoism came into being under "the Old Master," Lao-Tzu (possibly the most widely used of several alternate spellings). Swathed in a mantle of legends, the historical Lao-Tzu is difficult, if not impossible, to unveil. There are those who deny his very existence. For those who accept his historicity, it seems reasonable to sort these bare-bones essentials from the maze of lore surrounding him:

- he was a minor official of substantial intellect with an unchallenging (read: boring) position in the court of the Chou emperors;
- he elected to live a simple life;
- he looked for more profound meaning for his own life through a deeper comprehension of the universe as he understood it;
- at one point in his life, he encountered K'ung Fu Tzu (Confucius).

As the story goes, Lao-Tzu, wearied by lack of acceptance of his teachings, picked up and left, traveling toward Tibet on a water buffalo. Along his route, he encountered a man at an outpost who begged him to remain or, if he would not, to at least leave behind his wisdom in writing. After three days, Lao-Tzu completed a concise compilation, the *Tao Te Ching,* the *Way and Its Power* (Grove/Atlantic, 1972). So beloved is this seminal text that quotations from it are found nearly everywhere in China and in Chinese literature.

Initially, Taoism was more philosophy than religion, and one branch of the tradition remains so today. In all probability, Lao-Tzu drew on much older nature worship, seeing behind the created world an indiscernible force, which he called Tao. The harmonious balance he saw displayed in nature could, he thought, be made to bring order and stability to human affairs as well. His goal was to improve life as it is lived in the here and now. Aspirations for an afterlife were secondary if they merited consideration at all.

Balancing one's individual life or the shared existence of the people according to nature's equilibrium is called *wuwei,* literally "no action." The Beatles song *Let It Be* contains something of the same philosophy. In practice, *wuwei* means something closer to "minimal action," precluding unnecessary struggle against what must be seen as the natural current. At the core of every person is *Ch'i,* the "breath of life," the "air of survival." It falls to each person to nurture this *ch'i* in every manner possible. For this reason, physical health and exercise are given emphasis comparable to virtue. Here the Three Jewels are accented: compassion, moderation, and humility. Precipitous action is avoided because, believing as they do in the balance of all things, Taoists might use the modern dictum "Don't rock the boat." Taoists insist that human nature is innately compassionate, that people tend toward good. So goodness shown to another without hope of reward, more often that not, will elicit a similar response.

The harmonious balance of the universe is typified in Taoism by *yin* and *yang*. Illustrated by the *t'ai chi* symbol, a circle in which the dark side *(yin)* is juxtaposed with the light side *(yang)* with a small amount of each apparent in the other, this is perhaps the finest example of the harmonious dualism discussed earlier. It is not a question of yang being superior to or more desirable than yin or vice versa. It is merely a matter of keeping the two in equilibrium: male and female, light and dark, cold and heat, life and death. The opposites are not seen as competitive with one another but complementary. Humans upset the balance, and from this imbalance all manner of ills beset the world. Thomas Merton interpreted it this way: "The world is a sacred vessel which must not be tampered with or grabbed after. To tamper with it is to spoil it, and to grasp it is to lose it."

Taoist principles, especially since they essentially espouse a philosophy more than religion, find their way into many other traditions, including Christianity. A Catholic theology professor, a Taoist priest, and a Chinese-American humanities professor found surprising parallels between Christianity and Taoism and published them in what they call "an experiment in inter-traditional understanding," *The Tao of Jesus* by Joseph A. Loya, Wan-Li Ho, Chang-Shin Jih (Paulist Press, 1998). Without ignoring their considerable differences, the wisdom of the two faiths converges in more areas than many would imagine, demonstrating yet again how much each of us stands to benefit from respectfully learning from the other.

Some Taoist appearances on the contemporary scene seem humorous until they are examined more closely. Benjamin Hoff saw Taoist thought coming from Pooh—yes, *that* Pooh—and proceeded to create two short works to prove his point, *The Tao of Pooh and The Te of Piglet* (Viking/Penguin, 1994). In his introduction, Hoff claims to have been involved in a discussion of the Great Masters of Wisdom. In the course of the debate, he read to the group a short passage:

"What's that?" the Unbeliever asked.

"Wisdom from a Western Taoist," I said.

"It sounds like something from Winnie-the-Pooh," he said.

"It is," I said.

"That's not about Taoism," he said.

"Oh, yes it is," I said.

"No, it's not," he said.

"What do you think it's about?" I said.

"It's about this dumpy little bear that wanders around asking silly questions, making up songs, and going through all kinds of adventures, without ever accumulating any amount of intellectual knowledge or losing his simpleminded sort of happiness. *That's* what it's about," he said.

"Same thing," I said.

Taoism continues to intrigue while at the same time defying satisfactory definition. Merton may have spoken for us all when he said: "If there is a correct answer to the question, 'What is the *Tao?*' it is: 'I don't know.' "

Confucius Says . . .

Some years back, "Confucius says . . ." jokes were making the rounds, each comprised of some inane observation on human behavior. What a disservice to turn the astuteness of so great a mind into fortune cookie wisdom.

K'ung Fu Tzu—Confucius to us—was born in 551 B.C.E. in the days of the same Chou dynasty that shaped Lao-Tzu. The moral laxity of the period may have contributed to the musings of the two men whose thoughts long survived it. Born into an aristocratic family and broadly educated, Confucius, like Lao-Tzu, found himself trapped in an unimportant administrative job unworthy of his talents. His need for greater fulfillment led him into teaching. He established a school where he taught history and the principles of good government to upper class young men. One of his writings, *The Analects,* preserves some of the give and take between teacher and students which he experienced over the years. By the way, *The Analects* is sometimes called *The Sayings of Confucius* and no doubt gave rise to all those "Confucius says . . ." quips. On a less facetious note, this work demonstrates once more the tendency of people in all times and places to preserve the sayings of those they revere.

Years of observation, especially years spent in the court of the emperors, brought home to Confucius the undeniable truth that life was far from perfect. His teaching, then, in the manner of Gautama and Lao-Tzu and often the biblical prophets, concerned itself with issues where, in more contemporary jargon, the rubber hits the road. In concert with the Buddha and the Old Master, his interest lay with people rather than gods.

His views on the transmigration of the soul, however, were nothing like Gautama's. Reincarnation is completely absent from Confucian thought. At death, a person becomes an honored ancestor. The funeral service is often conducted by a Buddhist or Taoist priest, occasionally even a member of the Christian clergy. An altar is found in many Confucian households where the spirits of deceased ancestors are installed.

Confucius and Lao-Tzu had this much in common with the biblical prophets: they all had a terrible time getting their message heard, never mind accepted. The Confucian call to the crumbling Chou dynasty and to all those suffering as a result was to reform, to return to China's golden age as described in the writings of the ancients. Certain Confucian writings are actually titled *The Way of the Ancients.* For Confucius the teacher, hope lay primarily in education accompanied by social ethics. To this end, one of Confucius's most lasting contributions was his editing and commentary on the time-honored *Book of Changes,* or *I Ching,* a Chinese classic still very much in use. Confucian morality is frequently divided into six categories:

- **Li:** courtesy, propriety, manners; in other words, proper behavior
- **Hsiao:** familial love, especially between parents and children
- **Yi:** uprightness; righteousness from which the cosmic energy, *te,* flows
- **Xin:** reliability and honor
- **Jen:** the greatest Confucian virtue, involving humaneness, good-heartedness, the kind of harmonious relationship with others also advocated by Taoism
- **Chung:** good citizenship

Confucius would today be termed a pacifist or, at least, a dove, believing as he did that learning the art of peace would bring greater good than continuing to teach the art of war. If he were among us now, Confucius might sigh and lament the sad fact that the world still has not learned this lesson, that people still don't listen. Yet, more listened than he perhaps realized. His wise counsel continues to be sought in his writings.

Adherence to the models listed above has not only shaped individual Chinese lives but over time has formed in large part the nature of the Chinese people. Although Confucianism is practiced by as few as six million people today, it will always retain an influence far exceeding those numbers simply because roughly one in five persons on this planet owes his or her formation to it.

Shintoism: The Way of the Gods

Across the Sea of Japan, another "way" governed the lives of the people for centuries. Its name, strangely, is Chinese in origin, *Shin tao,* the Way of the Gods. Long before its formal beginnings (c. 500 B.C.E.), this tradition sprang from primordial roots in animism. Animists believe that spirits indwell all living things, not only the animate (humans, beasts, birds, sea creatures), but the inanimate as well (trees, all forms of plant life, even water and stones). These gods, or *kami,* numbered as high as eight million. Their realms were roughly divided into gods of the sky and gods of the soil. Life for humans was to a great degree determined by the interaction between the two domains.

Animism was not the only force molding Shintoism, however. Equally as important was the fierce devotion to Japan itself. The Japanese considered their land the center of the world, not an unreasonable conclusion for an island nation. Shinto lore tells of a kami couple who gave birth to the islands. Their children became deities themselves with their daughter assuming the role of sun goddess. She became the primary deity, the rising sun became the nation's symbol, and from her, it was believed, the Japanese royal family was directly descended. The land was not only treasured, it was precious. Its limits clearly defined by the crashing sea on every side of every island, the demarcation of Japan's territorial resources was immediately obvious. Every square foot was of inestimable value.

This would probably have been felt just as deeply had Japan had boundless acreage because it wasn't simply the geography that was valued, it was those who peopled it. Shintoism taught that the souls of individuals themselves became kami after death. Those who ranked higher in life would rank higher in death. The emperor, therefore, with his divine lineage, ranked highest of all both in life and in death. The last Japanese monarch laying claim to divine status was Hirohito, who occupied the throne during World War II. One of the stipulations of the surrender agreement ending that war was that Hirohito would make a radio address to the nation, repudiating his divine status. It has been said that this announcement was nearly as devastating to the Japanese people as the loss of the war itself.

Imbued by kami, all of life and all of nature has a sacredness. Every human is kami's child. Harking back once more to the Second World War in the Pacific, allied ships and planes were harried by the *kamikaze,* suicidal pilots who crashed their planes, often loaded with explosives, into warships. It was hard for Western minds to comprehend the kind of devotion that would lead to such sacrifices. Kami, coupled with *kaze* ("wind"), is usually translated "divine wind," which is the way the young pilots saw themselves as they plunged to their deaths in defense of their beloved homeland. Spotlighting warlike aspects only is terribly unfair to Shinto, which traditionally has promoted the same kinds of peaceful harmony found across the sea in the Chinese faiths.

Shintoism is not heavily theological. Its Four Affirmations are more pragmatic than religious:

◆ **Tradition and the Family:** Here again one finds noticeable similarities with Taoism and Confucianism. Such devotion to family and to the family's honor has contributed to maintaining low crime rates.

◆ **Reverence for Nature:** To be close to nature is to be close to the gods, the kami. The beauty of Japan's gardens attest to this belief. Even urban Japanese avail themselves of immaculately groomed parks and may have in their apartments Bonsai trees, perfect miniatures of the real things.

- **Misogi (Personal Hygiene):** If the old adage "Cleanliness is next to godliness" found a place in the Western world, the Japanese have made of it an art form. Hand washing and bathing are indispensable components of daily routine, especially prior to entering a shrine.

- **Matsuri:** The honoring of kami, among them ancestors, is interwoven into everyday life and is expressed flamboyantly during Shinto festivals.

Shinto shrines dot the land, each devoted to a particular kami. One enters such a shrine through a *tori,* a special gateway marking the line between this world and the world of the gods. It is expected that followers will visit shrines especially during those times of life generally seen as rites of passage for special priestly blessings. *Origami,* paper of the spirits, adorns many Shinto shrines. This lovely art form, which has become popular in the Western world in recent years, is designed from folded paper. The paper is never cut out of respect for the tree who gave its life to make the paper.

Shintoism did not take the usual path of branching into several major divisions until the nineteenth century. Since then, Shintoism has been comprised of:

- **Jinja:** Here are preserved the aboriginal forms of Shintoism from primeval times. The vast majority of shrines are Jinja. Until the end of World War II, Jinja was closely associated with State Shinto, complete with emperor worship.

- **Kyoha:** This arm of Shintoism is made up of thirteen sects founded in the nineteenth century by individual worshippers.

- **Folk:** This group really does not observe Shintoism in any religious sense but may participate in certain rituals and practices.

The three are not mutually exclusive. It is not unknown for a member of one to place a votive offering at the shrine of another. This is in keeping with Shinto respect for other religions generally. And although Shintoism has holy writings, most date from as late as the eighth century C.E. and none are scriptural in the same sense as the Bible or the Qur'an.

How many Shinto practitioners are there today? It's virtually impossible to determine, given the flexibility of public practice allowed. Educated guesses run from three million at the low end to more than one hundred million at the high. No matter what the exact numbers may be, one thing is undebated: Shintoism has had and continues to exert a powerful influence over Japanese character.

Conclusions?

Our time spent with the five great religions of the Far East has again been much too brief, and it would be wrong to draw hard and fast conclusions from these introductory remarks. A little light has been shed on vital areas such as their concept of god(s), their ethical and moral codes, and their history—but only a little. Utilizing some of the works cited in the text, you may wish to delve more deeply into some or all of these faith traditions. You may find, as I have, that in doing so you will come to a more comprehensive grasp and appreciation of your own faith and will nurture a growing respect for religions you once thought totally alien.

Our conclusion could easily be that of the bishops of the Second Vatican Council in their *Declaration on the Relationship of the Church to Non-Christian Religions:*

> There is absolutely no ground, then, to offer anyone less than full dignity and respect. Therefore, we outrightly reject and abhor any discrimination against anyone based on race, color, condition of life, or religion. We beg all Christians to be at peace and to maintain good relations with all peoples.

A Handy-Dandy Checklist

In becoming better acquainted with other religions, asking the following questions can be helpful:

- What are the major beliefs and/or principal values of this religion?
- What are its important practices?
- What are the elements of its prayer or spirituality?
- What can we as (Catholic) Christians learn from this faith to enrich our own?

- What can followers of this religion learn from (Catholic) Christianity to enrich their own tradition?
- What do you find most appealing about this religion and why?
- What do you find least appealing about this religion and why?
- How can knowledge of this faith be useful in situations encountered today?

CHAPTER THIRTEEN

Pushing Through
the Curtain of Death

O f the Three Big Questions, the one which is by turns the most intriguing and the most disturbing is the last. Where are we going? Some say nowhere; it all ends with our last breath. But historically, those are the minority. Humankind has apparently harbored some notion that death is not as final as it appears for so long that there is evidence of it even among humanoids, those not usually considered human in the fullest sense of the word.

Neanderthals, who lived between 100,000 and 50,000 B.C.E., placed flint tools, food, even flowers in graves, implying that the dead would have need of these in the life to come. Their successors, the Cro-Magnons, practiced these customs as well, adding to them second burials of bones once the flesh had disintegrated, a habit found much later in a host of societies, including many ringing the Mediterranean Sea. Cro-Magnons sometimes painted these bones red, symbolizing the blood which they apparently recognized as the life force. Other examples could be cited, but these are sufficient to illustrate the common occurrence of a rudimentary idea that life continues past death.

Long Life in the Here and Now

In light of modern Christian theology, one would almost naturally expect belief in life eternal to have been its cornerstone always. One would be wrong. The complexity of this dogma required slow, patient development over tens of centuries. God has afforded humanity the same kind of consideration human parents grant their children. Basic lessons must be mastered first. Once these are absorbed and intellectual development permits a deeper grasp, it's time to introduce intermediate material. Maturity finally makes it possible to present advanced information. Even then, comprehension will never be complete for, in this area at least, the student will never surpass the teacher.

Among God's most endearing characteristics is his willingness to accept humans, individually or collectively, where they are and as they are, not where God wishes they were or as they could be, but where they really are and as they really are at a particular moment in their history. We may not recognize this as often as we should, but God is incredibly courteous.

Our Hebrew ancestors in the faith can be forgiven if their glimmerings of afterlife shed very little light. The second creation account may have something to do with this. "[T]hen the LORD God formed man from the dust of the ground, and breathed into his nostrils the breath of life; and the man became a living being" (Genesis 2:7). Had you lived three to four millennia ago, what conclusion would you have drawn from these words? Man (Adam) is basically a chunk of earth who lives only because of the animating breath of God. When this breath is withdrawn at death, man goes back to being a chunk of earth. Is that all there is? Yes.

If this is the case and there's no hope of going anywhere later, then life's primary object has to be to remain here as long as possible. In the early stages of the relationship between the biblical patriarchs and their unfamiliar and often baffling God, it was believed that the greatest of all blessings was long life. "Live long and prosper" predated *Star Trek* by a good many centuries. The exaggerated ages show the extent to which these people, and others like them, were believed to be favored by God.

With their hopes securely pinned to long life, our spiritual forebears would have been interested in retirement planning. Their twin concerns match closely our own. Anyone who plans to stick around this planet awhile will necessarily require two things to make life tolerable, much less enjoyable: health and wealth. The bestowal of these, too, came to be seen as indicating divine approval; their lack, divine disapproval. To be impoverished, to be physically impaired, to suffer from a chronic ailment, i.e., leprosy, was evidence of God's displeasure. Such a person had clearly been guilty of serious sin or, if not that particular person, then surely a parent or ancestor for whose transgressions this person must now atone.

What the Neighbors Believed

Early Israelite thought could have drawn on better formed philosophies at either end of the Fertile Crescent. Egypt, where later Israelites spent some four centuries, had an extremely intricate theory of life after death. The Egyptian *Book of the Dead* lays this out in detail. Aristocrats, especially royalty, could extend their existence through mummification. Still, this elaborate belief system seems to have had little impact on Hebrew/Israelite/Jewish thinking. This may be attributable to the pantheon of deities involved which offended the monotheistic sensibilities of Abraham's descendants.

It would appear that Abraham's home turf had far greater influence here. The Sumerian idea was that the only type of survival which could be expected after death would be found in a one-size-fits-all abode into which every person was eventually swept, there to lie in an inert semi-existence. When the concept of afterlife began to evolve in the Hebraic mind, it was to this model that they turned.

Nether World vs. Netherlands

If you recall, the cosmology of the ancient Near East featured a flat earth, supported by pillars and crowned by the dome of the firmament. In this worldview, the abode of the dead was located below the earth's surface in that shadowy realm of darkness plunging into the depths of the unknown. It is referred to biblically either as Sheol or the nether (archaic for "under") world. While confusing this with the present-day Netherlands is apt to get you in Dutch, the origins of the terms are surprisingly similar. Today's Netherlands are largely areas which would be under the sea were it not for some fancy engineering footwork. The biblical nether world is an amorphous domain below the surface of the earth, also encroached upon by water.

Ah, the prototype for hell, you may observe. Not yet. You're skipping ahead. Initially, the abode of the dead was precisely that: the place people went when they died—everybody, without exception. There was no moral component to it whatsoever. The godly and the ungodly, everybody went, but not one moment sooner than absolutely necessary. No one anxiously anticipated entry into Sheol. ". . . and the ground opens its mouth and swallows them up, with all that belongs to them, and they go down alive into Sheol" (Numbers 16:30b). "If I look for Sheol as my house, if I spread my couch in darkness, if I say to the Pit, 'You are my father,' and to the worm, 'My mother,' or 'My sister,' where then is my hope? Who will see my hope? Will it go down to the bars of Sheol? Shall we descend together into the dust?" (Job 17:13–16) "For in death there is no remembrance of you; in Sheol who can give you praise?" (Psalm 6:5)

"Down" into the "darkness" of the "pit." Scarcely consistent with the expectations of modern Christians! But these weren't modern Christians. They weren't modern Jews either. They must be met on their own turf and respected there. As the centuries rolled and the Chosen became better acquainted with their previously unknown God, attitudes began to shift. It seemed incongruous for the God they were experiencing to countenance identical fates for everyone, taking no account of their faithful service or lack thereof. In the interest of justice, some differentiation had to be made.

Returning to the accepted cosmology of the age, if the abode of the dead lay beneath the flat earth, the abode of the gods (or, in the case of the Israelites, God) was positioned above the firmament. Up and down are constants in this universe, but not in ours. Retaining this imagery today perpetuates an obsolete mentality which restricts, among other things, our concepts of God and human immortality. The good go up, and the bad go down? It's hard to make this stick when confronted with the latest photographs from the Hubble telescope. Growing beyond outdated ideas leaves us free to consider insights scientists and theologians present to us today.

Heaven or Heavens?

Heaven (singular) and heavens (plural) are just the same, only different. Oddly, the plural may predate the singular. The heavens initially had much the same meaning as the firmament, that great expanse overhead traversed by sun and moon, dotted by stars and clouds. "In the beginning when God created the heavens and the earth . . ." (Genesis 1:1). ". . . and the windows of the heavens were opened" (Genesis 7:11b). "The LORD will open for you his rich storehouse, the heavens, to give the rain of your land in its season and to bless all your undertakings" (Deuteronomy

28:12a). "The heavens are telling the glory of God; and the firmament proclaims his handiwork" (Psalm 19:1). Nonetheless, the heavens are clearly the dwelling place of God; there is little, if any, intimation that mere mortals may hope to reside there as well. Heaven, singular, will come to designate humanity's final destination, the realm of God.

There and Then Emerges from Here and Now

Hope continued to focus on the here and now. "Do not fret because of the wicked," advises the psalmist; "do not be envious of wrongdoers, for they will soon fade like the grass, and wither like the green herb. Trust in the LORD, and do good; so you will live in the land, and enjoy security" (Psalm 37:1–3). More time is required before a coherent concept of ongoing life begins to emerge. When it does, it can be partially ascribed to the Greeks, whose philosophy saw humanity not so much as animated clay as encapsulated spirit. From this perspective, death does not extract the life force; it releases the spirit. Eventually, what would become Christian belief saw the issue not as either/or but as both/and. It takes body, mind, and spirit to make up an authentic human being. If this being is to survive death, all three components must somehow survive as well. But that's some distance down the road.

By the time the hands on the historical clock had moved to the sixth century B.C.E., a new vision had been born. This can be taken quite literally in Ezekiel's famous symbolic account of the dry bones (Ezekiel 37:3–14). In this apocalyptic illusion, God shows the prophet a field strewn with bleached bones:

> "Mortal, can these bones live?" . . . "O Lord GOD you know." . . .
> Thus says the Lord GOD: I am going to open your graves, and bring you up from your graves, O my people; and I will bring you back to the land of Israel. And you shall know that I am the LORD, when I open your graves, and bring you up from your graves, O my people. I will put my spirit within you, and you shall live, and I will place you on your own soil; then you shall know that I, the LORD, have spoken and will act," says the LORD.

The emphasis is still on life in this world, but the notion of some sort of positive afterlife is definitely there. One of the first notes of a future resurrection chorus may have sounded here, albeit a somewhat general, all-encompassing one.

Daniel, another book awash in apocalyptic imagery, puts a more personal spin on it. The tales told in Daniel had probably been around awhile before finding their way into the written word in the third to second century B.C.E. Among them is a story of the end of the age (which also, coincidentally, forms the end of the book):

> "Many of those who sleep in the dust of the earth shall awake, some to everlasting life, and some to shame and everlasting contempt. Those who are wise shall shine like the brightness of the sky, and those who lead many to righteousness, like the stars forever and ever" (Daniel 12:2–3).

As might be expected, the latest books of the Hebrew canon provide the most developed concept of afterlife. In the mid-second century B.C.E., Judas Maccabeus, the "hammer" who swept Greeks from the battlefield and their Hellenistic influence from the Jewish Temple, made his own memorable contribution to this developing theology. Upon inspecting the bodies of his fallen comrades strewn across the battlefield, Judas was dismayed to find many of them adorned with amulets of pagan gods. After offering fervent prayer,

> [H]e also took up a collection, man by man, to the amount of two thousand drachmas of silver, and sent it to Jerusalem to provide for a sin offering. In doing this he acted very well and honorably, taking account of the resurrection. For if he were not expecting that those who had fallen would rise again, it would have been superfluous and foolish to pray for the dead. But if he was looking to the splendid reward that is laid up for those who fall asleep in godliness, it was a holy and pious thought. Therefore he made atonement for the dead, so that they might be delivered from their sin (2 Maccabees 12:43–45).

Here, too, is found biblical justification for the Catholic doctrine of purgatory since, as previously noted, prayer for the dead would be fruitless were they definitively consigned to either heaven or hell. Because they belong to the Deuterocanonical books which are part of the Septuagint, the Books of Maccabees are not found in modern Bibles using only the Hebrew canon.

The Deuterocanonicals also contain the Book of Wisdom. Thought to have been composed in the Jewish community living in Egyptian Alexandria close to 100 B.C.E., this is in all probability the final biblical work written. Originating in the city founded and named for Alexander the Great, the Book of Wisdom, not surprisingly, reflects a Hellenistic outlook and was drafted in Greek. The first reading used in Catholic funeral liturgies is frequently Wisdom 3:1–9:

> But the souls of the righteous are in the hand of God, and no torment will ever touch them. In the eyes of the foolish they seemed to have died, and their departure was thought to be a disaster, and their going from us to be their destruction; but they are at peace. For though in the sight of others they were punished, their hope is full of immortality. Having been disciplined a little, they will receive great good, because God tested them and found them worthy of himself; like gold in the furnace he tried them, and like a sacrificial burnt offering he accepted them. In the time of their visitation they will shine forth, and will run like sparks through the stubble. They will govern nations and rule over peoples, and the Lord will reign over them forever. Those who trust in him will understand truth, and the faithful will abide with him in love, because grace and mercy are upon his holy ones, and he watches over his elect.

If the notion of resurrection was becoming more widely held by the time the Hebrew Scriptures ended, it was by no means universal. As the curtain rose on Jesus' experience in the early first century C.E., there was obvious disagreement on this matter on the part of the Pharisees and Sadducees, the two most prominent Jewish sects of the day (Acts 6:10).

Enter Jesus

At the outset of Jesus' ministry, ideas on afterlife had a long way to go to reach consensus. Most influential in the Jewish religious world at the time were the Pharisees, whose focus seemingly lay more on messianic expectations and the establishment of an independent Jewish state than on states of life following death. The smaller Sadducee sect, which numbered many priests and prominent laymen among its members, rejected the idea of afterlife out of hand. Hellenistic Jews (those profoundly affected by Greek philosophy) were most inclined to believe in the immortality of the soul and the continuation of human life in some type of ideal setting.

Jesus raised this debate to an unprecedented level by insisting that, not only could his followers look forward to unending life, but that life would be lived in union with the loving God who was his Father. This is particularly evident in the gospel of John where eternal life and unity of Father and Son are dominant themes. The term *life* is used twenty-seven times in the fourth gospel, and ten of these are preceded by the adjective *eternal*. On four occasions, John speaks of resurrection. Several of John's characteristic *I am* statements have to do with life:

- "I am the bread of life" (6:35, 48).
- "I am the resurrection and the life" (11:25).
- "I am the way, and the truth, and the life" (14:6).

Only John recounts the raising of Jesus' friend Lazarus. Castigated by Lazarus' sister Martha for not arriving on the scene in time to save her brother:

> Jesus said to her, "Your brother will rise again." Martha said to him, "I know that he will rise again in the resurrection on the last day." Jesus said to her, "I am the resurrection and the life. Those who believe in me, even though they die, will live, and everyone who lives and believes in me will never die. Do you believe this?" (11:23–26).

Martha assents. But then, she's known Jesus up close and personal over an extended period. Now that humanity has known Jesus over a period of a couple of millennia, do we believe this? Do we even understand it?

When I have put the question of resurrection to groups of Catholic adults, the most common responses miss the mark considerably. Some understand resurrection as applying solely to Jesus, but it is obvious from

Jesus' comments to Martha that this is not the case. Others see resurrection as referring to the survival of the disembodied soul after death. But
Jesus was not a disembodied soul when he appeared to his disciples
following his own resurrection, a point he was most anxious to make to
his frightened followers:

> "Look at my hands and my feet; see that it is I myself. Touch me
> and see; for a ghost does not have flesh and bones as you see that
> I have." And when he had said this, he showed them his hands
> and his feet. While in their joy they were disbelieving and still
> wondering, he said to them, "Have you anything here to eat?"
> They gave him a piece of broiled fish, and he took it and ate in
> their presence (Luke 24:39–43).

Jesus' demonstration must have provided graphic proof since those
watching would have been well aware of the impracticality of feeding a
spirit who is sadly lacking teeth, an esophagus, a stomach, and a digestive
tract.

Are we to believe, then, in the resurrection of our physical bodies?
This is what Jesus tells us according to all four gospels. However, a full
decade before any written gospel came to be, Paul dealt with the issue
movingly in chapter 15 of his First Letter to the Corinthians. The
excerpts that follow are shameless teasers whose purpose is to send you
running to your Bible to read the chapter in its entirety:

> Now if Christ is proclaimed as raised from the dead, how can
> some of you say there is no resurrection of the dead? If there is
> no resurrection of the dead, then Christ has not been raised; and
> if Christ has not been raised, then our proclamation has been in
> vain and your faith has been in vain (15:12–14).

The terminology is strong and unambiguous. Startling as it may be
for us to hear that so much of our foundational belief system rests with
Christ's resurrection, even short reflection shows it to be true. Jesus'
teachings are not discounted, but the issue here is not what Jesus *taught*
but who Jesus *is*. And who Jesus is after his resurrection is no longer the
historical Jesus, but the cosmic Christ. Never in this chapter does Paul

use the name Jesus unless in conjunction with Christ. If God has not raised Christ from the dead, Paul insists, then God has been misrepresented as well (1 Corinthians 15:15–18). "If for this life only we have hoped in Christ, we are of all people most to be pitied" (15:19).

Having laid out the negative arguments, Paul turns to the bright side: "But in fact Christ has been raised from the dead, the first fruits of those who have died" (15:20). He then embarks on a short theological dissertation involving the nature of Christ's role, ending with, "The last enemy to be destroyed is death" (15:26).

Our New, Improved Selves

Dialogue about our own resurrection usually results in the question, Will I still be me? In a word, yes. Life once created is never destroyed. As the Preface of the funeral liturgy reminds us, "Life is changed, not ended." Speculation as to whether we'll look like ourselves is another matter. Which self are we talking about? The seven-pound lump of squalling, red fury which first saw the light of day? The tenuous tot starting kindergarten? The teen torn between acne and academics? The young professional ready to take the world by storm? The newly married idealist? The much more realistic parent striving to make ends meet? The empty nester? The retiree? These and many other selves surface in the course of a lifetime.

Paul turns pragmatic:

> But someone will ask, "How are the dead raised? With what kind of body do they come?" Fool! What you sow does not come to life unless it dies. And as for what you sow. you do not sow the body that is to be, but a bare seed, perhaps of wheat or some other grain. But God gives it a body as he has chosen, and to each kind of seed its own body. Not all flesh is alike (15:35–39a).

> So it is with the resurrection of the dead. What is sown is perishable, what is raised is imperishable. It is sown in dishonor, it is raised in glory. It is sown in weakness, it is raised in power. It is sown a physical body, it is raised a spiritual body (15:42–44a).

> Listen, I will tell you a mystery! We will not all die, but we will all be changed, in a moment, in the twinkling of an eye, at the last

trumpet. For the trumpet will sound, and the dead will be raised imperishable, and we will be changed. For this perishable body must put on imperishability, and this mortal body must put on immortality. When this perishable body puts on imperishability, and this mortal body puts on immortality, then the saying that is written will be fulfilled, "Death has been swallowed up in victory. Where, O death, is your victory? Where, O death, is your sting?" (15:51–55).

For those who believe in Christ, death is never the final answer; life is—more life, better life, life with infinitely greater possibilities than anything we are able to envision. For Christians, then, despair in the face of death is not an option because despair sees no hope. For Christians, sadness and grief at parting are normal and natural, but beyond these we see reunion and great joy. Where some, even in the formative stages of our own belief system, saw death as a brick wall, impossible to breach, scale, tunnel under, or skirt, we see a curtain through which we push to begin the fulfillment of the life for which we were created.

Jesus was himself no stranger to the wrench of being parted from loved ones by death. Led to the tomb of his friend Lazarus, "Jesus began to weep" (John 11:35). Not even the knowledge that he would momentarily have Lazarus back with him was enough to entirely blunt Jesus' grief. Here, too, there is a lesson for us as Joyce Rupp points out in *Praying Our Goodbyes* (Ave Maria Press, 1988):

> If we were left with Jesus' emptiness and desolation, if we had only our kinship with him in his goodbyes, it would not be enough to sustain us in our own leave-taking. We would draw comfort, but we would not have the hope of a future hello. The beauty of the paschal mystery, the mystery of passing over from death to life, of moving from goodbye to hello, is that it ends with hello. If Calvary is the deepest goodbye that anyone has ever known, then the resurrection is the greatest hello that anyone has ever proclaimed.

Christianity is, then, the most hopeful of religions. The resurrection proclamation can be summarized using the word *LIFE* as an acronym: **Life Is For Ever!** How this life will be lived we cannot say in much detail, and if we possessed the details, there is little likelihood we would be able to grasp them from our current perspective. It might be comparable to attempting to explain this world to a child about to be born into it. How to define colors? How to portray the sea? How to describe music? Such efforts are doomed since the *in utero* infant has no frame of reference. Perhaps the sure and certain knowledge that we will live forever in the presence of the God we have gradually over centuries come to discern is all we really need to know of heaven, just as the shock of the realization that we will live forever separated from this God is all we really need to know of hell.

What we can clearly see is that theology of afterlife, completely missing in the earliest Hebraic traditions, evolved by the time of Jesus into an intensely hopeful foundational tenet of Christian faith. And so it remains as we are reminded every Sunday of the liturgical year. Falling as it does on the first day of the week, the Christian Sabbath constitutes a continuous commemoration of Jesus' resurrection and, by extension, our own. No longer do we feel bound by a life/death continuum. For us who believe we will follow where the cosmic Christ has led, it will ever be life/death/LIFE!

Olam Ha-Ba: The Jewish World to Come

Does contemporary Jewish belief in afterlife parallel that of Christianity? Yes, no, and maybe. Jesus' teaching, the essence of Christian thought, must necessarily be factored out when comparing the two traditions. Even so, one would imagine certain similarities should remain inasmuch as Christianity stands on the broad shoulders of its Jewish parent, and Jesus was in every way Jewish himself. Kinship in this area does exist, but often it's a distant relationship.

The emphasis on this life's blessings which figured so prominently in the early Hebrew Scriptures remains very much a part of Jewish thought today. Jews tend to accent the improvement of the life they're living and soft pedal concerns about afterlife. As a result, the door is left open to a variety of conceptions and opinions, none of which is accepted unanimously throughout the Jewish community. While some of the Orthodox understand the souls of the just to be rewarded in something very like the Christian heaven, others believe these souls to be reincarnated again and again, and still others advocate a waiting period in a kind of staging area for the coming of the Messiah. The souls of the unjust may be subjected to torment or may simply cease to exist.

The concept of resurrection of the dead, introduced late in the Hebrew Scriptures and upheld by the Pharisees, is a longstanding tradition in Judaism, but the concept differs notably from its Christian counterpart. For Jews, this resurrection will occur during the messianic age, called in Hebrew *Olam Ha-Ba,* the "World to Come." This term can be used to denote a spiritual afterlife as well. It is believed that the Messiah will usher in a utopian period of peace and prosperity. When this occurs, the righteous who have died will be resurrected in order that they may enjoy the fruits of their labors. Each person's place in the Olam Ha-Ba is predicated upon his or her actions in life, but life is not to be lived with a view to "earning" a more meritorious position. Like Christians, who also do not believe it possible to earn their way to heaven, Jews insist that doing good in the service of God and others is sufficient reward.

Olam Ha-Ba can also be interpreted as a higher state of being to be lived by the good in *Gan Eden.* While this does translate to the "Garden of Eden," it does not refer to the biblical home of Adam and Eve, but rather a place of blissful perfection. Although some believe Olam Ha-Ba to be reserved exclusively to Jews, others maintain that the righteous of all traditions may expect to share in it. Only the pure may expect to go to Gan Eden immediately following death. For most, there is a stop in *Gehinnom* or *Gehenna.* The ancient *Sheol* also turns up in reference here from time to time. Precisely what this place is remains unclear. Some characterize it as a place of temporal purification, not unlike the Catholic purgatory. Others believe it to be a time of attitude adjustment when the choices made in life are finally seen free of distortion and understanding is unclouded, also reminiscent of purgatory. Contrition is the natural result. After a period not to exceed twelve months, the soul is released.

Christians may find it surprising that the notion of reincarnation is not foreign to Judaism, and it is true that many Jews do not accept it. Its advocates, notably the Hasidic branch of the Orthodox, defend the idea by saying that it helps explain the time-honored tradition that every Jewish soul of every time and place was in some sense present when

Moses brought the tablets of the Law down from Sinai and was party to accepting the Covenant. Jews rejecting reincarnation construe the tradition as meaning that, because the soul is created prior to the body, unborn souls were somehow present at Sinai.

Judaism, then, accommodates considerable diversity with regard to eschatology. The afterlife, while meaningful, does not form the hub around which modern Judaism revolves.

Allah's Day of Judgment

The issue of life after death is unquestionably central to the world of Islam. "How can you deny God, since you were dead and God gave you life; and will then kill you, and then bring you to life; then you will be returned to God." "Be they Muslims, Jews, Christians, or Sabians, those who believe in God and the Last Day and who do good have their reward with their Lord. They have nothing to fear, and they will not sorrow" (*Qur'an: The Cow*, 28–29 and 62).

No thought of reincarnation surfaces in Islamic belief. Life is a fleeting, one-time opportunity which, if lost, will not come again. Muslim philosophy is in this respect in keeping with that reflected in the Letter to the Hebrews: ". . . it is appointed for mortals to die once, and after that the judgment . . ." (Hebrews 9:27). The choices made in life will determine the fate of the soul after death in the heavens or hells realistically described in the Qur'an. Those who live enslaved to their passions during this transitory existence are sure to rue that decision in the end. Those martyred for their faith, however, may expect immediate admittance to paradise.

This determination of the soul's ultimate fate will be made on a Day of Judgment marking the end of this world when all of humankind will be resurrected to undergo the judgment of Allah. For Muslims, this culmination of human history is so essential that they see belief in God as irrelevant without it. Only then can the full justice and mercy of God be manifest. Acutely aware of their accountability for their decisions and actions, Muslims tend to be extraordinarily self-disciplined.

Among the reasons cited for belief in an afterlife whose rewards or penalties are commensurate with life choices are these:

- such a belief has been consistently preached by the prophets;
- societies professing this belief tend on the whole to be morally stable;
- human capacity for rational thought naturally leads to this conclusion;
- the divine attributes of justice and mercy are meaningless without it.

Near Eastern Eschatology

The religions of the Near East, then, all espouse an afterlife in some form, their ideas sometimes intertwining, sometimes veering off onto conspicuously different paths. Their points of commonality are condensed by Huston Smith in *Forgotten Truth* (HarperCollins, 1976):

> Body dies, but the soul and spirit that animate it live on. . . . At death man is ushered into the unimaginable expanse of a reality no longer fragmentary but total. Its all-revealing light shows up his earthly career for what it truly was, and the revelation comes at first as judgment. The pretenses, rationalizations, and delusions that structured and shaped his days are now glaringly evident. And because the self is now identified with its Mind or vital center rather than its Body . . . Mind's larger norms, to which the embodied ego paid little more than lip service, now hold the balance. It is thus that in hell man condemns himself; in the Koran it is his own members that rise up to accuse him. With [forgiveness] the balance is restored and the distortions, too, are seen to have had their place . . . the Mind recedes as the Body earlier did at death, and the self . . . passes on to the Soul's immortal center which is now freed for the beatific vision. Lost in continual adoration and wonder, it abides in the direct presence of the Living God who is Being Itself. Beyond this, where the film that separates knower from known is itself removed and the self sinks into the Spirit that *is* the Infinite. . . . Ah, but we can say no more. We have reached the Cloud of Unknowing, where the rest is Silence.

Far Eastern Eschatology

The understanding of time as cyclical has had a profound impression on Far Eastern beliefs concerning death and afterlife. The Western notion of a particular person surviving whole and intact in some form perpetually is entirely foreign. As Huston Smith puts it: "In the Hindu view, spirit no more depends on the body it inhabits than bodies depend on the clothes they wear or the houses they live in. 'Worn-out garments are shed by the body. Worn-out bodies are shed by the dweller.' (*Bhagavad-Gita*)." *Atman,* a bit of *Brahman,* is the animating soul which moves up and down the karmic scale until eventually attaining *moksha,* union with the ultimate reality. When this occurs, some Hindus reserve the hope that some trace of atman may remain, thus preserving a certain apartness. Most, however, believe it is absorbed into the universal soul.

This unyielding doctrine of the impermanence of the world and all it contains carries over into a related tradition, Buddhism, but there are differences. Buddhism sees the human being as an interactive, ever changing blend of thoughts, feelings, and perceptions. The resulting energy situates itself in a new body upon the death of the old. Some hold that this action takes place immediately; others believe it takes forty-nine days. In any case, the new life is dependent upon the same kind of karmic considerations found in Hinduism. Gautama may have lifted this idea from his ancestral faith although there is evidence that samsara was not a belief widely held by Hindus during Gautama's lifetime and that Buddhists may in the long run have had more influence on Hindus in this regard than the other way around. The categorical destination is Nirvana for Buddhists, Brahman for Hindus.

For an "enlightened" opinion of the nature of nirvana, we turn again to Huston Smith:

> The question of a realized soul's existence after death is a case in point. If the Buddha had said, "Yes, it does live on," his listeners would have assumed the persistence of our present mode of consciousness which the Buddha did not intend. On the other hand, if he had said, "The enlightened soul ceases to exist," his hearers would have assumed that he was consigning it to total oblivion, which he also did not intend. On the basis of

this rejection of extremes we cannot say much with certainty, but something can be ventured. The ultimate destiny of the human spirit is a condition in which all identification with the historical experience of the finite self will disappear, while experience as such will not only remain but be heightened beyond recognition.

As an inconsequential dream vanishes completely on awakening, as the stars go out in deference to the morning sun, so individual awareness will be eclipsed in the blazing light of total realization. Some say "the dewdrop slips into the shining sea." Others prefer to think of the dewdrop as opening to welcome the sea itself. If we try to form a more detailed picture of the state of *nirvana,* we shall have to proceed without the Buddha's help, not only because he realized almost to despair how far the condition transcends the power of words, but also because he refused to wheedle his hearers with previews of coming attractions. A thousand questions remain, but the Buddha is silent.

The twin pillars of Chinese philosophical tradition, Confucianism and Taoism, do not often focus their eyes on the skies, preferring instead to deal with more earthly matters. Reverence for ancestors, vital to Chinese practice, was seen by Confucius as secondary to the claims of real live people. He spent little time speculating about what might lay beyond death. "Recognize that you know what you know, and that you are ignorant of what you do not know. Hear much, leave to one side that which is doubtful, and speak with due caution concerning the remainder. . . . You do not yet understand life. How can you understand death?" This does not mean Confucius banished all thought of the supernatural. He believed in some kind of cosmic power for good and that, because of this, human nature was called to be just and righteous. But a mystic he was not.

One of the greatest exponents of Taoist thought from the third century B.C.E., Chuang Tzu, opined:

Life is the companion of death, death is the beginning of life. Who understands their workings? A person's life is a coming together of breath. If it comes together, there is life. If it scatters, there is death. And if life and death are companions to each other, then what is there for us to be anxious about?

Final Destination?

Of the Three Big Questions, the third, must of necessity remain the most clouded. Scientific spheres from astronomy to archaeology are almost daily broadening our understanding of where we came from. Great minds from every religious tradition continue to add to the contributions of their forebears, clarifying what should be expected of the life we live in this world. But thus far, neither scientists nor religious philosophers are able to provide a clear picture of our final destination. As we have seen, ideas of what may lay ahead are sharply divided, debunking yet again the cavalier notion that it doesn't matter much which religion one practices as they are all pretty much alike. Their differences are many, and we ignore them at our peril. They are important and must be addressed intelligently and respectfully.

As Christians, however, we can certainly lay claim to the most hopeful eschatology offered by the great world faiths. As the individual persons we are today, we shall in time face death. When we do, we will not find there an impenetrable wall, but a gossamer curtain which we push through like the ultimate birth experience to begin the life for which we were created with the loving God who waits for us. The life begun here goes on and on for **Life Is For Ever!**

Now the Fun Begins

A s our time together nears its end, it is my hope that you find yourself ravenously hungry. This modest manuscript has been able to set before you only a taste of the feast awaiting those willing to explore the world of religion. I have attempted to whet your appetite, enticing you to refill your plate again and again from the limitless banquet of delights at hand. Go back for seconds in the Hebrew and Christian Scriptures. Sample entirely new flavors from one or another of the world's great religious traditions.

As tempting as it may be to spend an inordinate amount of time at the dessert table, enjoying what is sweet and slides down easily, remember that the greatest nourishment lies in the main courses, which may require a substantial amount of chewing before they can be swallowed, let alone digested. At the end of such a meal, we are usually comfortably satisfied or stuffed—for the moment. We will hunger again, and although we are not promised a permanent surfeit during this life, we are never asked to settle for bread and water or, worse yet, pureed baby food. "Blessed are you who are hungry now," said Jesus, "for you will be filled" (Luke 6:21a).

The daily hunger of the body is but one of many human hungers. If our bodies, minds, and spirits never hungered, we would probably never seek to be fed. Just as the strained peaches of infancy eventually give way to more solid fare, so what we were fed as children in religious education classes and schools should yield to a more mature menu. Paul was troubled by the Corinthians' failure to grow: "I fed you with milk, not solid food, for you were not ready for solid food. Even now you are still not ready" (1 Corinthians 3:2).

The road to maturity is never easy, always beset by growing pains. More than one case of heartburn can be expected. Working one's way through the religious smorgasbord for our discoveries will not always agree with us. As Catholics become increasingly familiar with their long and checkered history, they will encounter chapters which leave a very bad taste in their mouths, i.e., the Crusades, the Inquisition, forcible conversion, etc. The antacid of relief comes in the realization that we usually act more consistently with our God as we come to understand him better and in apologies which have been forthcoming in recent years from hierarchical circles as high as the papacy itself. This indicates that we are learning; we are maturing. Commenting on the role of Catholicism in the Crusades, sociologist Andrew M. Greeley had this to say:

> This is not a defense of holy wars . . . be they Islamic, Christian, or Zionist. As the pope has said, thank God we do not do things that way anymore. It is rather a defense of the complexities of the human story and an assertion that it is fruitless to claim moral superiority in the great drama of history. Quite the contrary, when someone apologizes for the past—by which they mean that they propose never to let the brutalities and the mistakes of the past happen again—people of good faith and good will will attempt to join in efforts for greater understanding.

The more we attempt to comprehend the God at the center of all human history and be faithful to this God, the less likely we are to repeat even well-intentioned errors of the past or, worse, devise new ones. We see the will of God in a more positive, less negative or fatalistic, light. Says Father Edward Hays in *The Old Hermit's Almanac* (Forest of Peace Publishing, 1997):

> What is frequently called God's will could also be called God's dreaming. God's vision for how creation and the world should be is a dream that has been shared with each of us. Prophets, visionaries, and mystics have been gifted with pieces of God's dream, helping to flesh out important pieces of the living vision for all of us.

In *White Smoke: A Novel about the Next Papal Conclave* (Forge/Tom Doherty Assoc., 1996), Father Andrew Greeley introduces his readers to a Spanish cardinal, Don Luis Menendez, who is on many people's short list of possible successors to the current pontiff. The fictional Don Luis's television address merits the careful consideration of grownup Catholics, Christians of other traditions, and sincere seekers everywhere:

> Above all we must not be afraid. . . . We must change in order to remain the same. We must not confuse what is essential in the Church with that which is mutable, no matter how ancient it may be. . . . No custom and no tradition which is not of the essence of our message, no matter how old, should escape reexamination. And no custom and no tradition, no matter how new, should be abandoned until we carefully consider the costs of doing so. We must be willing to experiment, to modify, to refine before we change.
>
> We must be open, sensitive, and above all hopeful. We must be ready to dialogue with everyone. . . . While we must certainly recognize the presence of evil in the world and the threats to human dignity and freedom that evil poses, we must also recognize the goodness and good will in the world and become partisans of goodness and good will. . . .
>
> So many of our lay people believe that ours is a church of rules, that being Catholic consists of keeping rules. They do not find an institution which is like that very appealing. Nor should they.
>
> In fact, we are a church of love. Our message from the Lord himself even today is the message that God is Love and that we are those who are trying, however badly, to reflect that love in the world. . . .
>
> More important for us today, however, is the reaffirmation that we exist to preach a God of love, we try to be people of love, and we want our church to be, insofar as we poor humans can make it, a church of radiant love.

A Prayer for Change

(Source Unknown)

L ord and source of all gifts, we rejoice in the fullness of your holy
generosity.

We thank you especially now for the gift of change, that gift of newness
that opens doors closed by habit and routine.

We bless you and thank you as well for that which is stable and
unchanging, for the ancient and traditional which give meaning to
the new and different.

We are grateful in this prayer for those persons who, through their gifts
of excitement and adventure, have taught us not to fear change, not
to resist the new.

We are thankful for your Son, your sacred Word, who spoke to us of
new wine for new wine skins and who calls us daily to a new
kingdom and to a new covenant.

May our hearts be ever-changing, ever in growth, as we journey to you,
our creative source . . . you who are forever fresh and new, yet
forever the same.

2000 Catholic Almanac, ed. Matthew Bunson, Our Sunday Visitor Press, 1999.

All Saints, Robert Ellsberg, Crossroad Publishing Co., New York, NY, 1997.

Ancient Wisdom Modern World, Dalai Lama, Little, Brown & Co., UK, 2001.

And God Said What?, Margaret Nutting Ralph, Paulist Press, Mahwah, NJ, 1986.

The Baltimore Catechism, reprint: Tan Books and Publishers, Rockford, IL, 1977.

Bhagavad Gita, Trans. Edwin Arnold, Heritage Press, 1965.

The Bible and the End of the World: Should We Be Afraid, Margaret Nutting Ralph, Paulist Press, Mahwah, NJ, 1997.

The Bible Companion: A Handbook for Beginners, Ronald D. Witherup, S.J., Crossroad Publishing Co., New York, NY, 1998.

The Book of Revelation: A Catholic Interpretation of the Apocalypse, John Tickle, Liguori Publications, Liguori, MO, 1983.

The Brothers Karamazov, Fyodor Dostoyevsky, Vintage Books, New York, NY, 1991.

Catholic Update: C0692, Virginia Smith, St. Anthony Messenger Press, Cincinnati, OH, 1992.

Catholic Update: C0993, Kenneth E. Untener, St. Anthony Messenger Press, Cincinnati, OH, 1993.

Catholicism, Richard P. McBrien, Harper SanFrancisco, San Francisco, CA, 1994.

The Constitutions, Vatican II in Plain English, Bill Huebsch, Volume 2, Thomas More Publishing, Allen, TX, 1997.

The Council, Vatican II in Plain English, Bill Huebsch, volume 1, Thomas More Publishing, Allen, TX, 1997.

The Decrees and Declarations, Vatican II in Plain English, Bill Huebsch, Volume 3, Thomas More Publishing, Allen, TX, 1997.

Desire of the Everlasting Hills, Thomas Cahill, Nan A. Talese / Doubleday, New York, NY, 1997.

The Diary of Adam and Eve, Mark Twain, Modern Library / Random House, New York, NY, 1996.

Discovering Our Jewish Roots, Anna Marie Erst, S.H.C.J., Paulist Press, Mahwah, NJ, 1996.

Divino afflante Spiritu, Pius XII.

The Dragons of Eden, Carl Sagan, Random House, Inc., New York, NY, 1978.

The Encyclicals of John Paul II, *Providentissimus Deus*, ed. J. Michael, C.S.B., Our Sunday Visitor, Huntington, IN, 2001.

The Essential Koran, Thomas Cleary, Castle Books, 1993.

The Essential Rumi, Coleman Barks, Castle Books, 1997.

Focus on Asian Studies, "Confucianism," Judith A. Berling, Volume II, Number 1, *Asian Religions*, 1982, pp. 5–7.

Forgotten Truth, Huston Smith, Harper Collins, New York, NY, 1976.

The Gifts of the Jews, Thomas Cahill, Nan A. Talese / Doubleday, New York, NY, 1998.

God After Darwin, John F. Haught, Westview Press, Boulder, CO, 2000.

God, The Oldest Question, William J. O'Malley, S.J., Loyola Press, Chicago, IL, 2000.

Gone with the Wind, Margaret Mitchell, reprint: Scribner, New York, NY, 1996.

The Good Earth, Ted Perry, Sacred Heart League, 1990.

Gospel Light, John Shea, Crossroad Publishing Co., New York, NY, 1998.

The Gospel of Gabriel, Edward Hays, Forest of Peace Books, Leavenworth, KS, 1996.

Great Religions of the World, Loretta Pastva, S.N.D., Saint Mary's Press, Winona, MN, 1986.

How Good Do We Have to Be?, Harold S. Kushner, Little, Brown & Co., New York, NY, 1996.

The Illustrated World's Religions, Huston Smith, Harper SanFrancisco, San Francisco, CA, 1994.

The Inner Game of Tennis, W. Timothy Gallwey, Random House, Inc., New York, NY, 1997.

Interpreting the New Testament: A Practical Guide, Daniel J. Harrington, S.J., Michael Glazier, Inc., Collegeville, MN, 1979.

An Introduction to New Testament Christology, Raymond E. Brown, S.S., Paulist Press, Mahwah, NJ, 1994.

An Introduction to the New Testament, Raymond E. Brown, S.S., Doubleday, New York, NY, 1997.

Living God's Word: Reflections on the Weekly Gospels, Year B, David Knight, St. Anthony Messenger Press, Cincinnati, OH, 1999.

Man's Search for Meaning, Viktor E. Frankl, Washington Square Press, New York, NY, 1984.

Meeting the Living God, William J. O'Malley, S.J., Paulist Press, Mahwah, NJ, 1998.

The Men and the Message of the Old Testament, Peter F. Ellis, C.SS.R., Liturgical Press, Collegeville, MN, 1976.

More Daily Prayers for Busy People, William J. O'Malley, S.J., Saint Mary's Press, Winona, MN, 1999.

The New Jerome Bible Handbook, ed. Raymond E. Brown, S.S., Joseph A. Fitzmeyer, S.J., Roland E. Murphy, O.Carm., Liturgical Press, Collegeville, MN, 1992.

The New Jerome Biblical Commentary, ed. Raymond E. Brown, S.S., Joseph A. Fitzmeyer, S.J., Roland E. Murphy, O.Carm., Liturgical Press, Collegeville, MN, 1990, 1968.

New Jerusalem Bible (NJB), ed. Henry Wansborough, Doubleday, New York, NY, 1985.

New Oxford Annotated Bible (NRSV), ed. Bruce Metzger, Oxford University Press, New York, NY, 1991.

Noah's Flood, William Ryan / Walter Pitman, Touchstone Books, New York, NY, 2000.

The Old Hermit's Almanac, Edward Hays, Forest of Peace Books, Leavenworth, KS, 1997.

One River, Many Wells, Matthew Fox, Jeremy P. Tarcher / Putnam, New York, NY, 2000.

A Popular Guide through the Old Testament, Mary Reed Newland, Saint Mary's Press, Winona, MN, 1999.

Prayers for a Planetary Pilgrim, Edward Hays, Forest of Peace Books, Leavenworth, KS, 1988.

Praying Our Goodbyes, Joyce Rupp, O.S.M., Ave Maria Press, Notre Dame, IN, 1988.

Praying with Pope John XXIII, Bill Huebsch, Saint Mary's Press, Winona, MN, 1999.

A Prophetic Voice in the City, Carlo Maria Martini, Liturgical Press, Collegeville, MN, 1997.

Responses to 101 Questions on Buddhism, John Renard, Paulist Press, Mahwah, NJ, 1999.

Retreat with John the Evangelist: That You May Have Life, A Raymond E. Brown, S.S., St. Anthony Messenger Press, Cincinnati, OH, 1998.

Revelation: Proclaiming a Vision of Hope, Wilfrid Harrington, O.P., Resource Publications, Inc., 1994.

Scripture from Scratch: Facilitator Manual, Virginia Smith / Elizabeth McNamer, St. Anthony Messenger Press, Cincinnati, OH, 1991.

Scripture from Scratch: N0295, Virginia Smith, St. Anthony Messenger Press, Cincinnati, OH, 1995.

Scripture from Scratch: N1097, Dianne Bergant, C.S.A., St. Anthony Messenger Press, Cincinnati, OH, 1997.

Scripture from Scratch: N1298, Lawrence Boadt, C.S.P., St. Anthony Messenger Press, Cincinnati, OH, 1998.

The Song of the Bird, Anthony de Mello, S.J., Image Books, New York, NY, 1984.

The Spirituality of Teilhard de Chardin, Robert Faricy, S.J., Winston Press, 1981.

The Tao of Jesus, Joseph A.Loya, Wan-Li Ho, Chang-Shin Jih, Paulist Press, Mahwah, NJ, 1998.

Summa Theologica, St. Thomas Aquinas, Trans. Fathers of the English Dominican Province, Christian Classics, Allen, TX, 1981, 1948.

The Tao of Pooh and the Te of Piglet, Benjamin Hoff, Penguin USA, New York, 1994.

The Ten Commandments: Sounds of Love from Mt. Sinai, Alfred McBride, O. Praem., St. Anthony Messenger Press, Cincinnati, OH, 1990.

Thoughts on the East, Thomas Merton / George Woodcock, New Directions Publishing Co., New York, NY, 1995.

To Life!, Harold S. Kushner, Little, Brown & Co., New York, NY, 1993.

When Bad Things Happen to Good People, Harold S. Kushner, Avon Books, Inc., 1981.

White Smoke: A Novel about the Next Papal Conclave, Andrew M. Greeley, Forge/Tom Doherty Associates, Inc., New York, NY, 1996

Why Be Catholic?, William J. O'Malley, S.J., Crossroad Publishing Co., New York, NY, 1993.

Why Religion Matters, Huston Smith, HarperCollins, New York, NY, 2001.

Written That You May Believe, Sandra M. Schneiders, Crossroad Publishing Co., New York, NY, 1999.

Zen and the Art of Motorcycle Maintenance, Robert M. Pirsig, Reprint: Harper Trade, New York, NY, 2000.

Zen for Beginners, Judith Blackstone / Zoran Josipovic, Writers and Readers Publishing, Inc., New York, NY, 1986.